YALE STUDIES IN POLITICAL SCIENCE, 2

Published under the direction of the Department of Political Science

JAMES HARRINGTON
1611–1677

*from a portrait attributed to A. Van der Venne in the
National Portrait Gallery, London*

AN IMMORTAL
COMMONWEALTH

The Political Thought of James Harrington

by CHARLES BLITZER

New Haven, Yale University Press, 1960

To my parents

Contents

Introduction

IN THE AUTUMN OF 1656 James Harrington's *Common-wealth of Oceana* was first advertised to the public in the pages of the *Mercurius Politicus*.[1] Although it was in a very real sense an occasional work, written in the belief that it contained the only sure prescription for curing England's chronic constitutional ills and dedicated to Oliver Cromwell in the hope that he would undertake to effect this cure, the *Oceana* has for three centuries been recognized as an important part of the history of western political thought. The reasons that have been adduced for according it this status have varied widely: the fathers of the American Revolution found it an eloquent and persuasive vindication of government by laws and not by men; French reformers of the era of the First Republic admired it as a model of rational constitution-making; Marxists have been pleased to find in it an anticipation of the doctrine of historical materialism; and recent social historians have identified it as the *locus classicus* of the theory of "the rise of the gentry."[2] While this variety of interpretations may in itself suggest something of the richness of Harrington's thought,

1. *Mercurius Politicus, comprising the sum of foreign intelligence, with the affairs now on foot in the three nations of England, Scotland, & Ireland.* Number 334 (October 29–November 6, 1656), "An Advertisement of Books Newly published."
2. See Judith N. Shklar's excellent article, "Ideology hunting: the case of James Harrington," *American Political Science Review*, September 1959, 662–92; and "Storm over the gentry," by J. H. Hexter, *Encounter*, May 1958, 22–34 and extensive correspondence in subsequent issues.

it also suggests that any new commentator would do well
to make clear at the outset his own point of view and his
own method of approach.

What follows has been written in the conviction that the
political theories of past ages can profitably (perhaps, most
profitably) be treated as constituting moments in a continuing process of intellectual and institutional development. Although this is a process for which it would be
foolish to hypothesize any particular *terminus ad quem*—
now more than ever we are aware of the fragility of our
beliefs and institutions—nevertheless it is a process whose
temporary culmination is the world we live in. The ideas
by which we order our experience and the institutions by
which we order our actions are no more to be understood
apart from their development through time than are our
common language or our individual psyches. When we
seek to reconstruct our political heritage, in both its theoretical and its practical aspects, no evidence is more valuable
than that provided by the political theorist, who at the same
time reflects the problems and preoccupations of his age
and helps to shape its attitudes, who is at once a part of
historical development and a commentator upon that development. As patient and agent in the historical process
he doubly repays our attention.

Such an approach has certain consequences for the study
of political thought. It means that we will not be concerned
primarily with judging whether a political theory is correct
or incorrect in some absolute sense, either morally or em-
pirically. The question of whether Locke's constitutional
commonwealth is ethically more desirable than Hobbes's
absolutist state, or the question of whether Hobbes's account of primitive human existence is anthropologically
more accurate than Locke's, are at best peripheral. At the
center of attention are, rather, questions such as these:
what does the Hobbesian system reveal of the character

of seventeenth-century absolutism, its origins, its justification, its consequences; what do Locke's writings tell us
about the conditions and the state of mind that led to the
imposing of constitutional limitations on the modern state?

A second consequence of such an approach is the focusing
of our attention on certain decisive moments and figures
in the history of political thought. Thus, despite the arguments of critics such as C. Northcote Parkinson,[3] we do
not hasten to consult the writings of the great sages of
Africa and the Orient; interesting as these doubtless are
in themselves, by no stretch of the imagination can they
be considered as part of the development of our political
tradition. And even within this tradition we are led by the
historical approach to concentrate upon those figures—not
always inherently the greatest—whose writings are most
directly related to, and thus most revelatory of, critical
institutional and intellectual developments. While it would
be folly to argue that in the overall scheme of things Mar-
siglio of Padua was greater than Dante Alighieri, the student of political thought who is concerned to understand
the emergence of secular political institutions at the close
of the Middle Ages will quite properly devote more attention to the *Defensor Pacis* than to the *De Monarchia*.

The relevance of these points to Harrington's political
thought should be apparent. If it is necessary to point out
that the mid-seventeenth century was precisely such a critical moment in western political development, the same
issue of the *Mercurius Politicus* that first advertised the
Oceana reminds us forcefully of the fact. In a dispatch from
Westminster, dated November 3, we read: "Divers strange
and absurd pranks having been plaid lately by James Naylor
the Quaker, at Bristol, he is sent for up by Order of the
Parliament." The ensuing persecution of Naylor at the

3. *The Evolution of Political Thought* (N.Y. 1958), pp. 7–8 and
passim.

hands of parliament, and the desperate but unsuccessful attempts of Cromwell to intervene in the name of the religious liberty guaranteed by the Instrument of Government, led to the adoption of the Humble Petition and Advice in the spring of 1657. The establishment of a second legislative chamber, and the almost simultaneous offer of the Crown to Cromwell, mark the beginning of the process that culminated in the restoration of the Stuart monarchy in 1660. Was the traditional monarchical form, then, the last, best hope of protection against the unbridled exercise of political power? Was it necessary in order to achieve such protection to recreate the very tensions and conflicts that less than a generation before had led to the destruction of the monarchy? Most Englishmen evidently thought so. But some, among whom Harrington was pre-eminent, thought differently; and these men were soon proved correct by the course of events.

More important than his correctness, however, was the fact that Harrington was concerned with precisely these issues of sovereignty and constitutionalism, the issues that were at stake in this critical moment. Unlike the conservative, tradition-bound constitutionalists of his time, he explicitly recognized the impossibility of a return to the old order of "government by confusion," and argued persuasively the necessity of a clear-cut decision about the location of sovereign power in a healthy and stable political system. But, unlike the absolutists of his time, he also insisted that such sovereignty could and should be made compatible with a system of restraints upon the arbitrary and invasive use of the power of government. It is as one of the first and most forceful advocates of this distinctively modern form of constitutionalism that Harrington most strongly commands our attention.

If we examine the grounds for Harrington's advocacy of this form, we are immediately reminded that his was an

age of intellectual as well as political turmoil. His deep
concern with the problem of what constitutes "demonstration" reflects the fact that this, the most fundamental of
methodological questions, was very much an open question in the mid-seventeenth century. On the one hand, this
was to be for Harrington the source of what was in effect
a problem of communication. Utterly sure of the final correctness of his own position, he tried unstintingly to win
the approval and support of his contemporaries. But how
was this to be done? How, and in what terms, were they to
be convinced? There were still many for whom the appeal
to traditional authority remained decisive, while others
searched assiduously for proof from the Word of God. At
the same time, the "new philosophy" was winning impressive victories on all sides, and its disciples demanded deductive proofs and empirical demonstrations. The age that
produced Francis Bacon and William Harvey, as well as
John Bunyan and Praisegod Barebones, Thomas Hobbes
as well as Robert Filmer, was one in which the dramatic
confrontation of new and old posed almost insuperable
obstacles to the maintenance of a true intellectual community. Indeed, so complex was the situation that any simple classification of "old" and "new" does violence to the
facts of the age. Harrington's own theoretical system, containing as it does elements of the most diverse character,
bears witness to his desire to synthesize the teachings of
classical antiquity, the lessons of history—both sacred and
profane—and the techniques of modern scientific investigation. To this extent he was, indeed, the child of his
times. But in his pioneering efforts to create a method appropriate to the study of political reality he has also been
a source of inspiration to men of later ages who have shared
his concern with this continuing problem.

Perhaps partly as a result of Harrington's interest in
methodological problems, his writings are also notable for

their extraordinary historical detachment. When all is said
and done, it is this quality that most clearly distinguishes
them from the works of the great majority of his contemporaries. Living and writing in the midst of the most passionate political controversies, both on the Continent and
in England, he seems never to have lost his calmness of
temperament or his clarity of vision. And this despite the
fact that he was himself deeply committed to many of the
very principles and institutions that hung in the balance
during these troubled years. His great honesty, his broad
learning and his deep sensitivity led him to recognize that
the shattering events of his age were not simply the consequences of human wickedness, or even folly, but rather were
parts of an unfolding historical process. The English Civil
Wars resulted largely from hitherto unseen changes in the
condition of English society, and only in small degree from
the misguided policies of the Stuarts; the Thirty Years' War
was not so much a struggle between Protestant saints and
Catholic devils (or vice versa) as it was a bloody resolution
of the ambiguities of feudal constitutionalism. In recognizing these facts Harrington was not led to conclude that man
is impotent in the face of vast and inexorable historical
forces. Rather, he concluded that effective action in fur-
therance of human goals is possible, but only if that action
is guided by sure knowledge of the laws of politics. The determination to lay bare the true nature of political reality
in order that man may *act*—this is the spirit that informs
all of Harrington's writings and that above all else gives
them their genuine distinction.

I should like to express my gratitude to many friends both
at Harvard and at Yale for their advice and encouragement,
and I should like especially to acknowledge here three
sources of particular aid and comfort in the preparation
of this book: Carl J. Friedrich's kindness and patience and

wise counsel over many years deserve, I fear, a more ample repayment than I shall ever be able to make; John E. Pomfret, the Director of the Henry E. Huntington Library, and his splendid staff, did everything imaginable to ensure that my research would be both fruitful and delightful; Marian N. Ash, of the Yale University Press, deserves most of the credit for whatever order and clarity this book possesses.

Publication of this book has been facilitated by a grant from the Yale Fund for Young Scholars, for which grateful acknowledgment is made.

"There is nothing in this world, next the favor of God, I so much desire as to be familiarly understood."

Valerius and Publicola

CHAPTER 1.

The Aristocratic Commonwealthsman

"... some sober men came to me and told me, if any man in *England* could shew what a Commonwealth was, it was my self. Upon this persuasion I wrote. . . ."

Statement during interrogation
in the Tower of London

J AMES HARRINGTON clearly belongs in the class of political theorists whose ideas were shaped by the pressure of personal and historical circumstances. All his political writings, from the *Commonwealth of Oceana* in 1656 to the posthumously published *System of Politics,* bear the stamp of these circumstances. They are unmistakably the work of an English gentleman who has a profound respect for the traditional virtues of his class; of a convinced republican who has been the friend of kings; of an erudite classicist and historian who is determined to create a science of politics; of a gentle and tolerant man who has lived in an age of violence and bigotry; of a private citizen who is obsessed with the importance of political life. How, we may ask, did Harrington come to possess these qualities and to hold these attitudes? An answer must be sought in the history of his family and the story of his formative years.

In June of the year 1657 an English Royalist, whose name we know only as J. Lesley, read James Harrington's recently published *Oceana* and was moved to write its author a stinging letter of rebuke—a letter that has survived through the centuries, bearing the scribbled annotation, "A Slap on the Snout of the Republican Swine that rooteth up Monarchy." The warmth of Mr. Lesley's reaction is not to be explained solely, or even chiefly, by the abhorrent republicanism of the book. What he found intolerable was the spectacle of James Harrington willfully and publicly betraying the class into which he had been born. "Good man!" he wrote, "what moveth James Harington to provoke the wrath of kings? His own lineage is derived from the blood of the Anointed." After a lengthy and not always accurate account of the close relations between the Harringtons and the kings and queens of England, he continues:

Yourself was caressd by the blessed martyr Charles,
and honoured with his wordes, and even his princelie
favours from his own hands on the scaffold. And shall
then any one branch of such noble stock, endowed
with such rare gifts and graces, as all have been for
the most part, and so many of you countenanced by
kings, shall any espouse such evil principles as you have
now set forth in your book. . . . You cannot be a good
man, for, Fear God, and Honour the King, are both
in one place, and support each other as the corner
stones of religion and royalty. But you have dishon-
oured both, and blasted a long line of ancestors re-
nownd for both, and stirred up the ill affections of all
the noble families to whom you stand in alliance.[1]

For all its ill temper and all its exaggerations, Lesley's
letter has the virtue of reminding us that an account of
Harrington's life would be inadequate if it did not include
at least a cursory consideration of the family and the social
class into which he was born. In an obvious sense this statement might properly be made about any historical figure,
but in the case of Harrington it seems to possess a special
relevance. Not only did he live in an age and a society in
which social position and family connection were matters
of great moment, but also he was himself singularly sensi-
tive to the historical and political implications of just these
sociological facts. One might argue persuasively, as Tawney
has indeed done,[2] that Harrington's brilliant and percep-
tive account of the social history of England in the centuries
preceding his own is in essence the history of his family

1. The letter is printed in a collection of family papers compiled
by Sir John Harington, under the title *Nugae Antiquae;* it may be
found on pages 82–85 of the London edition of 1769.
2. R. H. Tawney, "Harrington's Interpretation of His Age," *Proceedings of the British Academy,* 27 (London, 1941).

writ large. If only for this reason, it is appropriate that we should turn our attention to that family.

A recent historian[3] has traced the Harrington family back to one Osulf of Flemingby, who settled in Cumberland during the reign of Richard I; Osulf's son appears in contemporary records as Robertus de Hafrinctuna, a style which in the next generation changes to "de Haverington." From this time forth, the history of the family can be followed without a break. For some three centuries the Lancashire branch of the family claims our attention: these Harringtons were strong, willful, and ambitious men, men who worked and fought for great stakes with skill and courage but all too seldom with either good judgment or good luck. These were the Harringtons who fought for Henry IV against the Percies, who stood with Henry V at Harfleur and Agincourt; but they were also the men who supported the Yorkist cause in the Wars of the Roses, were attainted for treason in 1458, were almost wiped out at the battle of Wakefield, fought at the side of the unlucky Richard III at Bosworth, and were once more attainted in the first year of the reign of Henry VII. Dramatic as this record is, and exciting as it must have been to recall in later generations, it does not tell of the kinds of actions calculated to lay firm foundations for the future prosperity or greatness of the family. After the debacle of Bosworth Field the Harringtons of Lancaster pass into obscurity and are replaced in the family history by their quieter and less ambitious, although more successful, cousins of Rutlandshire. The story of the Harringtons now becomes one of modest country life, of the gradual accumulation of property, of regular public

3. Ian Grimble, *The Harington Family* (London, 1957). My account of the early history of the family draws heavily upon the fruits of Grimble's extensive and admirable researches. I have, however, elected to use the more common modern spelling, "Harrington."

service, enlivened by occasional flashes of brilliance or ec-
centricity. The gentry have superseded the great warriors of
medieval times and the gentle virtues of prudence, learning,
and good management have taken the place of courage,
daring, and prowess in battle.

By its very nature the history of the Rutlandshire Harringtons is lacking in dramatic interest. Any attempt at a
continuous narrative would necessarily degenerate into a
succession of complicated marriage settlements, or an account of the steady acquisition and occasional loss of manors
in and about the county, or a catalogue of sheriffs, members
of Parliament and minor courtiers. Tolstoy's judgment
about happy families would seem to apply equally well to
prosperous ones—they have very little history, and that
hardly worth the telling. To avoid such a tedious chronicle,
we may be content simply to note some landmarks in the
progress of the family. In 1492, for example, Robert Harrington became the first of his name to hold the office of
High Sheriff of Rutlandshire; by the seventeenth century
we find the sixth Harrington High Sheriff collecting ship
money in the county for Charles I. The historian of the
family has described in some detail the "series of purchases
with which the Haringtons supplemented their marriage
settlements, to build up one of the largest landed fortunes
in England."[4] The climax of this process was reached about
the time of the first Sir James Harrington of Exton (1511–
1592), who managed to add five substantial manors to the
large estate he had inherited, an accomplishment all the
more impressive for the fact that Sir James held no crown
offices. An industrious if not completely reliable scholar of
the late seventeenth century once calculated that the descendants of Sir James included among their number no
fewer than eight dukes, three marquises, seventy [sic] earls,

4. Ibid., p. 65.

nine counts, twenty-seven viscounts, and thirty-six barons.[5]
This record will perhaps seem less improbable when we
observe that Sir James's wife Lucy, a sister of the poet Sir
Philip Sidney, bore him eighteen children, of whom eleven
married; among the husbands of the eight daughters we
find the Earls of Manchester and Dunmore, Lord Camden,
Lord Hastings (later Earl of Huntingdon), and Lord Dud-
ley.

By the year 1600, Sir James's eldest son John was described as being "able to dispend yearly betwixt £5000 and
£7000 of good land," an income equal to that of "the best
barons."[6] And in fact John was within three years to become a baron, an honor bestowed upon him by James I at
his coronation, and to be appointed tutor and guardian of
Elizabeth, the king's only daughter. In the event, this proved
to be a costly honor and one that strained even the lordly
financial resources of the new baron. An annual allowance
of £1500, and later of £2500, did not begin to cover the
expenses of the princess' household. By February of 1613
Lord John of Exton was in debt to the extent of £40,000;
in recognition of his loyal services he was granted the royal
patent to coin brass farthings but, as the Venetian ambassador reported, "after it had been granted and confirmed by
the Council it was suspended on account of the immense
profit."[7] Harassed by debts and exhausted by the responsibilities arising from the marriage of Princess Elizabeth to

5. James Wright, *History and Antiquities of Rutlandshire* (London, 1684), p. 52.

6. Thomas Wilson, *The State of England 1600* (Camden Society,
1936), p. 23; quoted by H. R. Trevor-Roper in "The Gentry 1540–
1640," *Economic History Review Supplements, 1* (Cambridge, n.d.),
23.

7. Venetian Calendar 1610–1613, p. 524; the ambassador's estimate
that Lord Harrington made some £20,000 from this privilege while
it lasted, Grimble believes to be "a complete exaggeration" (*The
Harington Family*, p. 163).

the Elector Palatine, Lord Harrington died in Germany in
August of 1613 on his way back to England after seeing the
royal couple settled in their new home.

The paradoxical, but by no means unusual, combination
of royal favor and financial crisis that characterized the life
of the first Baron Harrington marked a turning point in
the fortunes of his family. His son John, the second Lord
Harrington of Exton, strove manfully to pay his father's
debts, and even sold Exton in order to do so—but in vain.
Within a year he, too, was dead and the debts remained.
His untimely death moved Donne to write a nicely balanced
elegy of 258 lines, mourning the loss of a friend and cele-
brating the salvation of a soul:

> At that gate then Triumphant soule, dost thou
> Begin thy Triumph; But since lawes allow
> That at the Triumph day, the people may,
> All that they will, 'gainst the Triumpher say,
> Let me here use that freedome, and expresse
> My griefe, though not to make thy Triumph lesse.

Whatever its metaphysical or theological implications, the
death of John spelled the financial ruin of the Harringtons
of Rutlandshire. It remained only for Lucy, his sister and
coheir, to deliver the *coup de grâce*. For although thrift and
prudent management might conceivably still have sufficed
to re-establish the family's financial position, Lucy, Countess of Bedford, was hardly the woman to undertake the
task. By almost limitless extravagance and never-ending
self-indulgence she managed to dissipate utterly the grad-
ually accumulated properties of her ancestors. Within thir-
teen years of her father's death the major branch of the
Harringtons of Rutlandshire had virtually ceased to exist.

At almost precisely the same time the career of the most
famous of the Harringtons, Sir John of Kelston (1561–
1612), the translator of *Orlando Furioso* and inventor of the

water closet, came to a close. The origins of Sir John's family, and therefore also its precise relation to the other Harrington lines, remain shrouded in obscurity. It is clear, however, that this is the branch of the family that made its way in the world not through courage or prudence, but through wit, artistic ability, and the enjoyment of royal favor. Alexander Harrington (died c. 1539), the grandfather of Sir John, was rumored to be the illegitimate son of the Dean of York, but there seems to be no evidence to support the rumor. We know only that he lived in Stepney and that he was the friend of many Tudor poets and of the musician Thomas Tallis, who taught his son the forms of musical composition.

This son, John, made his way to the court of Henry VIII and soon became established as one of the most gifted and popular of court poets. According to Lesley's letter of 1657, "The great King Henry the VIIIth matched his darling daughter to John Harrington, and, though a bastard, dowered her with the rich lands of Baths priory; and Queen Elizabeth affected these faithful servants so much, as to become godmother to their son, and make him a knyght for his wit and his valour." The matter of John's marriage is as mysterious as is his ancestry; Lesley is quite correct, however, in suggesting that his son (by a second marriage) was a favorite of the Queen. Her interest in the young man seems to have resulted first from her gratitude for his father's loyalty during the difficult years preceding 1558. Thus when the boy was fourteen and away at Cambridge, his royal godmother sent him a copy of a speech she had delivered in Parliament in defense of her decision to remain unmarried; in the covering letter she wrote:

> Boy Jack: I have made a clerk write fair my poor words for thine use, as it cannot be such stripplings have entrance into Parliament assembly as yet. Ponder them

in thy hours of leisure, and play with them till they enter thine understanding; so shalt thou, hereafter, perchance, find some good fruits hereof when thy god-mother is out of remembrance; and I do this, because thy father was ready to serve and love us in trouble and thrall.[8]

In the course of time, however, the Queen came to look with favor upon the young man who signed himself "your Highness' saucy Godson" for his own sake rather than for his father's. She feigned horror when he circulated his translation of the improper twenty-eighth book of Ariosto's *Orlando Furioso,* but punished him merely by banishing him from court until he should have translated the whole huge work.

This was published in 1591 and was followed in the next year by the work that established its author's immortality, *The Metamorphosis of Ajax.* Predictably, another scandal resulted from the publication of a book on so unseemly a subject; threats of the Star Chamber were heard when it began to be rumored that Harrington had satirized various court figures, including no less a personage than Leicester. But once again the Queen intervened, sending her godson away from court to protect him from the rigors of the law. For seven years Harrington remained at his estate of Kelston, near Bath. Finally in 1599, at the express instructions of the Queen, he was summoned thence to accompany Essex on his expedition to Ireland. In recognition of his valor and loyalty he was knighted on the field by Essex, becoming Sir John of Kelston—although the Calendar of State Papers has fallen victim to the prank of an unknown seventeenth-century wag and solemnly records the title as Sir Ajax Harrington. The last years of Sir John's life need not con-

8. Grimble cites *Nugae Antiquae* (1779 ed.), *1,* 127–28 in *The Harington Family,* p. 109.

cern us here, save for the fact that they confirm the impression that his earlier success and prosperity had been due to the Queen's friendship and protection. In 1603, the year of the accession of James I, we find him in prison for debt; the last nine years of his life were lived in poverty and obscurity, a gloomy conclusion to a glorious story, and one that almost exactly parallels that of the Rutlandshire Harringtons.

Clearly, by the beginning of the seventeenth century the great days of the Harrington family had passed. Its last truly eminent member, the political theorist with whom we are here concerned, was born at the moment when its fortunes were at their lowest ebb. But this should not lead us to conclude that the importance of the family connection had become negligible. In his *Commonwealth of Oceana* James Harrington suggested the chief sources of his family's continuing distinction when he wrote that a nobility or gentry "may be defined divers wayes, for it is either ancient riches, or ancient virtue, or title confer'd by a Prince or a Common-wealth."[9] Observing that by "virtue" Harrington means essentially public service, we may say that through the centuries his family had amply fulfilled each of these requirements. Indeed, as we have seen, its history thoroughly documents the various means by which an English family could hope to achieve distinction: by valor, by good management of its estates, by wit and learning, by royal favor. And distinction, once achieved, was not to be destroyed overnight simply by a reversal of fortune. Certainly the family no longer enjoyed its former wealth or influence, but various attributes—tangible and intangible—remained to become part of the birthright of James Harrington.

9. *James Harrington's Oceana,* edited with notes by S. B. Liljegren (Heidelberg, Carl Winters, 1924), p. 119. All citations of the *Oceana* refer to Liljegren's magistral edition.

James Harrington was born on Friday, January 3, 1611,
at Upton Hall in the village of Upton, Northamptonshire.
His father was Sir Sapcote Harrington, Knight, of Rand in
the county of Lincoln, a nephew of the first Baron Harrington of Exton and a cousin of the prodigal Lucy, Countess
of Bedford. James's mother was Jane Samuell, the daughter
of Sir William Samuell of Upton, in whose home he was
born. Since he was born into a society governed by strict
rules of primogeniture—rules that he was later to subject
to searching criticism—it is of great importance to note
immediately that James was his parents' first child; when
his father died in 1630 he became heir to all the family
property. Despite the rapid disintegration of the estates
of the senior branch of the family, it would seem that Sir
Sapcote possessed a considerable fortune, including properties the income from which enabled his heir to live in
comfort for sixty-six years while contributing to the support
of a brother, two sisters, two half-brothers, and two half-
sisters.

Almost nothing is known of the first years of Harrington's
life. His earliest biographer and great admirer John Toland
mentions his "Inclination and Capacity to learn whatever
was propos'd to him" and a "natural gravity" exceptional
in a child[10]—but of course these are precisely the qualities
that one might retrospectively attribute to a child who is
known to have become a scholar in later life. We do know
that Harrington's childhood was spent in the tiny Lincoln-

10. See pp. xiii–xiv in Toland's "Life of James Harrington" in
*The Oceana and other works of James Harrington, Esq., Collected,
Methodiz'd and Review'd, with An exact account of his Life prefix'd,
by John Toland. To which is added An Appendix, containing all the
Political Tracts wrote by this Author, omitted in Mr. Toland's edition*
(3rd ed., London, for A. Millar, 1747). This, perhaps the most widely
available edition of Harrington's works, is referred to hereafter simply
as *Coll. Works.*

shire village of Rand, where his father's monument may still be seen in St. Oswald's Church. If it is true that he was an unusually serious boy, he might well have been forcibly struck by certain conditions outside the confines of his own family's comfortable country existence. Neither the romantic images conjured up by the name of Lincoln Forest, nor the loveliness of the English countryside as we see it today, should blind us to the often harsh and brutal realities of the rural life that surrounded him. Lincolnshire was the scene of disastrously bad harvests in 1621 and 1622, Harrington's tenth and eleventh years. In 1623 Sir William Pelham sent his father-in-law a description of conditions in the county: "Theare are many thousands in thease parts whoo have soulde all they have even to theyr bedd straw, and cann not gett worke to carne any munny. Dogg's flesh is a dainty disch, and the other day one stole a scheepe, whoe for meere hunger tore a legge out, and didd eate itt raw."[11] In 1630 and 1631, the former being the year of the death of Harrington's father, thousands were carried off by simultaneous plague and famine. In 1631, for example, one-third of the population of the village of Louth died and 493 bodies were buried in July and August alone. When a quarter of a century later Harrington wrote that "he who wanteth bread, is his servant that will feed him,"[12] he was indulging in no idle metaphor, but rather was giving a sober description of one aspect of seventeenth-century rural life as he had observed it.

But it was not only the grim side of country life that was presented to the eye of the young Harrington in Lincolnshire. While men of the lowest degree suffered horribly at the mercy of forces they could not control, others were able

11. Pelham to Sec'y Conway, April 21, 1623; quoted in Charles Brears, *Lincolnshire in the 17th and 18th Centuries* (London, 1940), p. 15.
12. *Oceana*, p. 14.

through energy, intelligence, or sheer good fortune to bring
about the most striking improvement in their condition.
Nor was this a purely random or haphazard process; in it
modern historians have detected a pattern—a pattern that
was apparent to Harrington three centuries ago. "The Dissolution of the Monasteries," writes the most recent historian of Lincolnshire,[13] ". . . brought about one-eighth of
the land in the county into the market and provided a
golden opportunity for the families which had prospered
by trade to acquire landed estates. Robert Carre, a wealthy
wool merchant, bought a great estate including Sleaford,
and his grandson owned land in more than sixty villages in
the county. . . . But above all, prosperous Lincolnshire yeo-
men added to their property and climbed the social ladder.
The outstanding instance is that of the Cust family. Henry
Cust was a yeoman in 1617, Samuel Cust an esquire in 1662,
Richard Cust a baronet in 1677. . . . Many of these new
landowners worthily played their part in public life and
shouldered the ever-increasing burden of government."
Once again the coincidence between local and presumably
familiar events of Harrington's youth and his later writings
is too striking to require much comment. As we shall see,
what is most impressive in Harrington's later intellectual
life is his ability to discern the pattern underlying the
events and to incorporate it into his general theory. All
this, however, is still far in the future.

The question of Harrington's education is a puzzling
one. The available records indicate that he received only
two or three years of formal schooling, at Oxford and the
Middle Temple. Yet we know that he was a man of for-
midable learning; his mastery of classical and modern languages alone would be sufficient to suggest long years of
study, to say nothing of his extensive knowledge of litera-

13. Brears, *Lincolnshire*, p. 4.

ture, theology, and history. The best guess would seem to be that his brief period of formal training was no more than an interlude between intensive private education as a child and years of self-education as a young man. We do know that he entered Trinity College, Oxford, as a gentleman commoner in the year 1629. Here he was, for a time at least, a pupil of the renowned William Chillingworth, an extraordinary man who was soon to be converted to Catholicism and then to return to Protestantism as a notable latitudinarian. In his later years Chillingworth devoted his energies to arguing that sectarian differences are not matters of fundamental importance; his *The Religion of Protestants a Safe Way to Salvation* (1637) bears comparison with Grotius' *De veritate religionis Christianae* (1627) as a landmark on the road to religious toleration. Despite the fact that Harrington was at Oxford prior to Chillingworth's brief Catholic period, his own latitudinarianism and advocacy of toleration reflect something of the spirit of his tutor.[14]

While Harrington was still at Trinity, and still legally a minor, his father died; his mother had died several years earlier. The socage tenure of his estate allowed him to select his own guardian, and he chose his maternal grandmother, Lady Samuell. In going to Trinity College Harrington had followed in the footsteps of three of Lady Samuell's four sons; in October of 1631 he once again emulated these uncles by enrolling as a student in the Middle Temple. One feels that he must have been somewhat halfhearted in both actions. Just as he had left Oxford without taking a degree, so too he abandoned the study of law after only a few weeks. Evidently both his new guardian and his financial condition allowed him considerable freedom; eschewing further

14. For a somewhat different view, see the essay by A. E. Levett in *Social and Political Ideas of the 16th and 17th Centuries,* ed. F. J. C. Hearnshaw (New York, 1949), p. 176. Also, see below, pp. 165–69.

experiments with formal education he set out to travel on the Continent. Whether he embarked on his travels with the specific purpose of investigating politics we cannot tell, although it seems unlikely. Toland does tell us that after his return he "was often heard to say, that, before he left *England,* he knew no more of Monarchy, Anarchy, Aristocracy, Democracy, Oligarchy, or the like, than as hard words wherof he learned the signification in his Dictionary."[15] The mere fact that Harrington was twenty years old, financially independent, and intellectually alert is perhaps sufficient explanation for his desire to travel. But we should not forget that at this time the Thirty Years' War was entering its dramatic third phase; in September of 1631 Gustavus Adolphus had won his great victory over Tilly at Breitenfeld, arousing the hopes of Protestants throughout Europe. Is it too fanciful to suggest that Harrington's restlessness at Oxford and the Middle Temple might have been due to eagerness to observe at first hand, or even participate in, these momentous events? It would seem not, for immediately upon arriving in the Netherlands, early in 1632, he enlisted in the English volunteer regiment that had been raised by the Earl of Craven. The fact that the Earl had been Harrington's contemporary at Trinity College raises the possibility that this whole affair had been prearranged. In any case, the young Englishman soon found himself actively engaged in the attempt to recover the Palatinate for the Protestant Elector, Frederick V.

At this point in the story we are faced with another coincidence. The Elector's wife Elizabeth, the tragic "Winter Queen" of Bohemia, was of course the daughter of James I, who had been raised and educated by Harrington's great-uncle. Thus Harrington possessed a personal motive for dedicating himself to the mission of Craven's regiment. The

15. *Coll. Works,* p. xiv.

regiment marched from the Hague and arrived at Frank-
furt-am-Main on the tenth of February, 1632. There a parley
between the Elector and Gustavus Adolphus made clear the
Swedish King's unwillingness to cooperate and doomed the
enterprise to failure. A march of some three hundred miles
in midwinter can hardly have been a pleasant introduction
to the Continent or to the glories of military life, and now
to make things worse it had turned out to be fruitless,
lacking not only a successful conclusion but even the excitement of battle. By the time the expedition had returned
to the Hague, however, Harrington had achieved something—he had won the friendship and respect of the Elec
tor. Soon he had become a favorite of the whole royal family
in exile. The young daughters of the Elector, we are told,
grew especially fond of him, "his Conversation being always extremely pleasant, as well as learned and polite."[10]
This accords well with Aubrey's characteristically vivid and
telegraphic description: "He was of a middling stature,
well-trussed man, strong and thick, well-sett, sanguine,
quick-hott-fiery hazell eie, thick moyst curled haire, as you
may see by his picture. In his conversation very friendly,
and facetious, and hospitable."[17] Impressed by what he had
seen of the young Englishman, the Elector decided to en-
trust him with the management of his affairs in England, a
considerable honor and a grave responsibility at the age of
twenty-one.

In the culturally and economically flourishing Netherlands Harrington had had an opportunity to observe the
struggle of the Protestant provinces against both foreign
control and the attempted centralization of the House of
Orange. When, after journeying through Flanders, he
reached France, the contrast must indeed have been strik-

16. Ibid.
17. John Aubrey, *Brief Lives,* ed. A. Powell (London, 1949), p. 266.

ing. In the combination of Louis XIII and Richelieu he
was able to observe two of the most able and successful
architects of the modern monarchical state. His later warnings to the English that if they did not set their house in
order France would come to rule the world indicate that he
was duly impressed with the efficiency, if not the desirability, of the political institutions that were being created
across the Channel. As we shall see, it was this appreciation
of the immense potentialities of rationalized and centralized
political institutions that more than anything else distinguished Harrington from the other republican and constitutional theorists of his day. Having seen the wonders of
the already great French monarchy, he could no longer be
content with a government that "subsisted by confusion."
The real question was whether political efficiency necessarily required political absolutism. And if France demonstrated the advantages of efficiency, the next country Harrington visited suggested to him the possibility that these
advantages might be gained by other and more desirable
means.

From France Harrington traveled to Italy, arriving in
Rome during a special papal jubilee.[18] His visit to that
city is noteworthy only because it produced an amusing
and rather revealing anecdote. It seems that Harrington
went with several other Protestants on Candlemas to watch
Pope Urban VIII perform the ceremony of consecrating the
candles. In order to obtain one of the consecrated candles
it was necessary for the visitor to kiss the Pope's toe. Although we are told that Harrington greatly desired to have
a candle, presumably as a souvenir of his trip, he refused to

18. The fact that Harrington arrived during a jubilee does not
allow us to pin down the precise time of his visit to Rome. Unfortunately, Urban VIII declared no fewer than seven extraordinary
jubilees during his long pontificate. Harrington's visit must, however,
have occurred in either 1634 or 1636.

perform the necessary obeisance. His fellows felt no such scruples and returned to England with their candles. Later some of them told Charles I of Harrington's behavior. The King is reputed to have said to Harrington that he might have kissed the Pope's toe simply "as a respect to a temporal Prince," whereupon Harrington replied that "since he had the honor to kiss his Majesty's hand, he thought it beneath him to kiss any other Prince's foot."[19] Charles, we are told, was highly pleased by the youth's loyal and witty reply, which is said to have been the origin of the close friendship that grew up between the two. In any case, the story does indicate that Harrington had met the King before setting out on his European journey.

Much the most significant part of this journey was Harrington's sojourn in Venice; of all the places he visited, this city had undoubtedly the greatest influence on the development of his political thought. Despite the fact that the greatness of Venice had sharply declined by the middle of the seventeenth century, the city and its institutions made an ineradicable impression upon the young traveler. Toland tells us that: "He prefer'd *Venice* to all other places in *Italy*, as he did its Government to all those of the whole World, it being in his Opinion immutable by any external or internal causes. . . . Here he furnish'd himself with a Collection of all the valuable Books in the *Italian* language, especially treating of Politics, and contracted acquaintance with every one of whom he might receive any benefit by instruction or otherwise."[20] Anyone who has read any of Harrington's works will be inclined to accept the accuracy of this account. It is easy to imagine the young Englishman assiduously inquiring into the workings of the Venetian government and providing himself with the *opera omnia* of Machiavelli, Giannotti, and Contarini. We know that

19. *Coll. Works,* p. xv.
20. Ibid.

he was permitted to observe the intricate and stately process of balloting in the Grand Council; given his obvious penchant for clever and complex mechanical contrivances it is easy to understand the fascination the experience held for him. It is suggestive, as Russell Smith points out,[21] that Harrington was impressed by the government of Venice rather than by its architecture or its canals. Whatever his original motives for traveling, it is apparent that his interest in things political had been firmly established by this time.

Perhaps because he felt that in Venice he had seen the best that Europe could offer, or perhaps for other reasons, Harrington soon returned to England, taking with him not only his collection of political treatises but also a substantial knowledge of the workings of modern governments. The things he saw in Europe and the conclusions he drew from them were to remain with him for the rest of his life, constituting a major influence in the shaping of his thought.

The England to which Harrington returned already showed ominous signs of the impending conflict between king and parliament. The Petition of Right, the assassination of Buckingham, and the stormy session in Commons in January of 1629 when Eliot's resolutions were read, all had strengthened Charles I's determination to dissolve Parliament. On March 10, 1629, the momentous step was taken; for eleven years no Parliament was to meet in England. But in his attempt to impose on his subjects the absolutist government that flourished in France the King was beset by endless problems. In 1634, hard pressed by growing financial difficulties, Charles extended the hated ship-money tax to the entire country; in the same year John Hampden's dramatic legal protest against the tax won great popular support. Year by year the situation drew nearer to the perhaps already unavoidable crisis. It was inconceivable that

21. H. F. Russell Smith, *Harrington and His Oceana* . . . (Cambridge, 1914), p. 4.

anyone as deeply interested in political affairs as Harrington should long remain aloof from these events.

Unfortunately, our knowledge of Harrington's activities in the period between his return from the Continent and the end of the Civil Wars is fragmentary in the extreme. We do know that for some time he was a member of the royal household, having been appointed a Gentleman of the Privy Chamber Extraordinary in reward (so the story goes) for his remark about paying homage to the Pope. In this capacity he accompanied the King to Scotland during the first Bishops' War in 1639. On September 8, 1641, he lent the government £100 "for the Affaires of Ireland," that is, in connection with the bloody quelling of the Irish rebellion. A year later he lent an additional £800. In the autumn of 1642 the House of Commons ordered repayment of the first loan, plus five pounds, six shillings and eightpence interest. Actually, the major significance of these transactions is that they establish the fact that Harrington was at this period still living at Rand.[22]

After the start of the Civil Wars we find Harrington busying himself on behalf of the Elector Palatine, whose agent he had become. In August of 1644 he reported to the Committee of Both Kingdoms on the arrival of the Elector at Gravesend.[23] On February 17 of the next year he sent to Parliament a "Humble Remonstrance concerning the affairs of the Elector Palatine, stating the former orders of the Parliament and the Committee of the Revenue on the subject, the obstructions to their execution and the distressed condition of his Highness."[24] Upon receiving Harrington's petition the House of Commons appointed a com-

22. Commons Journals, 2, 783, 834.
23. This is, of course, not Frederick but his successor, Charles Louis. Calendar of State Papers (Domestic) for August 1644.
24. Historical Manuscripts Commission, *13th Report,* Appendix, Part I (London, 1891), p. 210.

mittee including among its members the elder Henry Vane, John Evelyn, and Sir Ralph Ashton (the husband of Harrington's sister Elizabeth), and further "Ordered, that Two Thousand Pounds, out of the first Monies that shall come in at the Committee of Accompts, next after the Assignments and Engagements already passed upon that Committee, shall be advanced and paid to Mr. James Harrington Esquire, upon Account, for the Supply of the urgent Necessities of the Prince Elector."[25] The lack of evidence to the contrary would seem to suggest that Harrington spent these momentous years in quiet retirement on his Lincolnshire estate, only occasionally bestirring himself in the interest of the Elector. In Toland's words: "His natural inclinations to study kept him from seeking after any public Imployments."[26]

Soon, however, Harrington was to place himself in the very center of political activity. At the beginning of the year 1647 the Scottish army surrendered the defeated Charles I to Parliament in return for back pay amounting to four hundred thousand pounds. A Parliamentary commission was sent to bring the King from Newcastle, where he was held captive, to London; some thought that the commission might perhaps be able to arrange a political settlement with the King. The commission left London on January 12; although the distance was only two hundred miles, the journey in midwinter took ten days. At some point along the route Harrington joined the party and continued north with it, partly out of curiosity and partly in the hope that he might be of help in effecting a reconciliation between the King and Parliament.

Where, then, did his sympathies lie in the great struggle that had rent English society? Unquestionably he was in principle a parliamentarian. Anthony Wood tells us that

25. Commons Journals, *4,* 58.
26. *Coll. Works,* p. xvi.

at the beginning of the wars he "sided with the presbyterians."[27] We know that in 1645 he had been active in collecting money in Lincolnshire for the parliamentary cause, and that in 1647 and 1648 Parliament had named him "commissioner for the parts of Holland" in Lincolnshire.[28] Nevertheless, we also know that during these troubled years he remained personally devoted to the King. Thus he was, as he doubtless recognized, in a peculiarly appropriate position to serve as a mediator.

By the time the Parliamentary commission reached Newcastle, Harrington had been chosen to wait upon the King; shortly thereafter the King appointed him a Groom of the Bedchamber. Thus he had succeeded in winning the favor and trust of both parties to the great political conflict of his time, and might with reason have felt that the peace of England rested momentarily in his hands. In fact, his position was impossibly ambiguous. It seems clear that by 1647 any reconciliation of the King and his enemies, especially those in the New Model Army, was not to be expected. Harrington was being forced to make a choice between the two—but this he steadfastly refused to do. Torn between his intellectual commitment to republicanism and his emotional commitment to the person of the King, he sought a solution that would allow him to maintain both loyalties. Even his human relationship with Charles reveals Harrington's dilemma. Speaking of precisely this period, John Aubrey tells us that "the King loved his company, only he would not endure to hear of a Commonwealth; and Mr. Harrington passionately loved his Majesty."[29] It requires little imagination to visualize Harrington, "in his

27. Anthony Wood, *Athenae Oxonienses*, ed. P. Bliss (London, 1817), *3*, 1119.

28. *Acts and Ordinances of the Interregnum*, ed. C. H. Firth and R. S. Rait (London, 1911), *1*, 662, 740, 969, 1086.

29. *Brief Lives*, ed. Oliver Lawson Dick (Ann Arbor, 1957), p. 124.

conversation very friendly and facetious and hospitable,"
trying to persuade Charles of the advantages to be gained
by compromise. Small wonder that years later he was to describe the King as "stiffe in disputes."[30] On the other hand,
his efforts were equally unstinting in the other direction—
"he made use of his Interest with his Friends in Parlament
to have Matters accommodated for the satisfaction of all
Partys."[31]

Thus as events moved nearer to their tragic culmination
Harrington continued his attempts to effect a reconciliation. In November of 1647 the King escaped to Carisbrooke
Castle on the Isle of Wight; Harrington either accompanied
him on this flight or joined him later, in time to participate
in the negotiation of the abortive treaty of Newport. Once
again he took upon himself the role of mediator: "During
the Treaty in the *Isle of Wight,* he frequently warn'd the
Divines of his acquaintance to take heed how far they prest
the King to insist upon any thing which, however it concern'd their Dignity, was no essential point of Religion; and
that such matters driven too far wou'd infallibly ruin all
the indeavours us'd for a Peace."[32] Wise counsel indeed,
but perhaps too late in the winter of 1647.

As is so often the case, it was the stronger party that made
further compromise impossible. Harrington's continuing
attempts to maintain friendly relations with both the King
and his opponents finally earned him the suspicion of the
latter. When Charles, once again a prisoner, was moved
from Wight to Hurst Castle in December, a forcible attempt
was made to discharge Harrington from his service. Toland
tells us that this was done because Harrington had "supported some of the King's arguments against the Parliamen-

30. *Oceana,* p. 49.
31. *Coll. Works,* p. xvi.
32. Ibid.

tary Commissioners at Newport."[33] Happily, a more detailed account of these events has survived in Thomas Herbert's *Memoirs of the Last Two Years of the Reign of King Charles I;*[34] since this is the earliest firsthand description of Harrington's behavior in a political situation it is worth quoting at some length:

> During his Majesty's Confinement at Hurst-Castle, it so happened, that Mr. Harrington, being one Morning in company with the Governour and some other Officers of the Army, he fell into some Discourse with them concerning the late Treaty at Newport, wherein he magnifi'd the King's Wisdom in his Arguments with the Commissioners upon the Propositions and Satisfaction the Parliament had in his Concessions, and probability of a happy Event, if this Force in removing him had not interven'd, and made an unhappy Fracture, which created Parties; enlarging upon his Majesty's learned Disputes with Mr. Vines, and the other Presbyterian Divines, with such Moderation, as gained Applause from all those that heard them argue: which Discourse, how inoffensive soever, and without Exception, at any other time and place, it appears that Truth is not at all times seasonable nor safe to be spoken, as by Mr. Harrington's Example was evidenced; for those captious Persons with whom he held Discourse, being full of Jealousies, and apt to wrest his Words to the worst Sense, they withdrew a little, and at their return told him plainly, They were dissatisfied with what he had said. He pray'd them to instance wherein. They reply'd, In all Particulars; which, when he began to repeat for his own Justification and their better Understanding, they interrupted

33. Ibid., pp. xvi–xvii.
34. (London, 1813), pp. 128–30.

him, and told him in plain terms, They could not suffer his Attendance any longer about the King. With
which Proceeding and Dismiss, without acquainting
him with the occasion, was ill resented by the King,
who had Mr. Harrington in his good Esteem, being a
Gentleman qualifi'd with special Parts, and having
found him trusty, his Service was the more acceptable;
but blam'd him nevertheless for not being more wary
amongst Men, that at such a time were full of Jeal-
ousies, and very little obliging to his Majesty.

There is a certain irony in the picture of Charles I urging
Harrington to behave in a moderate and politic fashion—
something that he himself was seldom if ever able to
achieve. Nevertheless, it would seem that Harrington's position had finally been shown to be untenable. He contrived
to remain in the King's service for a short time, and when,
at Windsor, he was required to swear that he would neither
assist nor conceal the King's escape, he firmly refused to
turn his back on his friend. As a consequence of his refusal
he was discharged and detained in custody until Major
General Ireton obtained his release. On the thirtieth of January, 1649, he was present at Whitehall to witness the execution of his "beloved friend" Charles I.

The death of Charles I marked the beginning of a new
and more important period in Harrington's life. That the
change was not immediately apparent can be explained
simply in terms of the great shock which Harrington received from the execution of his friend and his king. Even
ten years later Aubrey was to report that he "oftentimes
heard him speak of King Charles I with the greatest zeale
and passion imaginable, and that his death gave him so
great grief that he contracted a disease by it."[35] For several
years after 1649 Harrington seems to have been undecided

35. *Brief Lives* (Dick ed.), p. 124.

as to his future course. Evidently he considered becoming
a poet, but we are informed that "his muse was rough."[36]
At least we do know that he temporarily ceased his political
activities; undoubtedly his failure to achieve some compromise that might have saved Charles had greatly discouraged
him.

Toland tells us that following Charles' execution Harrington took to his library and was thought by many to be
melancholy. Probably this judgment was correct. But after
the experiment with poesy had been abandoned, we once
more find him turning to political affairs—this time on a
more theoretical level. If Harrington's temporary absten-
tion from politics can be explained by the execution of
Charles I, so too can his return to this field. There can be
no doubt of his abiding interest in political matters, but
there can also be no question that his personal relationship
with Charles was politically embarrassing to him. Not only
did tact prevent him from forcefully expressing his republican ideas, it also won him the suspicion of those with
whom he would normally have agreed. Now that Charles
was dead there was nothing to keep Harrington from devoting himself to the propagation of his republican principles. The immediate explanation of Harrington's return
to the world of politics is to be found in his friendship with
Henry Nevill. An author himself, and later an exponent of
Harringtonian ideas in Parliament, Nevill is reputed to
have been responsible for the writing of Harrington's first
and most important work, *The Commonwealth of Oceana*,
which he began in 1654.[37] Aubrey tells us that "Mr. Henry
Nevil persuaded him to improve his proper talent, viz. Po-

36. Ibid.
37. We can infer this date from Harrington's statement that the
writing of the *Oceana* took about two years. See his "Epistle to the
Reader," *Oceana*, p. 5.

liticall Reflections. Whereupon he writ his Oceana."[38]

Actually, there are several theories concerning the circumstances under which the *Oceana* was written. Aubrey seems to have subscribed to the view, apparently originated by Hobbes, that Henry Nevill actually helped Harrington with the writing of the book. Thus, "Mr. T. Hobbes was wont to say that Mr. Nevil had a finger in that pye, and 'tis like enough."[39] Aside from being the only evidence that Hobbes was at all aware of Harrington's work, this theory is of little interest. Harrington's frequent assertions, in a different connection, that the writing of a book can be the work of only one man would seem to belie the accuracy of the theory.[40] Russell Smith feels that Harrington wrote the book "in response to a request for some public protest against the Instrument of Government."[41] Although this is a very plausible explanation, such speculation would seem to be more interesting than fruitful, and might perhaps even be misleading. Harrington himself explained that he wrote the book in order to prove, against "the usurper Cromwell," that a true commonwealth was possible in England. But since this explanation was offered during Harrington's inquisition by the Royalists in 1661 we may perhaps doubt its disinterestedness. It certainly appears rather paradoxical in view of the fact that the book was dedicated to none other than "the usurper Cromwell," although of course in more respectful language. Without seeking any more specific cause, we may conclude simply that the *Oceana* was written during this period of political turmoil in order to express its author's suggested remedies.

38. *Brief Lives* (Dick ed.), p. 124.
39. Ibid.
40. See, for instance, *Oceana*, p. 59: "a Book or a Building hath not been known to attaine to perfection, if it have not had a sole Author."
41. *Harrington and His Oceana*, p. 7.

Having completed the book late in 1656, Harrington was quite naturally anxious to have it published. It was therefore delivered to a printer[42] probably early in August of 1656. At this point, however, we learn of various difficulties which arose as a result of official suspicions. Evidently fearing that the work would be seized before it could be published, Harrington apportioned the actual printing among three firms. As he put it, "a Spanell [i.e. spaniel] questing hath sprung my Book out of one Presse into two other."[43] The event proved Harrington's fears well founded. Before publication, and perhaps even before the printing had been completed, the book was in fact seized by the authorities. All Harrington's attempts to secure its release proved ineffectual. At last in desperation he remembered that Cromwell's favorite daughter, Lady Claypole, "acted the part of a Princess very naturally, obliging all persons with her civility, and frequently interceding for the unhappy."[44] Therefore, although he did not know the lady, Harrington determined to call on her for help.

Toland gives us an amusing account of their interview: while waiting in the anteroom for Lady Claypole to appear, Harrington took to playing with her small daughter, and was holding the child in his arms when she appeared.

> Whereupon he stepping towards her, and setting the Child down at her feet, said, "Madam, 'tis well you are com at this nick of time, or I had certainly stolen this pretty little Lady." "Stolen her," reply'd the Mother, "pray, what to do with her? for she is yet too young to becom your mistress." "Madam," said he, "tho her charms assure her of a more considerable Conquest, yet I must confess it is not love but revenge that

42. Livewell Chapman was the original printer.
43. *Oceana*, p. 8.
44. *Coll. Works,* p. xix.

prompted me to commit this theft." "Lord," answer'd
the Lady again, "what injury have I don you that you
should steal my Child?" "None at all," reply'd he, "but
that you might be induc'd to prevail with your Father
to do me justice, by restoring my Child that he has
stolen." But she urging that it was impossible, because
her Father had Children enough of his own; he told
her at last it was the issue of his brain which was mis-
represented to the Protector, and taken out of the Press
by his order.[45]

Impressed by this gambit, Lady Claypole promised to do
what Harrington wished, providing that his "child" contained nothing that would be prejudicial to her father.
Harrington assured her that "it was only a kind of Political
Romance," that he would be quite willing to dedicate it to
Cromwell, and that she would be given one of the first
copies. On these assurances Lady Claypole agreed to inter-
cede with her father, which in fact she did.[46]

45. Ibid. Quotation marks added.

46. The chief source for this account is Toland's biography of
Harrington, appearing as a preface to his editions of the *Collected
Works*. The whole question of the events surrounding the original
publication of the *Oceana* is a difficult one. The great scholar S. B.
Liljegren believes that the actual printing of the book took place
between the entry in the *Stationers' Register*—Sept. 19, 1656—and
the advertisement in the *Mercurius Politicus*—Oct. 29, Nov. 6, 1656;
viz. his *Oceana*, p. xi. Although the book was unquestionably printed
before the latter date, I doubt that the entry in the *Register* indicates
the day on which the printing began. My reason for this is the fact
that the *Register* mentions that the book is dedicated to Cromwell.
If we accept the story of Harrington's difficulties with Cromwell, and
of Lady Claypole's intercession, then it is obvious that the original
work on the book, which was interrupted by Cromwell's agents, must
have occurred before Sept. 19, since by that date the book had already
been dedicated to the Lord Protector. Actually, Liljegren does not
accept this story, and therefore his interpretation is wholly consistent.
I see no reason not to accept Toland's account, particularly in view

On the nineteenth of September, 1656, the following entry appeared in the *Stationers' Register:*

> Livewell Chapman Entered . . . under the hand of Master Thrale, a booke entituled *The Commonwealth of Oceana,* dedicated to his highnes the Lord Protector of the Commonwealth of England, Scotland & Ireland by James Harrington.[47]

This constitutes the first official notice of the existence of Harrington's work. Whether it is an announcement of the publication of the work, or simply of the delivery of the manuscript to the printer, cannot definitely be determined. It is true that the weekly newspaper *Mercurius Politicus* during the week October 29–November 6 listed the *Oceana* in its "Advertisement of Books newly published," but this does not preclude the possibility that the book had been published six weeks earlier. In any case, this listing of the book makes it possible for us to state definitely that the book was published sometime shortly before November 6, 1656.

The original edition of the *Oceana* is in large quarto, consisting of about 280 pages. Possibly because of the difficulties attending its printing, the book contains several errors of pagination and some two hundred textual errors. There are two title pages, the first containing the name of the work, an introductory quotation from Horace,[48] and the name of the publisher; the second title page contains the

---

of Harrington's remark about the "spanell questing" and the fact that the *Oceana* did appear with a separate title page containing the dedication to Cromwell. Probably this is a question which can never be satisfactorily answered, and fortunately it is not a vital one.

47. P. 503.
48. Horace, *Satires,* I, 1, 68 ff.

name of the work, the dedication to Cromwell, and the
author's name. It seems quite likely that this second title
page was added by Harrington after his interview with Lady
Claypole; if this is true, we may wonder whether it was
Harrington's original intention to publish the book anonymously.[49] Although its contents will be discussed in detail
below, we may here consider briefly the general form of
this work. Its title, *The Commonwealth of Oceana,* refers
to an imaginary polity which Harrington describes at great
length. For this reason it has been usual to include the
book among the political utopias, but in fact this would
seem to be a dubious classification. The author makes no
attempt to conceal the fact that Oceana is England, although it is an England transformed by his pen into a
Harringtonian commonwealth. Indeed, his introductory
quotation from Horace informs his English readers that
"mutato nomine, de te Fabula narratur." If we mean by a
utopia a state of ideal perfection, Oceana is not a utopia.
It is, rather, an improved England—but still an England
limited in its perfection by many inescapable political and
historical facts. It can perhaps more profitably be compared
to the "best possible states" of Plato and Aristotle, among
others, rather than to More's "nowhere."[50] The work itself
is divided into four sections. The first is an extended discussion of the general principles of politics, the second describes the creation of the Commonwealth of Oceana, the
third embodies an account of the structure and function of
this Commonwealth, and the fourth shows some of the
consequences of such a government. The work is large,
ponderous, and rather badly written. As one acute observer

49. Russell Smith erroneously states (*Harrington and His Oceana,*
p. 11) that the *Oceana* was published without the author's name. It
is probable that he overlooked the second title page.
50. For a similar view, see Russell Smith, *Harrington and His
Oceana,* pp. 12–13.

has said, "The reader who survives [Harrington's] discussion of the constitution of the Sanhedrim is unlikely to reproach him with lack of sobriety."[51] But the fact remains that in it Harrington did manage to express, in more or less definitive form, all the ideas which characterize his political thought.

The publication of the *Oceana* marked the beginning of the most active and productive period of Harrington's life. It is no exaggeration to say that, with the exception of the writing of the *Oceana* itself, everything that Harrington achieved and everything for which he is remembered was accomplished during the four years between 1656 and the restoration of the monarchy. For this reason, we would do well to break off our narrative at this point and consider briefly what sort of person Harrington was when he entered this most fruitful period of his long life. In 1656 Harrington was forty-five years old and apparently financially independent. As the oldest of his parents' eight children he felt a certain responsibility for his brothers and sisters and "made it his . . . care so to provide for each of 'em as might render 'em independent of others, and easy to themselves."[52] He seems never to have been gainfully employed, his inheritance being apparently sufficient to provide not only for his own needs but for those of the entire family. "He was of a very liberal and compassionat nature, nor could he indure to see a Friend want any thing he might spare; and when the Relief that was necessary exceded the bounds of his Estate, he persuaded his Sisters not only to contribute themselves, but likewise to go about to the rest of their Relations to complete what was wanting."[53] As the oldest son of a solid and prosperous gentle family he enjoyed an assured

51. Tawney, "Harrington's Interpretation of His Age," p. 13.
52. *Coll. Works*, p. xv.
53. Ibid., p. xvi.

social position and was connected with many of the most
important families in England. His two sisters married into
the Ashton and Evelyn families, and his younger brother
was a successful architect and an early member of the Royal
Society.[54] Among his friends were many men of considerable importance—Henry Nevill, John Wildman, Andrew
Marvell, and John Aubrey were perhaps the most outstanding. In addition, Harrington had been an intimate of the
late King Charles and was, in a sense, an employee of the
Elector Palatine. In short, we may say that Harrington's
social position was eminently respectable and that he associated naturally with the intellectual and political leaders
of his time.

Furthermore, it seems that personally Harrington was
an extremely attractive figure. He impressed almost every-
one he met with his wit, his manners, his tolerance, and his
considerable learning. A study of the *Oceana* indicates
something of the breadth and depth of its author's learning.
He had a thorough knowledge of Greek, Latin, and Italian,
and could read Hebrew, French, and German. He had read
extensively in the Scriptures and theology, as well as in
classical literature and history. As a political theorist he
was well versed in political writings, from Plato through
Hobbes, and had an impressive background in European
history. We will examine more closely the extent of Harrington's reading when we come to consider the sources of
his thought; for the present it will suffice to note the general
area in which he specialized. From this we may conclude
that, educationally as well as personally, he was well prepared for the career on which he embarked in 1656.

Little is known of the *Oceana's* reception. Toland tells
us that Lady Claypole showed her copy to Cromwell, who

54. Ibid., p. xiii.

commented, "the Gentleman had like to trapan him out of his Power, but what he got by the Sword he would not quit for a little paper Shot."[55] This is not precisely a characteristic Cromwellian statement, however, and its authenticity is very doubtful. Probably it was invented by a friend of Harrington's who wished to explain the Lord Protector's lack of interest in the *Oceana* in a light favorable to the author.[56] We do know that Lady Ashton, Harrington's sister, sent a copy of the book to an Anglican clergyman of her acquaintance named Dr. Ferne. On November 4, 1656, Ferne wrote to Lady Ashton expressing his displeasure with her brother's book, especially with its religious implications. "And lamentable it is," he wrote, "to see so many (especially Gentlemen of good Parts) so opinionate, so boldly meddling in Matters of Religion, as if they had forgot, or did not understand their Article [sic] of the Catholick Church."

Probably pleased to receive this attention, unfavorable though it was, Harrington immediately wrote to Dr. Ferne, enclosing a list of questions prompted by the doctor's criticisms. Ferne replied and Harrington then answered his further objections. Finally on January 3, 1657, Harrington published the entire exchange—in which he, of course, had had the last word—in a pamphlet entitled whimsically *Pian piano*.[57] In the preface to this pamphlet Harrington made a statement which may perhaps help us to understand why his interest in political affairs manifested itself in writing rather than in political activity. "I seldom talk with him that does not confute me," he said, "nor ever read that which did not confirm me: Wherefore if I be glad to take a man in black and white, you will not blame me."[58] It might be that this inability to argue successfully was the

55. Ibid., p. xx.
56. Toland himself is a likely candidate.
57. *Coll. Works,* pp. xxiv and 549 ff.
58. Ibid., p. 549.

result of the "tolerance" and "politeness" for which Harrington was noted. The correspondence with Ferne and the publication of *Pian piano* mark the first public reaction to Harrington's magnum opus, and in them we can detect the beginnings of several significant trends. Already we can see that Harrington's work aroused immediate opposition. It is interesting to note that his initial antagonist was a clergyman who took exception chiefly to the religious parts of the book. This episode is our first indication too of Harrington's apparent delight in arguing the principles of political theory.

The year following the publication of Harrington's first writings was marked by continuing political experimentation. The so-called "Humble Petition and Advice" (March–May, 1657) altered the constitution of the Protectorate by adding a second house to the Parliament, reducing the powers of the Protector, and establishing toleration for all trinitarian Christians except Episcopalians and Roman Catholics. On the eighth of May, after considerable soul-searching and political calculation, Cromwell rejected the title of king which had been urged on him.

In these circumstances Harrington's work achieved a certain prominence. Early in March the weekly newspaper *Mercurius Politicus* began a series of "Letters from Utopia" devoted to ridiculing various proposals for the establishment of a new form of government in England. Quite naturally Harrington received his share of attention. The meticulous attention to detail which made the *Oceana* such a dull book also made it a perfect target for this sort of humor. In one of these letters[59] the author pictured the landing in Utopia of "a jolly crew of the inhabitants of the island of Oceana in the company of the learned Author

59. *Merc. Pol.*, No. 352, March 5–12, 1657.

himself," and as a necessary remedy proposed the appointment of "a State Droll . . . as a most necessary officer to
correct all that presume to Print or Dispute about Models of
Government." In the fifth, and last, of these "Letters" the
following passage appeared:

> The Agrarian-Wits of the five and fiftieth order, of
> the Commonwealth of Oceana, do humbly conceive,
> That no Government whatsoever is of any Weight but
> in their Balance, and that if you go to Venice to learn
> to Cog a Die with a Balloting Box you'll soon get
> money enough to purchase a better Island than Uto-
> pia, and there you may erect a commonwealth of your
> own. For (SIR) you are to know, its no great charge,
> when the accompt is cast up, as it is set down by the
> learned Author and founder of our most famous
> Oceana . . .

After an account of the cost of balloting apparatus in Oceana, amounting to a total of £339,000 and following Harrington's account exactly, the "Letter" concludes: "In the
mean time you may take notice, That we have quitted the
Island of Utopia for a time and perhaps for ever, being now
landed in Oceana to carry on the Plantation of that Country, where the learned Discoverer has promised to settle Dr.
Ferne in a fat Bishoprick, if he please but to wright [sic]
against him. For my part, I have done with him, and all the
Builders of Castles in the aire."[60]

The effect of such satire is hard to assess; it was clearly
designed for an age that was much concerned with the
business of colonization. And doubtless the reference to
Dr. Ferne was not lost on those who had seen how Harrington had managed to turn the doctor's criticisms to his own
advantage in *Pian piano*. But the most important fact about

60. Ibid., No. 356, April 2–9, 1657.

these "Letters" is that they indicate that Harrington had, by the spring of 1657, become something of a public figure in England. Certainly their brand of humor presupposes some knowledge of Harrington's writings, both in general and in detail. Thus, regardless of whether he had been successful in convincing his countrymen, Harrington had brought his ideas to their attention.

In the spring of 1657 the first serious reply to the *Oceana* was published. It was the *Considerations on Mr. Harrington's Commonwealth of Oceana* written by Matthew Wren, son of the former Bishop of Ely. Evidently Wren had been sent a copy of Harrington's book by Dr. Wilkins, the warden of Wadham College who was to be instrumental in the founding of the Royal Society. In his introductory Epistle he thanks Wilkins "for the occasion you have given me of reading the Commonwealth of Oceana; which book I finde to be so much the Discourse of good companies, that not to have seen it would expose a man to much shame." Wren's tone in dealing with Harrington is civil, but he soon voices the criticism which has been echoed by subsequent generations: "There are in it many things deserving of praise: a sprightly expression, and a sort of oratory well becoming a Gentleman, good remarques out of ancient and modern histories, and a judgment not ill founded upon past and present policie, were it not for a certain violence in seeking to draw all things into servitude to his Hypothesis." Like the author of the "Letters from Utopia," Wren adopts an essentially pragmatic, antidogmatic position and effects a certain contempt for mere theorizers about politics:

> I beseech you Sir, are not we the writers of politiques somewhat a ridiculous sort of people? Is it not a fine piece of folly for private men sitting in their cabinets to rack their brains about models of government? Certainly our labours make a very pleasant recreation for

those great personages who sitting at the helm of affairs have by their large experience not onely acquired
the perfect art of ruling, but have attained also to the
comprehension of the nature and foundation of government: To them I believe we shall appear just as
wise as the philosopher who read a lecture of the duty
of a good commander before the greatest captain of
his age.

After these civilities, Wren gets down to the serious business of disputation, attacking Harrington on twelve specific
points drawn from the Preliminaries of the *Oceana*. The
attack was an intelligent one and the objections which it
raised were of a fundamental nature, relating less to Harrington's political arguments than to the metaphysical
foundations of his work. For example, dealing with Harrington's discussion of the passions, Wren writes, "seeing
the whole force of the argument rests upon the similitude
of government with the soul of man, we may be instructed
what the soul is, and what the whole philosophy belonging
to it. And then and not before, will it be the time to consider how far the similitude between that and government
will hold true." Here Wren has put his finger on what is
unquestionably the weakest aspect of Harrington's book:
its rather casual and unsophisticated use of philosophical
terms. Again, in commenting on the discussion in *Oceana*
on the subject of "the common interest": ". . . the question
being, whether there be any such primary interest of mankind differing from that of every particular man, he takes
it for granted that there is such a common right or interest
. . . without proffering any other proof than the testimonies
of Hooker and Grotius; Whose opinions cannot oblige us
beyond the reasons on which they are founded." Wren's
searching questions may be taken as typical of one reaction
aroused by the *Oceana:* an opposition by trained philoso-

phers, coming primarily from Oxford and specifically from
the group around Dr. Wilkins that was to become the nu-
cleus of the Royal Society.

At about the same time Harrington was subjected to another attack from a very different quarter. Two Protestant
clergymen, the Episcopalian Dr. Hammond and the Presby-
terian Dr. Seaman, had written books about the ordination
of the clergy. Copies were sent to Harrington to refute his
statements on the subject in the *Oceana,* in which he had
defended an extremely democratic view of the process of
ordination in the early church. The subject is a technical
one, revolving around the question of the exact meaning of
the words *chirotonia* and *chirothesia* in the Greek scriptures.[61] From our point of view it is significant simply as
an example of the second major source of opposition to
Harrington's writings. Because of the catholicity of his
sources, and his insistence upon using the Bible for historical evidence about ancient government, he managed to
ruffle the feelings of innumerable clergymen. Furthermore,
his own essentially pagan view of the position of religion in
his projected commonwealth was calculated to antagonize
all religious extremists in seventeenth-century England.
For these reasons, he soon began to be subjected to almost
continuous attacks from theologians of every variety, rang-
ing from Anglican bishops to Fifth Monarchy men.

In his *Considerations* Matthew Wren had slyly mocked
Harrington's fondness for controversy: "I am not ignorant
Sir with what artifice and importunity Mr. Harrington hath
courted opposition from others." True to this pattern, Harrington was quick to reply to both Wren and his clerical
critics in a large work entitled *The Prerogative of Popular
Government.* Although the exact date of publication of this
book cannot be determined, there is good reason to suppose

61. *Chirotonia:* voting by show of hands; election by the people.
Chirothesia: laying-on of hands.

that it first appeared in November 1657, just fourteen weeks
after the publication of Wren's attack. The book consists
of 281 pages and is divided into two approximately equal
parts. The first is devoted to Wren's criticisms, and is described as "containing the first Preliminary of *Oceana*, in-
larg'd, interpreted, and vindicated from all such Mistakes
or Slanders as have bin alleg'd against it under the notion
of Objections." As this suggests, Harrington's tone had become appreciably less mild and detached. It seems that
Wren's book had angered him, and that he was aware of a
growing opposition in the universities. In a rather sardonic
Epistle, he dedicated the first book of the *Prerogative* "to
the Mirth and Discourse of the University Wits" who, he
suggested, "are good at two things, at diminishing a Commonwealth and at multiplying a Louse."[62] The second half
of the book is devoted to an infinitely tedious discussion of
ordination, in which we may detect a growing anticlerical-
ism on Harrington's part. Although he had been skeptical
of religion before, now he claims to have discovered "the
Arcanum or Secret of that Antipathy which is between a
Clergy and a Popular Government, and of that Sympathy
which is between the Miter and the Crown."[63] We will
have occasion soon to examine the substance of Harrington's arguments as they developed during these years of controversy. For the moment it will suffice to note that with
the publication of the *Prerogative* he had embarked on the
task that was to occupy him for the remainder of his productive life—the repetition, enlargement, and defense of
the ideas of the *Oceana*.

We have no information concerning Harrington's activities during the remaining weeks of 1657. The next event
that provided him with an occasion to express his views was
the publication in February 1658 of a book entitled *The*

62. See below, pp. 90–91, for an echo of this sentiment.
63. *Coll. Works*, p. 380.

Stumbling-Block of Disobedience. Written by Peter Heylyn, though published anonymously, this book contained a
carefully reasoned attack on the doctrine of the right of
resistance to tyranny.[64] The author sought to support his
position by extensive references to Calvin's *Institutes,* a
potent ally during the Interregnum, and it was to this part
of his argument that Harrington turned his attention in his
reply, which was published early in 1658 under the title
*The Stumbling-Block of Disobedience and Rebellion Cun-
ningly imputed by P. H. unto Calvin, remov'd in a Letter
to the Said P. H. from J. H.* Once again his concern was to
support popular institutions by historical and scriptural
example, refuting his opponents and further publicizing
his own theories. Evidence of his success in the latter undertaking at least is to be found in a rather sinister note of the
proceedings of the Council of State for June 22, 1658; at
this meeting the Council ordered that a committee consisting of Sydenham, Fleetwood, Wolsley, Jones, the Lord
Chamberlain, Lisle, and Thurloe should "read those books
lately published by William Sanderson and Mr. Harrington, and report."[65] We do not know for certain the occasion
for this order, but it is likely that the Council's quarry was
Heylyn rather than Harrington; in any case, there is no
evidence that Harrington was in any way persecuted by the
authorities during these years.

Preoccupied though he was with politics and political
controversy, Harrington nevertheless managed to find time
to publish two volumes of verse translations from Virgil:
two eclogues and two books of the *Aeneid* in 1658, four
more books of the *Aeneid* in 1659. Peripheral as these may

64. Heylyn had been a lecturer in historical geography at Oxford
and a supporter of Archbishop Laud. The Council of State initiated
proceedings against him in 1658.
65. Calendar of State Papers (Domestic), 1658–1659, p. 71; see also
pp. 75–77.

seem to a study of Harrington's political thought, the fact
is that they are among the most interesting Harringtonian
documents. In the first place, Harrington found it impossible to keep his political theories out of his translations. In
the fourth book of the *Aeneid*, for example, we find him
translating the innocuous words *"Legiferae Cereri"* with
the following gratuitous couplets:

> Lawgiving Ceres that inventing corn
> Is she, of whom bright Empire first was born,
> While men, for Acorns tasting bread, began
> To parcel fields by Laws Agrarian,
> And thence (as lots have chanc'd to rise or fall)
> Became the prize of One, or Few, or All.

Again, to the translation of the eclogues he appends a series
of nine queries on the relation of property and power, and
a truly excruciating ode, "On the Political Ballance," complete with a footnote referring to two books of the Old
Testament.

More interesting, however, is the insight which these
books give us into Harrington's character and personality.
Here, for almost the first time, one begins to understand
why he was so often described by his contemporaries as a
singularly pleasant and witty young man; especially in the
prefaces to his *Essay upon Two of Virgil's Eclogues* his
true disposition shines through as it seldom does in his
political writings. Beginning with a gently ironic quotation
from Montaigne—"Ce ne sont pas nos folies qui me font
rire, Ce sont nos sagesses"—he proceeds to discuss in an
extraordinarily felicitous manner his views of literature,
and particularly of poetry. This Epistle to the Reader is so
much the most graceful and attractive of Harrington's
writings that it merits quotation at length:

> I have reason'd to as much purpose as if I had rimed,

and now I think I shall rime to as much purpose as if
I had reason'd. All's one, a man that hath nothing to
entertain himself withal but a pen, must be contented
as others be, or should be with their estates, whether
narrow or plentiful. Be a man's estate as narrow as it
will, his natural necessities require of the earth variety
of fruits; much more doth his delight that hath a garden, that it should produce him variety of flowers. A
man's study, unless it be Law or Theology, which commonly is his bread, is his garden, in which he may af-
firm a rose or a violet to be the best flower, and yet be
unwilling it should not be furnished with greater variety. Indeed not Nature only, but her Maker is apparently delighted with variety; his plantations of
heaven and earth are not indued or sowed with one,
but divers influences, or seeds, and his nearer resem-
blance the soul of man is impregnated with divers
faculties. The heavens and the earth have their seasons
to play with flowers as well as to work at harvest: and
the soul of man is well indued with phansie as with
reason and memory. . . . Phansie of her self (that is
where the other two do not check but obey her) produceth but a flower, which is Poetry. . . . it is clear
enough that poetry is not *the wine of Divels,* but a
sprightly liquor infused into the soul by God himself.

True to this debonair view of the poet's calling as one
dedicated primarily to pleasure and variety, Harrington's
few original verses are of the sort that are described as "Cavalier": elegant, lighthearted, filled with conceits. The following, which is perhaps the best, is called, "On Florella's
coming to be a maid of honour":

> When in Florella first I view'd
> The charms which more then I have ru'd,
> She past her time in speckled bowers

And dwelt among the Countrey flowers.
My wonder lending fame a wing
This beauty to the Court to bring,
The virgin streight began to wear
An heart as hard as she was fair.
So Divers from the deep invite
The hidden coral to the light,
When at the touch of air alone
The tender plant turns precious stone.

Strange lines for a serious republican political theorist to be publishing in the disturbed years of the Interregnum! But lines, at least, that will save us from the error of viewing Harrington as yet another dour sectarian or political fanatic. Certainly no one can deny his fundamental seriousness, or his genuine concern with political problems; but it is refreshing to find that these existed side by side with a delight in beauty and variety and an engaging lightheartedness. It is no exaggeration to say that the softening and civilizing effect of these qualities can be detected in Harrington's political writings, although there they tend to be buried beneath layers of wearisome erudition and unedifying polemic.

After his poetical *jeu d'esprit* Harrington returned once more to matters of primary concern. A few weeks after the death of Oliver Cromwell, in November of 1658, his next political treatise was published. It was called *Seven Models of a Commonwealth* and its subtitle informed the reader that it contained "Brief Directions Shewing how a fit and perfect Model of Popular Government May be made, found or understood." The first part of this pamphlet was devoted to a description of the "commonwealths"[66] of Israel, Sparta, Athens, Rome, Venice, Holland, and one fictitious com-

66. We will have occasion later to discuss Harrington's use of this term.

monwealth; the second part consisted of a brief description of "a model of a commonwealth fitted to the present state of this nation."[67] It is interesting to note that here for the first time Harrington explicitly omitted any description of the balloting system which he had treated so thoroughly in the *Oceana*. By this time he had obviously realized that an overattention to detail had made his first book both dull and somewhat ridiculous. As he explained in *Seven Models,* "The use of the Ballot, being as full of prolixity and abstruseness in writing, as of dispatch and facility in practice, is presum'd throout."[68] In his preface Harrington explained his reasons for writing this pamphlet: "There is nothing more apparent [he wrote], than that this Nation is greatly disquieted and perplex'd thro a complication of two Causes: the one, that the present state therof is not capable of any other Form than that only of a Popular Government; the other, that they are too few who understand what is the Form or Model naturally necessary to a Popular Government. . . . For these Infirmitys I shall offer som Remedy by a brief Discourse."[69]

Harrington's characterization of the situation as disquieted and perplexed was unquestionably accurate. Although Richard Cromwell had succeeded to his father's position with little confusion, it was evident that the form of government was far from being settled. In desperate need of money, Richard summoned a Parliament to meet on January 27, 1659. Although the elections were conducted with the usual Cromwellian machinations, fifty republicans managed to win seats. And of these fifty, at least ten were followers of Harrington, notable among whom was Henry Nevill.[70] We may pause here briefly in order to consider

67. *Coll. Works,* p. 531.
68. Ibid., p. 537.
69. Ibid., p. 524.
70. Russell Smith, *Harrington and His Oceana,* pp. 81 ff.

the exact nature of the Harringtonian position in 1659. In his speech opening the Parliament of 1656, Oliver Cromwell had attempted to classify the various bodies of political opinion in England at the time. First, of course, there were those who supported the Cromwellian program and there were the Royalists. But in addition there were three groups of "discontented spirits," as Cromwell called them. There were the Levellers, who had been willing to join with the Cavaliers in 1655; there were the Fifth Monarchy men, "of notions more scraphical"; and there were the disaffected republicans, who went "under a finer name or notion" and called themselves Commonwealthsmen.[71]

It was in this last group that Harrington and his followers belonged. What was their political program in 1659? In the first place, they made many gestures of friendship toward Richard and the Protectorate. "This man," said Nevill, "is, at least, actually, if not legally, settled the Chief Magistrate."[72] And, furthermore, the followers of Harrington took great pains to point out that the existence of a single chief magistrate was not incompatible with their aims. "We that are for a Commonwealth, are for a single person, senate and popular assembly."[73] Since the "single person" was already present in the person of Richard, the attention of the Harringtonians was directed toward the "senate and popular assembly." Specifically, they were interested in arranging the qualifications for election to the Commons and the composition of the "other house" in such a fashion as to reflect their notions of the balance of property.

71. W. C. Abbott, *The Writings and Speeches of Oliver Cromwell* (Cambridge, Mass., 1947), *4*, 260–79; and also C. H. Firth, *The Last Years of the Protectorate* (London, 1909), *1*, 6.

72. *The Diary of Thomas Burton, Esq.* . . . . (London, 1828), *3*, 132; for a more complete discussion see Russell Smith, *Harrington and His Oceana*, pp. 81 ff.

73. Ibid.

A more vivid appreciation of the Harringtonian position may perhaps be gained by noting the terms in which Nevill expressed himself in the Parliament of 1659. Essentially he argued that the composition of the new equivalent of the House of Lords, which was the chief political issue of the time, should reflect the balance of property in England. As we shall have ample occasion to see, this was one of the central points of Harrington's general theory of politics. Said Nevill:

> The Commons till Henry VII never exercised a negative voice. All depended on the Lords. In that time it would have been hard to have found in this house so many gentlemen of estates. The gentry do not now depend upon the peerage. The balance is in the gentry. They have all the lands. Now Lords old or new must be supported by the people. . . . The people of England will not suffer a negative voice to be in those who have not a natural power over them.[74]

But if the "other house" must be a House of Lords, what function can it perform? To this question Nevill replied that "the Other House may be such a House as is only preparatory to this, as, among popular assemblies in other commonwealths, there was an assembly to propound laws, and another to enact them, and a single person to put all in execution."[75]

This was all quite orthodox Harringtonian doctrine applied to the situation in hand with considerable skill. Another follower of Harrington in the Parliament of 1659 was Captain Baynes, the member from Appleby. Having considerably enriched himself by dealings in the property of dispossessed Royalists, he felt a strong personal interest

74. Burton, *Diary, 3,* 132.
75. Ibid., p. 321.

in Harrington's idea of balance.[76] And like Nevill he gave voice to this idea in the Parliament. Said he,

> All government is built on propriety [private property], else the poor must rule it. . . . The people were too hard for the King in property; and then in arms too hard for him. We must either lay a foundation in property or else it will not stand. Property is generally now with the people; the government therefore must be there. If you make a single person he must be a servant and not a lord; *major singulis, minor omnibus.* If you can find a House of Lords to balance property, do it. Else let a senate be chosen by the election of the people on the same account.[77]

In short, the Harringtonians devoted their energies primarily to the creation of an elective second chamber. Failing this, they at least insisted that no hereditary House of Lords should be able to veto popularly approved legislation. For the time being they were satisfied to concentrate on this limited program, working within the framework of the Protectorate.

While his followers were active in Parliament Harrington himself continued to develop and publicize his theories. When on April 22, 1659, Richard was persuaded to dissolve Parliament, Harrington sensed that the time had come for a fundamental change in the government of England. On May 2 he published a pamphlet entitled *Pour enclouer le canon*, setting forth his view of the situation.[78] The people of England, he felt, were at that time "twenty to one for Monarchy," but they were merely deceived by the name. Actually they desired to return to a "Government of Laws," which they erroneously thought must mean a monarchy.

76. See Russell Smith, *Harrington and His Oceana*, p. 81.
77. Burton, *Diary, 3,* 147.
78. *Coll. Works,* pp. 595 ff.

On the other hand, the army and "the most active Part of the People" were determined to establish a true commonwealth. And consequently a commonwealth would be established. But would it be an "equal commonwealth"? Only two things, Harrington said, could prevent the new commonwealth from being equal—"a Senate for Life, or an Optimacy."[79] Having presented this analysis Harrington proceeded to outline in two brief paragraphs the means by which an equal commonwealth could, and should, be established in England. Since it was probable on May 2 that the Long Parliament would be recalled, Harrington argued that that body should introduce the necessary measures. Aside from its close connection with political affairs, the most notable feature of this pamphlet is its unprecedented conciseness. Harrington obviously was determined to present his program in the simplest possible terms, and the contrast with his *Oceana* is striking.

On May 7 the Rump of the Long Parliament reconvened and Richard Cromwell was persuaded to resign his office. As a result of this encouraging turn of events the Harringtonians redoubled their efforts. On May 16 Harrington published one of his most effective works, a pamphlet entitled *A Discourse upon this Saying: The Spirit of the Nation is not yet to be trusted with Liberty; lest it introduce Monarchy, or Invade Liberty of Conscience.*[80] Here the author continued to insist that an equal commonwealth was the only form of government which could possibly be successful in England. After repeating once more the theories he had first expressed in the *Oceana,* he concluded: "If your Commonwealth be rightly instituted, Seven Years will not pass, ere your Clusters of Parties, Civil and Religious, vanish, not through any Force, as when cold Weather kills flies; but by the rising of greater Light, as when the Sun

79. Ibid., p. 598.
80. Ibid., pp. 601 ff.

puts out Candles . . . *England* shall raise her Head to ancient Glory, the Heavens shall be of the old Metal, the
Earth no longer Lead, nor shall the sounding Air eternally
renounce the Trumpet of Fame."[81]

Despite this impassioned plea, the Rump showed no
signs of being influenced by Harrington's proposals. Instead
of the requested elective senate the Parliament appointed
a thirty-one-member Council of State, twenty-one members
of which sat in Parliament. The principle of the unchecked
supremacy of the House of Commons would seem to have
won the day. But the Harringtonians were not discouraged
by this failure; rather they seem to have become all the
more assiduous in their efforts. A group calling itself
"Friends of the Commonwealth" put forth, "with Mr. Harrington's consent," a *Proposition In order to the Proposing
of a Commonwealth or Democracy.*[82] This was a suggestion
that the Rump should appoint a committee "to receive Mr.
Harrington's Proposals" for the establishment of an equal
commonwealth. It was further suggested that 103 persons
be added to the Committee of the House, representing all
shades of republican opinion. Among those listed, we find
these names: Mr. Thurloe, Mr. Prynne, Captain Baynes,
Sir George Booth, Praisegod Barebones, Major Wildam
[Wildman], Maximilian Petty, Mr. Baxter, Drs. Ferne,
Hammond, and Seaman, and Colonel Lilburn. Finally, it
was suggested that this Committee should meet at three
o'clock on Tuesday and Friday afternoons in order to act
as a constituent assembly. The reasons given for this novel
proposal were two: "It is the fairest way of proposing a
Government, that it be first proposed to Conviction, before
it be imposed by Power. . . . The persons herein nominated
being convinced, it must necessarily have an healing Ef-

81. Ibid., pp. 608–09.
82. Ibid., p. 620.

fect."[83] Evidently no one paid much attention to the proposal except Prynne, who suggested that Harrington should
be included in the Committee and that he should attend
its meetings with a rope around his neck.[84] The naïveté of
the entire procedure makes it difficult to believe that even
Harrington himself could have put much faith in the proposal.

While this was going on Harrington was engaged in the
writing of still another book, *The Art of Lawgiving.*[85] This
work, which was published early in June 1659, consisted of
three Books. The first contained a discussion of the general
principles of government, similar to the Preliminaries of
the *Oceana;* the second embodied a discussion of the Commonwealths of Israel and of the Jews; the third proposed a
model of government for England. In short, *The Art of
Lawgiving* followed substantially the same pattern as Harrington's earlier works. It is of particular interest because
it contains a fairly extensive criticism of the *Agreement of
the People* of 1647. In this work Harrington also had occasion to reply once again to his critic Matthew Wren. In February of 1659, Wren had published his *Monarchy Asserted,*
an attack on the *Oceana* from an essentially Hobbesian position. "In Sovereignty," Wren argued, "the diffus'd
strength of the Multitude is united in one person; which in
a Monarchy is a natural person; in a State, an artificial one
procreated by the majority of Votes. . . . This then is the
grand security of all Soverains . . . that the united forces of
their Subjects, with which they are invested, is sufficient to
suppress the beginnings of Seditions."[86] The idea of any

83. Ibid.
84. William Prynne, *An Answer to a Proposition* . . . (London,
1659); see Russell Smith, *Harrington and His Oceana,* p. 88.
85. *Coll. Works,* pp. 383 ff.
86. Matthew Wren, *Monarchy Asserted* . . . (Oxford, 1659), pp. 97–
99; see *Coll. Works,* p. 466.

such unitary sovereign was distasteful to Harrington, and furthermore he felt that Wren dealt with symptoms rather than causes of sedition. "Who reads Mr. Hobbs," he asked, "if this be news?"[87] Finally, in *The Art of Lawgiving* one finds one of the few intimations that Harrington might have become discouraged by his lack of success in persuading those in power to adopt his proposals. The motto which he chose for the book was, "If this Age fails me, the next will do me Justice." But however great Harrington's discouragement might have been, it most certainly did not lead him to abandon his efforts.

On the sixth of July, 1659, a "Humble Petition of Divers Well-affected Persons" was presented to Parliament by Henry Nevill.[88] It is said that this petition was written by Harrington, and this is quite probably true. In any case, the ideas it embodied were unquestionably Harringtonian. In effect it was simply a request that the Parliament establish a Harringtonian commonwealth in England, outlining the six steps which would have to be taken to this end. In presenting the petition Nevill stated that it would have been possible to secure "many thousand" signatures in its support if this had been desirable. On the very same day Parliament returned its answer:

> The House has read over your Petition, and find it without any private End, and only for the public Interest; and I [Thomas St. Nicholas, Clerk of Parliament] am commanded to let you know, that it lies much upon them to make such a Settlement as may be most for the Good of Posterity: and they are about that Work, and intend to go forward with it with as much Expedition as may be. And for your parts, they have

87. *Coll. Works,* p. 466.
88. Ibid , p. 541; see also *Merc. Pol.,* No. 277 [sic, actually No. 577], p. 576.

commanded me to give you Thanks; and in their Names I do give you the Thanks of this House accordingly.[89]

This expression of thanks was the only recognition Harrington and his followers received from the Parliament. The members of the Rump continued to "go forward" with their work, paying but slight attention to Harrington's schemes. This lack of interest on the part of Parliament may help to explain the fact that on July 21, 1659, Harrington published a pamphlet entitled *A Discourse Shewing, That the Spirit of Parlaments, with a Council in the Intervals, is not to be Trusted. . . .*[90] This pamphlet, the contents of which are indicated by its title, once again put forward Harrington's proposals for the solution of England's problems.

Undeterred by his continuing inability to win official support for his program, Harrington returned to his desk, whence he issued two more pamphlets in August of 1659. The first of these, *Politicaster,* was simply another attack on Wren's *Monarchy Asserted.*[91] It was in the form of a "comical discourse," and in addition to being somewhat wittier than most of Harrington's works it has the distinction of containing some of his most extensive remarks on questions of methodology. This pamphlet also refers to the fact that Harrington received no degree from Oxford, and alludes to an apparent conflict between him and various scholars at that university. The other work Harrington wrote during this month was a pamphlet entitled *Political Aphorisms.*[92] This is a collection of 120 short propositions concerning the problems of governments in general, leading to the inevi-

89. *Coll. Works,* p. 546.
90. Ibid., pp. 609 ff.
91. Ibid., pp. 579 ff.
92. Ibid., pp. 515 ff.

table conclusion that "the highest earthly Felicity that a People can ask, or God can give, is an equal and well-order'd Commonwealth."[93] As in the past, these works were little more than restatements of the original ideas of the *Oceana*, in different form and with slight occasional variations. But in both cases there is clear evidence that Harrington was seeking a broader popular audience, either through humor or by pithy condensation.

Evidently Harrington's technique of constantly repeating his basic ideas was successful in gaining for him some of the popular recognition he desired. Russell Smith has carefully documented the extensive interest in Harrington's proposals during precisely this period.[94] This interest is understandable, as is the fact that the remaining months of 1659 have been called "the golden age for the Harringtonians and all other doctrinaire politicians," simply in terms of the relation between governmental instability and political theory. After Booth's abortive rising in August the power of the army, under General Lambert, constantly increased. On the thirteenth of October Lambert expelled the Rump, and on the twenty-sixth the old Council of State was replaced by the military Committee of Safety. This, too, proved to be an unsatisfactory solution, and just two months later the Rump was restored.

During this period of intensified political activity Harrington published several minor works. The first, entitled *A Parallel of the Spirit of the People with the Spirit of Mr. Rogers,* was a reply to a pamphlet written by John Rogers, a supporter of the Long Parliament.[95] Even Harrington was aware of its unimportance, concluding: "Reader, I intreat

93. Ibid., p. 523.
94. *Harrington and His Oceana,* pp. 92 ff.
95. *Coll. Works,* pp. 614 ff.; Rogers' pamphlet was entitled *Diapoliteia* (London, 1659).

your Pardon; I know well enough that this is below me; but
something is to be yielded to the Times: and it hath been
the Employment of two or three Hours in a rainy Day."[96]
Also in October Harrington wrote *Valerius and Publicola,*
his only work in dialogue form. Here the author is out-
spokenly critical of the "spirit" of the English people and
complains because his advice has been heeded neither by
them nor by their government. When Valerius asks Publicola why he has not explained his "principles" to the
Parliament, Publicola, who is Harrington, replies, "I have
printed it over and over."[97] The only other works which
Harrington published during 1659 were a further translation of Virgil[98] and a pamphlet written to refute Henry
Stubbe.[99] Although it may seem odd that Harrington did
not write more during this disturbed period, we need not
look far for the explanation. The fact is that he had turned
to other, nonliterary, means of developing and publicizing
his ideas. In November of 1659 Harrington's famous Rota
Club was founded.

Actually, Russell Smith informs us, "as early as 1656
Harrington had conducted with more or less regularity a
campaign in support of his propaganda among the London
coffee-houses."[100] But it was not until the fall of 1659 that
the Club was officially founded. We may infer from the various contemporary descriptions that the Club had no fixed
membership, although certain persons seem to have attended its meetings quite regularly. Among these were Harrington himself, Nevill, Major Wildman, Francis Cra-

96. *Coll. Works,* p. 618.

97. Ibid., p. 491.

98. *Virgil's Aeneis,* a translation of Bks. 3–6.

99. *A Letter unto Mr. Stubs, Coll. Works,* pp. 575 ff.; Stubbe's work
had been called *The Commonwealth of Oceana put in the Ballance,
and found too light* (London, 1660).

100. *Harrington and His Oceana,* p. 101.

doc,[101] Edward Bagshaw,[102] William Croon,[103] Philip Carteret,[104] Maximilian Petty,[105] John Aubrey,[106] Sir John Hoskyns,[107] and Roger Coke.[108] The meetings of the Club were held in various London coffee-houses between November 1659 and February 1660. Aubrey described them in this way:

> He [Harrington] had every night a meeting at the (then) Turke's head, in the New Pallace-yard, where they take water, the next house to the staires, at one Miles's, where was made purposely a large ovall-table, with a passage in the middle for Miles to deliver his coffee. About it sate his disciples, and the virtuosi. The discourses in this kind were the most ingeniose, and smart, that I ever heard, or expect to heare, and bandied with great eagernesse; the arguments in the Parliament howse were but flatt to it. . . . The room was every evening full as it could be cramm'd.[109]

The popularity of these meetings can be attributed at least partly to the novelty of the balloting box which Harrington had introduced. An idea of its use can be gotten from a pamphlet called *The Rota* which Harrington wrote early in 1660.

101. A merchant, later Provost Marshal of Barbados.
102. A member of Christ Church, Oxford.
103. A physician.
104. A gentleman from the Isle of Guernsey.
105. According to Aubrey, "a very able man . . . who had more than once turn'd the councill-board of Oliver Cromwell, his kinsman."
106. Noted biographer of 17th-century English figures, author of *Brief Lives*.
107. A future president of the Royal Society.
108. Grandson of Sir Edward Coke.
109. *Brief Lives* (Dick ed.), p. 125.

At the ROTA. Decem. 20. 1659
Resolved, that the Proposer be desired, and is hereby
desired to bring in a Model of a Free State, or equal
Commonwealth . . . to be farther debated by this Society . . .

Resolved, that the Model being proposed in Print,
shall be first read, and then debated by Clauses.

Resolved, that a Clause being read over Night, the
Debate thereupon begin not at the sooner till the next
evening.

Resolved, that such as will Debate, be desired to bring
in their Queries . . . if they think fit, in Writing.

Resolved, that Debate being sufficiently had upon a
Clause, the Question be put by the Ballotting-Box, not
any way to determine of, or meddle with the Government of these Nations, but to discover the Judgment
of this Society, upon the Form of popular Government, in Abstract, or *secundum Artem*.[110]

Evidently the Club went about its business in a serious
and orderly fashion, carefully considering various proposals
over a considerable interval of time. Certainly this was
something more than an arena in which interested persons
could air their prejudices. In fact, it seems that the use of
the ballot box, which had been proposed by Harrington in
his *Oceana,* did not always produce results which pleased
him. Pepys describes one meeting of the Club at which
Harrington argued that the Roman government was unstable because those who owned property did not also exercise political power. The question was then put to a voice
vote and Harrington's conclusions were upheld by the
gathering; but later "it was carried by ballot, that it was

110. *Coll. Works,* p. 621.

a steady government, though it is true by the voices it had been carried before that it was an unsteady government."[111] Harrington, having been hoist with his own petard, was then instructed to prove his point at the next meeting.

Perhaps more than any of his writings, the Rota Club contributed to the spread of Harrington's ideas during his lifetime. The list of those who regularly attended its meetings is an impressive one; even Pepys paid eighteen shillings to "be entered of the Club."[112] But as Russell Smith points out, "It is not without interest to know the names of the principal Rota-men, but it is far more important to remember the number of casual spectators, who dropped in nightly to hear the speeches and watch the procedure."[113] Apparently the arguments were stimulating and the balloting was of interest at least as a curiosity. The number of pamphlets, poems, and songs written to ridicule the Rota Club gives us some idea of its status as a public institution.[114] Typical of these was a pamphlet published late in March, which purported to be the work of Harrington himself. It was entitled *The Censure of the Rota upon Mr. Milton's Book, entitled "The Ready and Easy Way. . . ."*[115] The spurious nature of the pamphlet is apparent from the signature and the name of the "publisher"—it is signed "Trundle Wheeler . . . Printed at London by Paul Giddy, Printer to the Rota, at the sign of the Windmill in Turn-again Lane." But despite this fact, its contents do confirm the other accounts of the procedure of the club. By lively discussions and the fascinating spectacle of balloting Harrington had

111. Samuel Pepys, *Diary,* ed. Wheatly (New York, n.d.), *1,* 15.
112. Ibid., p. 10.
113. *Harrington and His Oceana,* p. 103.
114. Ibid., pp. 103–07.
115. Strangely enough, this book has often been taken as an authentic work of Harrington; it is so listed, for instance, in the Harvard University Library catalogue.

succeeded, far more than in any of his writings, in stimulating widespread popular interest in his ideas. The last
months of 1659 unquestionably mark the zenith of his fame
as a political figure in England during his own lifetime.

Just as periods of political instability present singular
opportunities for the political theorist, so conversely when
the necessary decisions have been made these opportunities
diminish and the hopes they have aroused fade. Thus, as
the years of the Protectorate marked the period of Harrington's greatest activity, so the restoration of the monarchy
saw the rapid decline of his importance. We may date this
decline from the restoration of the Rump on December 26,
1659. In January his pamphlet *The Rota* appeared. In
February, directly following the arrival in London of General Monk, he published another short pamphlet entitled
*The Ways and Means Whereby an Equal and Lasting Com-
monwealth May be Suddenly introduced*. In effect this was
to be Harrington's last attempt to gain acceptance for his
program. He began by recognizing that "The Desire of the
People of England now runs strongly to have a Free Parlament." In that case, he continued, "Let there be a free Parlament." And he then proceeded to show how this could
lead to the establishment of a commonwealth of the sort he
desired. But even in this work Harrington was forced to
recognize the growing sentiment in favor of a restoration of
the monarchy: "If it be according to the Wisdom and the
Interest of the Nation upon mature debate, that there be a
King," he wrote, "let there be a King."[116] The last work
Harrington published during his lifetime was *A Word Concerning a House of Peers,* a brief essay written on February
20, 1660.[117] Here one sees quite clearly that the events of
1660 had discouraged the author and made him doubt that
he would succeed in his life's work. He begins by insisting

116. *Coll. Works,* p. 540.
117. Ibid., pp. 468 ff.

that the *real* danger to England lies not in any particular settlement but rather in halfway measures. If a monarchy should be established, he argues, his own position will triumph inevitably—in the long run. "If thro som secret Dictat . . . or a hast to make riddance [the monarchy is restored, its flaws] will be but the more perceivable by the Work when it coms to wearing or in practice; and the Flaws or Grievances being found insupportable, the next Parlament, thro the mere want of any other remedy, must introduce a Commonwealth."[118] When a man of Harrington's sanguine disposition is forced to transfer his hopes to a more distant future it is an almost sure sign of the hopelessness of his position.

At the same time, the Rota Club also ceased to meet. On February 20, 1660, the very day on which Harrington had finished his last pamphlet, Pepys attended what was probably the final meeting of the Club. He has described it in this way: "In the evening Simons and I to the Coffee Club, where nothing to do only I heard Mr. Harrington, and my Lord of Dorset and another Lord, talking of getting another place as the Cockpit, as they did believe it would come to something. After a small debate upon the question whether learned or unlearned subjects are the best the Club broke up very poorly, and I do not think they will meet any more."[119] Quite fittingly, this was also the day on which the Long Parliament finally was re-established. As the vestiges of the old constitution were restored, the theorist of the commonwealthsmen ended his active career. In Aubrey's words, "upon the unexpected turne upon Generall Monke's comeing-in, all these aierie modells vanished."[120] We may conclude our consideration of this part of Harrington's life by noting the last of his many prophetic

118. Ibid., p. 469.
119. *Diary, 1,* 43.
120. *Brief Lives* (Dick ed.), p. 125.

remarks about the England of his day. Says Aubrey, "I well remember, he severall times (at the breaking-up) sayd, 'Well, the King will come in. Let him come-in, and call a Parliament of the greatest Cavaliers in England, so they be men of estates, and let them but sett seven years, and they will all turn Common-wealthe's men.' "[121] The assurance with which Harrington uttered this prediction—a prediction that turned out to be remarkably correct in substance if not in timing—can be understood only by reference to his theories of politics and of history. It is to these that we will now turn.

121. Ibid.

CHAPTER 2.

The Study of Politics

"For in the Art of Man, being the imitation of nature, which is the Art of *God,* there is nothing so like the Call of beautifull order, out of Chaos and Confusion, as the Architecture of a well order'd Common-wealth."

The Commonwealth of Oceana

I T IS DIFFICULT in the mid-twentieth century to dis-
abuse oneself of the notion that the English somehow
possess a natural gift for governing themselves well. Try
as one will to reason it away, the attractive image of an instinctively moderate, sensible, law-abiding nation still lin-
gers. If this image were no more than an emotionally satis-
fying sentimentality, it might easily be ignored. Unfortunately it serves, as such images often do, as a substitute for
thought or real understanding. Mr. Podsnap's comfortable
assurance that the English constitution "Was Bestowed
Upon Us by Providence" and that "No Other Country is
so Favoured as This Country" has proved almost irresistibly
seductive. Only with a considerable effort is one able to
view the creation of this constitution, and in a very real
sense of modern constitutionalism too, as a genuine historical process. In making this effort it is perhaps useful to
recall that in the seventeenth century the English were
widely thought to be politically incompetent and irresponsible, while the French—the disciplined, rational, glorious
French—were conceded to have found the best solution to
the problems of politics. This judgment, grotesque as it may
seem to modern eyes, made perfectly good sense at the time.
Milton mentions "the fickleness which is attributed to us
as we are islanders," and, in a lovely phrase refers to "the
fluxible fault, if any such be, of our watery situation."

The mid-seventeenth century was of course the most hectic era in modern English history. A generation of tension
and hostility following the accession of James I led finally
to armed conflict between the Stuart monarchy and its enemies. The two decades between the outbreak of hostilities
and the restoration of the monarchy in 1660 saw a succession of events unprecedented in English constitutional history. The Civil Wars led to the imprisonment and ulti-

mately to the execution of Charles I—a king convicted of treason. The next eleven years were marked by a dizzying succession of constitutional experiments and factional disputes, as the groups that had succeeded in overthrowing the monarchy attempted to erect in its place some viable and acceptable form of government. As always, an *ad hoc* alliance based simply on shared hatred for a common enemy collapsed when that enemy had been destroyed and the hard work of creation was undertaken. Presbyterians and Independents, parliamentarians and soldiers of the New Model, secularists and religious fanatics very soon discovered that they had not been fighting for the same things at all.

It was during this period, and under these circumstances, that England became the first modern state to be governed by a written constitution—Oliver Cromwell's Instrument of Government of 1653. Designed to be "somewhat fundamental, somewhat like a *Magna Charta,* that should be standing and be unalterable," this document had to be amended substantially in less than four years. The establishment of a second legislative chamber, and the very tempting offer of the crown to Cromwell, suggest strongly that even as early as 1657 the English had begun inexorably moving back toward their traditional constitutional forms. If this was indeed the case, the explanation would seem to be that only these forms could elicit the allegiance requisite for the operation of a truly constitutional order—the only alternative to absolutism. The death of Oliver Cromwell in 1658 inevitably intensified factional disputes among the army, the Parliament, and the new Protector, Richard Cromwell. Finally, the return of General Monk to London, the recalling of the remnant of the unpurged Long Parliament, and the meeting of the Convention Parliament led to the restoration of the Stuart monarchy in the person of Charles II.

It is surely no coincidence that this disturbed era was also the time of the greatest flowering of English political theory. In order to appreciate the immense vitality of English political thought in the seventeenth century it is only necessary to recall the names of Filmer, Hobbes, Milton, Lilburn, Winstanley, Halifax, and Locke. The troubled years between 1640 and 1660 were also the most productive, giving rise, as Wormuth has noted, to "a body of political speculation which in volume, scope, and audacity was exceeded only by the literature of the French Revolution."[1] It seems clear that the relation between these political events and this vast body of political theory was a double one.

On the one hand, it may be argued that this awakening of interest in abstract political problems was itself among the *causes* of the political unrest of the time. Certainly if one includes among "political theorists" such doctrinaire political practitioners as James I, the most disputatious of kings, and Archbishop Laud, there can be no doubt of the truth of the contention. Even if one leaves these men aside, it can hardly be denied that the attempt to create a stable government in the period 1650–1660 was substantially hindered by the activities of numerous and vociferous factions held together almost solely by their members' agreement on questions of theory.

On the other hand, it is equally true that a major part of this outpouring of political speculation was a direct *consequence* of the unsettled state of English politics. In the mid-seventeenth century all the most fundamental problems of political theory, problems that had been regarded as satisfactorily settled for generations past, once more became open questions. Problems of the nature and forms of gov-

1. F. D. Wormuth, *The Origins of Modern Constitutionalism* (New York, 1949), p. 43.

ernment, of the basis of political obligation, of the extent and limitations of sovereignty, and of the nature of justice in its political, social, and economic manifestations were all raised in an urgent and compelling fashion. In the England of the Interregnum these were no longer "merely theoretical" questions; they were practical problems. Toward the middle of the century it became painfully clear that they would have to be solved, and that some stable form of government would have to be devised, if the horrors of anarchy were to be avoided. This was a fact which no thoughtful observer could possibly fail to recognize.

The effect of this state of affairs on the output of political theory was twofold. In the first place, the deeply unsettled condition of English politics served to stimulate the interest and to raise the hopes of many men who had long been concerned with political issues. Where everything is open to question, any theorist may be led to believe that there exists a chance of gaining acceptance for his own views. Undoubtedly there were many in England who looked upon the fluid political condition of their age as the answer to a lifetime of hopes; agreeing that the time was out of joint, each happily proclaimed that he had been born to set it right. In the second place, there were also many who during this period found themselves turning toward politics for the first time. The urgency of England's constitutional crisis was so frighteningly apparent that it was hardly possible any longer to maintain an attitude of indifference toward political affairs. An era of stability may lead men to remark "how small of all that human hearts endure, the part that kings or laws can cause or cure." During a period of near anarchy, such an attitude becomes, if not impossible, at least exorbitantly expensive.

"The Most Useful of Controversies"

The career of James Harrington provides an interesting illustration of this reciprocal relation between political unrest and political theory. There can be no doubt that Harrington was fascinated by politics before, and quite apart from, the political crisis of the mid-century. His trip to the Continent, and particularly his reactions to the Venetian Republic, are ample evidence of this. One may say that his friendly but pointed disputations with Charles I mark the high point of his early interest in government. The most significant fact is that the climax of England's constitutional crisis—the execution of Charles in 1649—served in the first instance to turn Harrington's attention away from politics. We have already had occasion to note that in 1649 he retired completely from public life and adopted an attitude of aloofness toward politics. But we also know that his *Commonwealth of Oceana* appeared in 1656, marking the beginning of his public career as a political theorist. An understanding of the causes of this shift from aloofness to active participation will provide us with an insight into the purposes of Harrington's political writings as well as some clues as to his view of the function of political theory.

We are fortunate to have, in the *Oceana,* what amounts to a description of this crucial period of Harrington's life.[2] This is the passage that tells of the decision of Olphaus Megaletor, the hero of *Oceana,* to devote his life to the solution of his country's political problems. The circumstances which Harrington recounts are such as to leave no doubt that the passage is in fact autobiographical, although this is nowhere made explicit. The time is shortly after the execution of the king, and the government consists of "a single assembly elected by the people and invested with the

2. The passage referred to here occurs in *Oceana,* pp. 54–59.

whole power of the Government, without any Covenants, Conditions, or orders whatsoever." The political situation is characterized as follows: "The parties into which this Nation was divided, were Temporal or Spiritual; and the Temporal parties were especially two, the one the Royalists, the other Common-wealths-men; each of which asserted their different Causes, either out of Prudence or Ignorance; out of interest or Conscience." In these circumstances Olphaus Megaletor, a man learned in the political thought and history of the ancients, "had so sad reflections upon the waies and proceedings of the Parliament, as cast him upon books, and all other meanes of diversion." One recalls Toland's statement that, following the execution of Charles I, Harrington "was observ'd to keep much in his Library, and more retir'd than usually, which was by his Friends a long time attributed to Melancholy or Discontent."[3] Finally, the story continues, Olphaus Megaletor happened to come upon the passage in Machiavelli's *Discourses* which describes the great and lasting achievements of Lycurgus in Sparta.[4] Harrington's account of the impact of this passage on Olphaus Megaletor is instructive: "My Lord Generall took so new, and deepe impression at these words of the much greater glory of Lycurgus, that being on this side assaulted with the emulation of his illustrious object, and on the other with the misery of the Nation . . . he was almost wholly deprived of his naturall rest, untill the debate he had within himself, came to a firme resolution." The resolution which Olphaus Megaletor—or James Harrington— reached took the form of a decision to apply his knowledge

3. *Coll. Works*, p. xvii.

4. *Discorsi* I, 2; "Licurgo . . . fece uno Stato che durò più che otto-cento anni, con somma laude sua, e quiete de quella città." This is obviously the passage which Liljegren erroneously cites as *Discorsi* I, 6 in his edition of the *Oceana*, p. 286.

of political theory and practice to the solution of England's political problems.

Although it would probably be a mistake to base any argument solely on the assertion that this anecdote is auto-biographical in a literal sense, it is nevertheless useful as a symbolic expression of Harrington's state of mind at the time when he began the writing of his *Oceana* and em-barked on his career as a political theorist. It will be noted that in the anecdote Olphaus Megaletor is moved by two considerations: his desire to emulate Lycurgus and his real-ization of the "misery" of Oceana. These were, in a very real sense, Harrington's motives in undertaking his study of politics; he wished a place among the masters of political wisdom and he desired to do something about the critical state of English politics. It is quite clear that these were, both in fact and in Harrington's mind, complementary motives. England's political problems would be solved, he felt, by the application of "political prudence," of which the ancients were the acknowledged masters. Actually, as Harrington's reference to Machiavelli reminds us, this hark-ing back to the classics of political thought in times of crisis is by no means uncommon in the history of political theory. We shall have occasion later to discuss Harrington's attitude toward the ancients, but for our present purposes the im-portant fact is that he undertook his study of politics and the formulation of his political theory from extremely prac-tical motives. Like Machiavelli, he was keenly aware of the political evils of his time and wished to remedy them. And furthermore, again like Machiavelli, he felt that the pri-mary evil was political instability; if the causes of this in-stability could be found and removed, all would be well with English politics. As Tawney has described Harring-ton's goal, "Constantly sought, and as constantly receding, stability, finality, permanence, and the end of 'disputes about Government, that is to say, about notions, forms and shadows,' had already, when his earliest work appeared, become an obsession, and remained a hope, though an ever more forlorn one, when he published his last."[5]

This quotation is particularly valuable because it suggests what was perhaps the central paradox of Harrington's approach to political theory. As we have seen, he believed that the raison d'être of political theory must consist in the fact that it tells men what to do next. But then the question presented itself, is it really useful to tell men what to do next? Is it not possible that men might know instinctively what is to be done? And in this case would not conscious political direction be superfluous, or even dangerous? One can sense Harrington's indecision on this point within the limits of a single sentence; in the *Oceana* he wrote: "A People when they are reduced unto misery and despair, become their own Polititians, as certain Beasts when they are sick become their own Physitians, and are carried by a natural instinct unto the desire of such herbs, as are their proper cure . . ."[6] This would seem to indicate quite clearly that Harrington believed in the existence of a sort of political *vis medicatrix naturae* which would make any conscious political theorizing unnecessary in times of crisis—so far as practical consequences are concerned. However, Harrington ended this very same sentence with these words: "but the people, for the greater part, are beneath the Beasts in the use of [these natural remedies]." Thus, although the people do have a natural tendency in emergencies to choose the proper political course, this faculty is by no means adequately developed to serve as a sure guide to their actions. And consequently it is the job of the political theorist to make good the deficiency.

5. Tawney, "Harrington's Interpretation of His Age," p. 6; Tawney here quotes Marchamont Needham, writing in the *Merc. Pol.* of March–April 1657.
6. *Oceana,* p. 138.

It is important to remember that this was by no means simply an intellectual puzzle for Harrington; it was bound up with the chosen course of his life. Having dedicated all his energies to the study of politics and the creation of a theory of politics, he had to believe in the importance of such a study. And in this case "importance" could mean nothing less than usefulness in solving present political problems. Consequently the thought that political problems might best be solved by some "natural," "instinctive," nonintellectual process was one that threatened the whole enterprise to which Harrington was dedicated. In the sentence quoted above he has managed to arrive at a compromise solution to his dilemma. But apparently it did not completely satisfy him; although he arrived at this position in his very first published work, his later writings contain many passages indicating that the problem continued to bother him.

In his *Art of Lawgiving,* for instance, Harrington embarks on a discussion that clearly seems destined to conclude with a condemnation of political theory and political theorists. In this passage he describes an incident from a play he had seen while traveling in Italy:

> A Country fellow came with an Apple in his hand; to which, in a strange variety of faces, his Teeth were undoubtedly threaten'd, when enter'd a young Anatomist brimful of his last Lesson, who, stopping in good time the hand of this same country Fellow, would by no means suffer him to go on with so great an Enterprize, till he had first nam'd and describ'd to him all the Bones, Nerves, and Muscles which are naturally necessary to that motion; at which, the good man being with admiration plainly chopfallen, coms me in a third, who, snatching away the Apple, devour'd it in the presence of them both.[7]

7. *Coll. Works,* p. 430.

The moral of this tale seems quite plain: the people often
accomplish unconsciously things which they would be completely unable to explain in theoretical terms. The hero of
the tale is certainly the man who finally eats the apple, the
man who knows what he wants to do and simply proceeds to
do it without unnecessary self-consciousness. The tragic
figure is the "Country fellow" who is so confused by the
young anatomist's question that he becomes unable to perform what would otherwise have been a simple instinctive
act. And the villain of the parable is surely the pedantic
young anatomist who is so impressed with his newfound
knowledge that he cannot refrain from corrupting the
native intelligence of the "Country fellow." In political
terms, Harrington seems to be saying that theory is not
only superfluous, since proper action is quite possible without it, but that it may actually be evil insofar as it interferes
with the natural intelligence of the people and paralyzes
their instinctive political will. That Harrington did at times
take a position very much like this will become apparent
when we consider the rules which he posited for the govern-
ance of the legislature of the Commonwealth of Oceana.[8]

But in his *Art of Lawgiving* he was unwilling to let the
discussion rest at this point. Having expressed the Burkeian
position so vividly, he then proceeded to contradict it. "If
the People, in this case wherof I am speaking, were naturally so well furnish'd, I had here learn'd enough to have
kept silence; but their eating, in the political way, of absolute necessity requires the aid of som political Anatomist;
without which, they may have Appetits, but will be chop-
fallen."[9] In other words, the art of politics is a great deal
more complex than the process of eating an apple. And consequently, although the latter will suffer from the presump-
tuous intrusions of expert theoreticians, the former "of ab-

8. See below, pp. 241 ff.
9. *Coll. Works,* p. 430.

solute necessity" requires theoretical guidance. Harrington furthermore makes it clear that this in no way contradicts his earlier reference to the correct political instinct of the people. The people, he now tells us, "may have Appetits," that is to say they may instinctively desire the right things, but between the desire and its successful gratification must come the guidance of the expert. All of which leaves the reader wondering why Harrington bothered to recount the anecdote in the first place. Again the answer seems to lie in his essential uncertainty concerning this very central problem. As in the previous instance he seems on the verge of condemning political theory—this time not only as useless but as positively harmful. But, having reached this point, he once again retreats. Quite understandably he is hesitant to undermine his life's work.

Actually, of course, this is one of the problems that must be faced by any political theorist whose interests are practical, and it has been dealt with in various ways by virtually every political theorist from Plato to the present. In Harrington's case the problem was aggravated by two factors. In the first place, he recognized that some of England's political problems had been caused by none other than the political theorists themselves. These political theorists—the ones who caused confusion by misleading the people—are doubtless represented by the young Anatomist in the parable of the apple. In the face of this unpleasant spectacle Harrington must have wondered whether he would really serve the interests of England by adding to the proliferation of political theories. In the second place, and perhaps more interestingly, Harrington's position was complicated by the necessity of combining in his theory certain distinct elements of determinism with a strong belief in the efficacy of rational inquiry and direction.

An analysis of the nature of Harrington's determinism must await our consideration of the substance of his political theory. For the present it must suffice to say that he believed that certain forces, primarily economic in nature, play a large part in determining the location of political power in a community at any given time. This he believed to be true quite apart from any voluntary human action. As Tawney has said, "His central conception [was] that institutions are not accidental, or arbitrary, or susceptible of change at will."[10] At the same time, however, Harrington also quite clearly believed that human will *is* important politically and should be directed in some rational fashion. How could these two beliefs successfully be combined? If rational human action is effective, what remains of determinism? If events are really determined by nonhuman factors, or by factors beyond human control, of what importance is rational action?

We have already noted two instances of Harrington's uncertainty about the utility of political theory. The issue as it relates to determinism was perhaps most clearly faced in his *Valerius and Publicola*. The subject of this pamphlet is not the abstract question of the utility of political theory, but rather the specific problem of the introduction of a "true commonwealth" in England. In the course of the dialogue, however, Harrington was forced to consider the relation between intellect and will on the one hand and determinism on the other. The question under discussion is whether, since a commonwealth is inevitable in England in any case, political discussion and theorizing are not simply irrelevant. In the words of Valerius we can hear Harrington attempting to justify his choice of a career as a political theorist:

> *Publicola.* Think you that a Plant grows the worse for not understanding the manner of its Vegetation?

10. Tawney, "Harrington's Interpretation of His Age," p. 9.

Valerius. A Plant is not a free Agent; but among Men who are free Agents, the Introduction of Government seems to be Arbitrary.

Publicola. What, where there is no more than *Hobson's* choice, this or none?

Valerius. It is true, that if they can have nothing else, they must at length have a Commonwealth; but tho they can have nothing else to be holding, yet they will be trying other things.

Publicola. There is all the mischief.

Valerius. And enough to ruin the Nation.[11]

Here Harrington has expressed what we may take to be his final view of the practical importance of political theory, particularly in relation to the political crisis of his time. Although men are "free agents," there can be no question of the ultimate and inevitable outcome of the Civil Wars—a "commonwealth" must eventually be established in England. Unfortunately this indisputable fact is recognized neither by the people of England nor by their political leaders. As a result much unnecessary conflict has already occurred. And the turmoil must continue, Harrington believed, until those endowed with political power finally come to recognize the true state of affairs. In these terms the proper function of the political theorist becomes apparent: being familiar with the principles of politics, and therefore able accurately to appraise the political situation at any moment in history, his responsibility is to explain this situation to the people and their leaders. By this means all futile struggle against the necessary order of things will cease, the inevitable will be accepted immediately, and peace and order will be restored. It was to this task that

11. *Coll. Works,* p. 476.

Harrington devoted his life, believing that "To leave to our selves and Posterity a farther purchase in Blood or Sweat of that which we may presently possess, injoy, and hereafter bequeath to Posterity in Peace and Glory, is inhuman and impious."[12]

To a considerable extent, then, Harrington believed that the function of the political theorist is to demonstrate to his contemporaries the precise requirements of political necessity. But he can do more, for the realm of determinism and necessity does not comprehend all of man's political life. There is also an area in which men are free to choose among various alternative possibilities, and here Harrington sees no reason to suppose the existence of any *vis medicatrix naturae,* of any innate human tendency to choose wisely or well. It is precisely in this area that the activity of the political theorist may be genuinely creative rather than simply descriptive or minatory. Although the distinction will be more apparent when we come to discuss the substance of Harrington's theory, its general outline can be seen in his whole approach to the business of theorizing about politics. The hesitation that reflects his determinism is finally overcome by his conviction that men and societies stand in need of expert guidance, particularly in the matter of designing and establishing the institutions best calculated to achieve their ends, given the requirements of political necessity. In the case of mid-seventeenth-century England, for example, the laws of politics have already determined that the only possible stable government will be a "commonwealth," a government in which power is widely diffused. It is, of course, desirable that this fact should be pointed out as quickly and as forcefully as possible. The outpouring of blood and sweat will be cut short if men can be persuaded to accept the inevitable; but, by definition,

12. *Political Aphorisms, Coll. Works,* p. 521.

the ultimate outcome will be in its essential features the same whether they accept it or not.

But this is not to say that the laws of politics leave men no leeway; given the necessity of popular government, a wide range of institutional arrangements is still possible. In Harrington's terms, not every "commonwealth" is an "equal commonwealth." Although the locus of power in a community, and thus the *general form* of its polity, must be treated as a given fact, it is the proper function of the political theorist to show how this power may best be exercised. Such a function necessarily involves a discussion of both institutional forms and ethical ends. In a characteristic passage, written in May of 1659, Harrington concludes a discussion of the institutions he is proposing to his countrymen with this sentence: "If you *must* have a Commonwealth, and you *will* have an equal Commonwealth, then (pardon my Boldness) after this or some like Manner must you do, because like Work never was, nor can be done any otherwise."[13] The distinction between "must" and "will" reveals the twofold nature of the theorist's role: recognizing both the requirements of necessity and the possibility of choice, he should describe the former and prescribe the latter.

Having arrived, after considerable uncertainty and indecision, at this justification of the social utility of political theory, Harrington found himself faced with yet another problem. He had begun with an interest in things political and with a conviction that England's political crisis urgently demanded some practical solution. He had then gone on to conclude that this solution could only result from conscious and rational guidance in accordance with the principles of political theory. To whom could England look for such guidance? It was immediately apparent to Harrington that

13. *Pour enclouer le canon, Coll. Works,* p. 600. Italics added.

the people themselves were not fitted to perform such a
function. True, they might be educated to recognize the
political facts of life; but this could never be a process of
self-education. As he expressed it, "that the Politicks can
be master'd without study, or that the people can have
leisure to study, is a vain imagination."[14] This is, of course,
strongly reminiscent of Aristotle's contention that tradesmen and mechanics can never participate in the business of
government simply because they lack the leisure which is
requisite to becoming a good citizen. And just because it
is so reminiscent of Aristotle we should note that Harrington's view is really quite different. The important thing is
that Harrington is not here speaking of participation *in*
government, but rather of that political theorizing which
is to determine the *form* of government. Once a proper
constitution has been established Harrington is willing, as
we shall see, to have the people participate in politics. But
for the moment he feels that it is necessary to look elsewhere
for that theoretical guidance which England so sorely needs.
Who, then, is qualified to provide such leadership? In Harrington's mind, as in the minds of many of his contemporaries, the choice in the first instance was between those actively engaged in political affairs and those who remain
private citizens.

The question first arose with the publication in 1657 of
Matthew Wren's *Considerations on Mr. Harrington's . . .
Oceana.* In this work, as we have already noted, Wren had
written:

> I beseech you Gentlemen, are not we the Writers of
> Politics somwhat a ridiculous sort of People? Is it not
> a fine piece of Folly for private men sitting in their
> Cabinets to rack their brains about Models of Gov-
> ernment? Certainly our Labors make a very pleasant

14. *Oceana,* p. 118.

recreation for those great Personages, who, sitting at the Helm of Affairs, have by their large Experience not only acquir'd the perfect Art of Ruling, but have attain'd also to the comprehension of the Nature and Foundation of Government.[15]

Wren's assertion that political leaders are superior to private citizens in the *theory* as well as the *practice* of government Harrington found intolerable. In his reply to Wren, in the first Book of his *Prerogative of Popular Government,* Harrington devoted particular attention to this criticism. He wrote, "To say that a man may not write of Government except he be a Magistrat, is as absurd as to say, that a man may not make a Sea-chart unless he be a Pilot. It is known that CHRISTOPHER COLUMBUS made a Chart in his Cabinet, that found out the *Indys.* The Magistrat that was good at his steerage never took it ill of him that brought him a Chart."[16] Harrington's point here seems to be that there are two distinct political functions, theorizing and ruling, one of which is clearly prior to the other both in importance and in time. The work of the theorist is in fact indispensable to the ruler, whose actions would have no meaning and no direction without it. The example of Columbus—whatever a modern reader may think of its implication that Columbus knew where he was going—does suggest the possibility that a single individual might perform both political functions; and this would seem to weaken Harrington's position to some extent.

15. "Epistle to the Reader," as quoted by Harrington, *Coll. Works,* p. 235.

16. *Coll. Works,* p. 235. It is interesting to note that Edward Dacres uses the example of Columbus in precisely the same way in the Dedication of his translation of Machiavelli's *Discourses* published in London in 1636. Perhaps this is further evidence of the influence of Machiavelli, this time in translation, on Harrington's view of the function of political theory.

In any case, Harrington's reply did not satisfy Wren, who in a later work argued that Columbus could not have made a chart of the Indies unless he had first been there. Wren concluded, "They who understand that *Christopher Columbus* must first have been at the Indies, before he could make a Card to teach others the Way thither, will go near to suspect Mr. *Harrington's* Abilities in modelling a Commonwealth, till he have spent some Years in the Ministry of State."[17] This, of course, was precisely the point at issue. Harrington, having virtually no practical political experience, was presuming to instruct his countrymen in the art of politics. On what grounds could he justify this presumption against the criticisms of Wren and his followers? In the first instance, Harrington adopted the rather offensively personal tactics of his attacker and accused Wren, probably with some justice, of seeking to win favor with those in power in England. Along these lines he constantly refers to Wren as "the Flatterer." But this, of course, had very little to do with the point at issue. Returning to the substantive argument, Harrington cited numerous examples to prove that no great political leaders had ever contributed significantly to political theory. "What modelling of Government hath been bequeathed unto the World, by all the Ministers of State in *France* . . . ," he inquired, "or by all the Ministers of State since *Henry* the Seventh in *England?*"[18]

The obverse of this argument was used by Harrington during his examination in the Tower of London in 1661, at the close of his career as a political theorist. Here Harrington was charged with "being eminent in Principles contrary to the King's Government, and the Laws of this Na-

17. Quoted by Harrington in *Politicaster, Coll. Works*, p. 582, from Wren's *Monarchy Asserted*.
18. *Politicaster, Coll. Works*, p. 582.

tion."[19] His examiners made no reference to the fact that
he was merely a private citizen, but in his reply Harrington
gratuitously raised this question, which seems to have
weighed on his mind. After referring to the formal charge
he added, perhaps with Matthew Wren in mind, "Som, my
Lord, have aggravated this, saying, that *I being a privat man
have bin so mad as to meddle with Politics: what had a privat man to do with Government?*" Replying to his own
question, Harrington proceeded to note that all the great
political theorists of the past—he lists Plato, Aristotle, Livy,
and Machiavelli—had been private citizens. In conclusion
he said, "My Lord, there is not any public Person, not any
Magistrat, that has written in the Politics worth a button.
All they that have bin excellent in this way, have bin privat
men, as privat men, my Lord, as my self." Thus Harrington
pointed out first that no political leaders have been great
political theorists, and second that no great political theorists have been political leaders. But this can hardly be
called a complete or effective defense of the position that
only private citizens *can* become eminent as political theorists, a position that Harrington eventually came to adopt.

Under Wren's constant prodding Harrington did present
a more convincing argument in support of his position. The
political theorist, he said, must have two qualifications. The
first of these is a thorough knowledge of "ancient prudence," that is, of the political writings of classical authors
and the political history of ancient peoples. Such knowledge, Harrington pointed out, is seldom found among
"ministers of state." Nevertheless, it is clear that this requirement does not logically rule out the possibility that
men of affairs may become competent political theorists,
just as Columbus had been both a map-maker and a navi-
gator; and quite clearly Harrington did wish to rule out

19. *Coll. Works,* p. xxxiii; see below, pp. 318–20.

that possibility. More pertinent, therefore, is his second qualification, namely that a political theorist must be "disengaged from all Parties." Such objectivity and disinterestedness were rare in the political life of seventeenth-century England, and Harrington believed that they were absolutely incompatible with an active role in partisan politics. In this way he attempts to demonstrate not only that political leaders *have* never been distinguished as political theorists, but also that they necessarily *can* never achieve eminence in this field.

The same point had been made even more forcefully and explicitly when Harrington discussed in *Oceana* the possible claims of those practical political experts who guide princes in the management of their affairs—what one today might call "braintrusters." Here he announces quite simply, "The Counsellours of Princes I will not trust, they are but Journy-men."[20] His point—and it is an important one—is that men such as these may gain occasional practical successes, but their guidance will not be certain in the long run precisely because it is not based on any firm theoretical foundation. He expresses this belief vividly in the following passage: "Their Counsellours do not derive their proceedings from any sound root of Government, that may contain the demonstration, and assure the successe of them, but are expedient-mongers, givers of themselves to help a lame dog over a stile; else how commeth it to passe, that the fame of Cardinal *Richelieu* hath been like thunder, whereof we hear the noise, but can make no demonstration of the reason?"[21]

Having shown that neither the mass of the people nor their political leaders are capable of providing the expert political guidance that England requires, Harrington wished to argue against the pretensions of two other groups

20. P. 118.
21. Ibid.

—lawyers and clergymen. Although this point is of only incidental interest, we may at least note the general argument. In both cases it seems that what he objected to were the vested interests and the inevitable bias of these groups. The lawyers were generally disliked by the more radical republicans of the Interregnum who looked upon them (with justification) as supporters of the status quo ante, at least in its legal ramifications. Harrington seems to have felt that "their incurable run upon their own narrow bias"[22] disqualified them from consideration as true political theorists. Indeed, it was inevitable that there should be little sympathy between lawyers, whose livelihood depended upon a knowledge of the ancient laws of England, and any political theorist who was willing to wipe clean the slate and construct a completely new system of law; the enmity of Bentham and Blackstone was clearly not the first such case in English history.

Harrington's view of the clergy as potential political theorists is understandable in somewhat similar terms. In this case one suspects that his position is close to that adopted by the French *politiques* of the preceding century—generally speaking, political order is the *summum bonum* and should never be endangered in the name of sectarian religion. As we shall have occasion to see later, Harrington's interest in religious matters was ancillary to his concern with politics, and consequently it was to be expected that he would object to the intrusion of religious questions into political affairs. But the clergy, whose primary interest was naturally religious, were committed to a position that inevitably subordinated politics to religion. And surely Englishmen of the seventeenth century had had ample opportunity to observe in practice the politically disturbing and divisive effects of religious controversy. Even more disturbing was the tend-

22. Ibid.

ency of clergymen of all persuasions to turn political principles into articles of faith, thus making secular theorists
appear as blasphemers. This, for obvious reasons, Harrington found intolerable. As he wrote during his controversy
with Dr. Ferne, "Where-ever the Clergy have gained this
Point, namely . . . that it is unlawful for Gentlemen . . . to
discourse . . . as well in the Matter of Church as State Government, neither Government nor Religion have failed to
degenerate into mere Priest-craft."[23]

Harrington had now argued that theoretically sound
leadership was vital to the solution of England's political
problems, and also that neither the mass of the people, nor
their political leaders, nor their clergymen and lawyers
could become effective political theorists. Who, then, remained to perform this demonstrably important function?
One is tempted to say that Harrington remained; but a
more accurate answer would be that what remained was
the class to which Harrington belonged. It was in this class
of moderately wealthy, well-educated gentlemen of leisure
that Harrington discovered the source of potential political
theorists. These are the men he names "Gentlemen" and
describes as "such as live upon their own revenues in plenty,
without engagement either unto the tilling of their Lands,
or other work for their livelihood."[24] Unlike the mass of
the people, the members of this class enjoyed sufficient leisure to permit a thorough study and mastery of "ancient
prudence." Unlike active politicians, they could remain free
of narrow party commitments. Unlike lawyers and clergymen, they had no particular professional bias. Thus the

23. *Pian piano, Coll. Works,* p. 551.
24. *Oceana,* p. 119; the definition is taken from *Discorsi,* I, 55—
". . . dico che gentiluomini sono chiamati quelli, ch' oziosi vivono dei
proventi delle loro possessioni abbondantemente . . ."; it is interesting
that Machiavelli continues, "Questi tali sono perniciosi in ogni Re-
pubblica."

gentry were able, at least potentially, to view the world of politics with the requisite degree of intelligence and detachment. As Harrington expressed it, "There is something first in the making of a Common-wealth, then in the governing of her, and last of all in the leading of her Armies; which, though there be great Divines, great Lawyers, great men in all professions, seems to be peculiar unto the Genius of a Gentleman."[25] We shall have occasion later to note the practical political implications of this statement; at present it will suffice to say that this same "genius" explains the peculiar ability of Harrington's class in the business of political theorizing. Those who possess this "genius," if they neither govern a commonwealth nor lead its armies, are eminently qualified for the study and formulation of the principles of politics. It should be noted that Harrington's trust in the gentry and his reliance on them were related to contemporary political and social circumstances. Of course this was Harrington's own class, and consequently it was the one with which he felt most in sympathy.

This brings us finally to something of a paradox, or at least a difficulty, in Harrington's argument. The reader will recall Plato's belief that the solution of political problems would come only when philosophers became kings or kings became philosophers; in his *Oceana,* Harrington cited this passage from the *Republic* with approval.[26] Certainly the philosopher-king ideal is one which must appeal strongly to any political theorist who is eager to see his ideas translated into practice; even so confirmed a believer in popular sovereignty as Rousseau made use of a wise and omnicompetent "legislator." But Harrington's own theory logically precluded any such solution; so long as kings remain kings it is logically impossible that they should be

25. *Oceana,* pp. 34–35.
26. P. 20.

philosophers, since active participation in politics is incompatible with philosophic detachment. On the other hand it is equally clear that Harrington did expect the work of political theorists to have an effect on politics. If this dualism between theoreticians and practitioners necessarily exists, how is the connection between the two to be made?

To some extent Harrington's career provides us with an indication of his solution to this problem. It is the responsibility of the theorist to place his ideas before the public with the greatest possible clarity, frequency, and persuasiveness. Furthermore he should be willing to modify his ideas to some extent in order to appeal to the powers that be. In the *Oceana* his appeal was to Cromwell: the highly flattering picture of Olphaus Megaletor was unquestionably designed primarily to impress the Lord Protector, to whom the work was dedicated. "This," Harrington tells him, "is the measure of glory you could achieve by putting my ideas into practice."[27] Here the pattern is much like that followed by Plato in his ill-fated experiments with Dionysius; instead of a philosopher-king there is to be a king guided by a philosopher. Harrington's attempt, like Plato's, was unsuccessful, and he subsequently sought to win the support of the newly recalled Long Parliament, of the army, and of Richard Cromwell. Toward the end of his career Harrington was willing to sacrifice parts of his scheme in order to gain acceptance for the rest, and finally he turned for consolation to the belief that future generations would vindicate his position. Much of the tragedy that surrounds Harrington's life stems from the fact that he was not content with the assurance that his theories were correct; although he most certainly was sure of this, he could not rest until he saw his ideas put into practice. And this he did not live to see.

27. See, for instance, *Oceana,* pp. 207–26.

"Political Anatomy"

Carl J. Friedrich has noted that the phrase "you have ordered everything according to measure, number and weight" was a favorite in the early seventeenth century, and points out how characteristic it was that the men of this period should express their scientific outlook by a quotation from the Bible.[28] It would be difficult to find a figure more typical of this period of transition than James Harrington. Like so many of his contemporaries, Harrington was greatly impressed by the achievements of the natural and mathematical sciences in the sixteenth and seventeenth centuries and wished to make use of the techniques which these sciences had developed. But at the same time he was unable to rid himself completely of the reverence for "authorities" which had characterized so much of European intellectual history. In a sense Harrington's search for a methodology is best understood as an attempt to reconcile these two elements. But in a somewhat broader sense Harrington may be viewed as a typical man of his age, striving to create for himself a system that would embody the best elements of the new sciences without doing violence to the sensibilities of an era which was still deeply religious.

In this consideration of the methods which Harrington felt to be appropriate to political theory it will be necessary for us to keep constantly in mind the objectives that motivated his study of politics. Harrington wished first to explain and then to eliminate the confusions and instability which characterized English politics in his time. Consequently his study of politics assumed a rather pragmatic form. The specific phenomena which he sought to explain were all of the same general order: the Civil Wars, the deposition and execution of Charles I, and the successive fail-

---

28. *The Age of the Baroque* (New York, 1952), p. 93.

ures of the Commonwealth and the Protectorate to solve
the problems facing them. In short, Harrington was concerned primarily with the phenomenon of political instability. In order to restore stability to the English political
scene he felt it necessary to discover the general principles
which could account for the strength or weakness of various
governments. Like all scientists he began with the assumption that such general principles do exist and are capable of
being discovered by human reason. His problem was to
hit on the method which would best guarantee their discovery, and he faced this problem quite explicitly.

In the first place, we may note that Harrington deliberately rejected the use in political theory of any form of abstract, deductive reasoning. This he characterized on various occasions as "geometry," "mathematics," and "natural
philosophy." In the realm of political theory he felt that
Hobbes was the outstanding practitioner of this method and
referred scornfully to Hobbes's attempt to erect a monarchy
in England "by *Geometry*" rather than by some more respectable method.[29] What was Harrington's reason for ob-
jecting to abstract logic or deduction? This question can
perhaps best be answered by reference to Harrington's
criticisms of John Wilkins, the founder of the Royal Society. Wilkins, in a book entitled *Mathematical Magic,* had
described various oddities which could be proved possible
by the use of mathematics.[30] Harrington immediately
seized on this as evidence of the essential impracticality and
irrelevance of mathematical methods and, by extension, of
all abstract reasoning. He chose to attack in particular one
of Wilkins' demonstrations, a proof that with a certain arrangement of ropes, sails, and pulleys, a single man could
uproot the strongest oak simply by blowing against a sail.

29. *Oceana*, p. 50; and also *Politicaster, Coll. Works*, p. 587.
30. John Wilkins (1614–1672), *Mathematical Magic or, The Wonders That May be Performed by Mechanicall Geometry* (1648).

This may be all very well mathematically, Harrington says, but it is quite irrelevant.

From Harrington's point of view the essential weakness of this sort of reasoning was that it inevitably tended toward oversimplification. Politics, he believed, is an essentially complex subject, similar in this respect to anatomy. And politics can only be understood by some method that will take account of this complexity. Deductive, abstract reasoning most certainly did not do this, he felt. Characteristic of this view is Harrington's description of Dr. Wilkins' attempt to apply his method to political problems: the Doctor, he said, "had an excellent faculty of [magnifying] a Louse, and diminishing a Common-wealth."[31] Now it is all very well to magnify a louse, if one cares for such an undignified occupation; but by diminishing a commonwealth one inevitably loses sight of the inherent complexity of political life. The immediate result of this is that men like Dr. Wilkins and Hobbes are able to formulate conclusions with comparative ease. Thus Harrington wrote: "There is between the Discourses of such as are commonly call'd Natural Philosophers [i.e. those who reason abstractly or deductively], and those of Anatomists, a large difference; the former are facil, the latter difficult."[32] But this "large difference" is of course only a superficial one. The important fact is that the results of this facile reasoning are bound to be inaccurate since they do not take into account all the manifold factors in any actual political situation. Harrington's opinion of Hobbes's theories, which we shall examine in greater detail below, is instructive in this respect. When, quite uncharacteristically, Hobbes bases his conclusions on historical evidence, Harrington is quite willing to argue with him. Otherwise he is content to go his own way, re-

31. *Coll. Works*, p. xxiv.
32. *Art of Lawgiving, Coll. Works*, p. 429.

ferring only casually to Hobbes's patently foolish attempts
to "make you a King by *Geometry*."[33]

If abstract, deductive reasoning and "mathematical"
demonstration are unsuited to the study of politics, what
method did Harrington propose to follow? Before we can
answer this question we must pause to note still another
controversy between Harrington and his old antagonist
Matthew Wren. Wren, in one of his books, had asserted that
there could not possibly be any true demonstration or proof
save by mathematical methods. Harrington could not let
this pass unchallenged, and in reply he cited two contemporary logicians, DuMoulin and Sanderson, asking, "Are
they not clearly on my Side then, that there may be Demonstration, and yet not mathematical?" He answered his own
question thus: "Why sure there may be, Sir; nay, and such
a Demonstration may be every whit as valid and convincing,
as if it were mathematical."[34]

By what method is this equally valid demonstration to
be made? Here, surprisingly enough, Harrington appealed
to the very man whose method he had formerly criticized—
Hobbes. Hobbes had earlier asserted that "All true Ratiocination, which taketh its Beginning from true Principles,
produceth Science, and is true Demonstration."[35] This
statement Harrington adopted as the basis of his "science
of politics." But we must hasten to point out that in his
hands it became very different from what Hobbes had intended it to be. For Hobbes this was simply the justification
of the deductive method—beginning with a true premise
and reasoning by logically sound stages one will arrive at
a true conclusion. But, as we have seen, it was against precisely such abstract reasoning that Harrington had earlier

33. *Oceana,* p. 50; and also *Politicaster, Coll. Works,* p. 587.
34. *Politicaster, Coll. Works,* p. 592.
35. Hobbes, *De corpore politico* (London, 1650), p. 63; quoted by
Harrington in *Politicaster, Coll. Works,* p. 592.

protested. How, then, was he able to accept Hobbes's basic methodological principle without also accepting Hobbes's deductive method?

The answer to this question is to be found in the principle which Harrington, ostensibly following Hobbes's instructions, adopted as his own methodological starting-point. The principle was this: "What was always so and no otherwise, and still is so and no otherwise, the same shall ever be so and no otherwise."[36] This principle, Harrington believed, is self-evident; it "admitteth of as little proof or denial, as that Fire burns." But in this form, it must be admitted, the principle really means very little. At best it appears to express a belief in some sort of uniformity in natural phenomena; but even this is not very clear. Fortunately, Harrington discussed this matter at greater length in his dialogue *Valerius and Publicola*. There he expressed his principle in a somewhat different form: "That what neither is, nor ever was in Nature, can never be in Nature."[37] When Publicola (Harrington's spokesman here) had made this statement, Valerius raised several objections. Since the "frame of a government," like the frame of a house, is a matter more of art than of nature, he asked, why are not innovation and variety possible in politics? Publicola replied that it was the "materials of a government," like the materials of a house, that were found in nature and consequently limited the possibility of innovation and variation. But Valerius was not content with this reply; he sought to disprove Publicola's assertions by means of examples. What of the sea between Sicily and Naples that formerly had been land, he asked, or Holland that formerly had been sea, or the new star in the constellation Cassiopeia? Were these not, in fact, new things in nature? Publicola replied that this was not the case; these were all simply new

36. *Politicaster, Coll. Works*, p. 592.
37. *Coll. Works*, p. 492.

instances of things old in nature. Said he: "the new and extraordinary generation of a Star, or of a Mountain, no more
causes a Star or a Mountain to be a new thing in Nature,
than the new and extraordinary generation of a Commonwealth causes a Commonwealth to be a new thing in Nature."[38]

The substance of Harrington's methodological principle
has now become somewhat clearer. The principle of the
uniformity of nature is not to be understood in any simple-
minded sense; particular institutions or arrangements are
not immortal or immutable, nor are new ones impossible.
Rather the uniformity pertains to the basic elements of
politics and to the laws which govern their behavior; these
are immortal and immutable. And it was precisely these elements and these laws which Harrington sought to discover.

We have now reached the point at which Harrington
and Hobbes part company. Both believed in the existence of
general political principles, but they differed on the question of how these principles were to be apprehended by the
student of politics. Hobbes believed that by starting with
a true principle, which is itself self-evident, one can arrive
at true conclusions simply by a logical process similar to
that used in mathematics. As we have noted, Harrington
cited this passage from Hobbes as a justification of his own
method, which was inductive rather than deductive. He did
this with the help of a rather unconvincing verbal trick.
Hobbes started with a self-evident principle and ended with
various "demonstrated" conclusions, which he reached by
"true ratiocination." It was this reference to true ratiocination that contained the key to Hobbes's method. Harrington ignored this and, by so doing, was able to give the impression that his own method followed logically from
Hobbes's requirements. But if these words are ignored, all

38. Ibid., pp. 494–95.

that remains are the starting-point and the result of Hobbes's method, and not the method itself. And it was precisely on the question of method that Harrington and Hobbes disagreed. It is perhaps unfortunate that Harrington felt it necessary to go through this performance in order to give the impression that he and Hobbes were in basic agreement, for it obscures the very important differences between them.[39]

What was the method Harrington proposed to follow in his political investigations? He began, as we have seen, with the assumption of a certain uniformity in nature. This uniformity was manifest not in specific institutions, but rather in the basic "materials" of politics and in the laws that govern their behavior. Comparing this belief in the uniformity of political "nature" with the assertion that fire burns, Harrington wrote: "I can no more prove the one than the other: wherefore if you can no more deny the one than the other, by the leave of your Mathematicians, this Principle is no less sure and certain than the best in their Art: and what *Ratiocination* I use in my Politicks, *that taketh not its beginning,* or is not legitimately and undeniably derived from this Principle, I am contented should go for nothing."[40] Harrington was quite safe in thus challenging his opponents, for it cannot be denied that all of his "politicks" was founded on a belief in the existence of such immutable political laws. Since these laws govern all political behavior, they may be discovered through study of this behavior. This, in fact, is the key to Harrington's methodology; it led him to an espousal of the principles of induction and empiricism.

39. Since it is obvious that Harrington was aware of the fundamental differences between his method and Hobbes's, one can only conclude that he was anxious to win for himself some of the prestige that the deductive method enjoyed in the mid-17th century.

40. *Politicaster, Coll. Works,* p. 593.

In matters of method Harrington took as his model the physiological investigations of William Harvey, discoverer of the circulation of the blood and one of the intellectual heroes of the seventeenth century.[41] Harvey was by no means original in the problem which he chose to investigate; studies of the heart and blood vessels date back at least to Hippocrates. In the twenty-odd centuries between the "Father of Medicine" and William Harvey many serious students of anatomy devoted considerable attention to these organs and to the problems their functioning raised. Many of them, and in particular Galen, Leonardo da Vinci, Realdus Columbus, and Fabricius, had come close to an accurate explanation of the function of the heart and the circulatory system. But even as late as Harvey's time three great errors persisted: the beliefs that the interventricular septum is porous, that the arteries contain air, and that the veins carry blood to the periphery of the body. So long as these errors persisted, no real understanding of the circulatory system was possible. Successive generations of students accepted these mistaken views simply on the authority of their predecessors, and consequently were unable to discover the proper explanation of the behavior of the heart and the blood.

Harvey's fame rests on the fact that, refusing to fall into this error, he arrived at an accurate description of the circulation of the blood simply by observing the functioning of the body. It has been said that Harvey's method was consciously modeled on the pattern laid down by Francis Bacon in his essay on *The Advancement of Learning*.[42] Al-

41. For an excellent short treatment of Harvey, see Archibald Malloch, *William Harvey* (New York, 1929).

42. This is suggested by Sir William Hale-White in his *Bacon, Gilbert and Harvey*, Harveian Oration for 1927 (London, 1927). Hale-White's attempt to demonstrate a direct connection between Bacon and Harvey is far from convincing, but there can be no doubt that Harvey's method was much like that suggested by Bacon.

though this connection has hardly been demonstrated, it is unquestionably true that Harvey did agree with Bacon concerning the importance of detailed observation and experimentation. There can be little doubt that his discovery resulted from the brilliant and imaginative interpretation of the results of his long and painstaking observation of the circulatory systems of various animals. In his own words, he proposed "both to learn and to teach anatomy, not from books but from dissections; not from the positions of philosophers but from the fabric of nature." The following passage, although lengthy, is so revealing of Harvey's approach as to be worth quoting in its entirety:

> But what remains to be said upon the quantity and source of the blood which thus passes is of so novel and unheard-of character, that I not only fear injury to myself from the envy of a few, but I tremble lest I have mankind at large for my enemies. . . . Still the die is cast, and my trust is in my love of truth, and the candour that inheres in cultivated minds. And sooth to say, when I surveyed my mass of evidence, whether derived from vivisections, and my various reflections on them, or from the ventricles of the heart . . . or from the arrangement and intimate structure of the valves in particular . . . with many things besides, I frequently and seriously bethought me, and long revolved in my mind, what might be the quantity of blood which was transmitted, in how short a time its passage might be effected, and the like. . . . [And] I began to think whether there might not be A MOTION, AS IT WERE, IN A CIRCLE. Now this I afterwards found to be true; and I finally saw that the blood . . . was distributed to the body at large, and its several parts. . . . Which motion we may be allowed to call circular.[43]

43. Harvey, *Prelictiones anatomiae universalis*, 4a–4b; quoted by Malloch, *William Harvey*, p. 11.

This, then, was the method by which Harvey arrived at his discovery of the circulation of the blood. In the first place, he began with a definite problem: to explain the workings of the heart, the blood, and the circulatory system, and their interrelation. He then proceeded to observe the available evidence. On the basis of this evidence and of his "reflections" on it, he was able to formulate a tentative theory. On the basis of this hypothesis further observations were made and the theory was "afterwards found to be true." By this Harvey of course means simply that the phenomena he subsequently observed were all satisfactorily explained by his theory.

Harrington proposed to follow this method in his study of politics. Indeed, he conceived the task of the political "scientist" to be identical to that of the anatomist. In his *Art of Lawgiving* he wrote:

> But the fearful and wonderful making, the admirable structure and great variety of the parts of a man's Body, in which the Discourses of Anatomists are altogether conversant, are understood by so few, that I may say they are not understood by any. Certain it is, that the delivery of a Model of Government (which either must be of no effect, or imbrace all those Muscles, Nerves, Arterys and Bones, which are necessary to any Function of a well-order'd Commonwealth) is no less than political Anatomy.[44]

Like the anatomist the political scientist is concerned primarily with description. But in either case this is not simply description of individual or singular phenomena; rather it must be description of interrelations and general principles. In both cases these general principles are to be discovered only by a study of particular evidence. In his

44. *Coll. Works,* p. 429.

Leviathan, Thomas Hobbes had complained that both Aristotle and Cicero had derived their general principles "not from the Principles of Nature, but transcribed them into their books, out of the practice of their own Commonwealths."[45] Such an objection was natural to one who, like Hobbes, followed the deductive, "geometric" method. Since Aristotle and Cicero had generalized on the basis of their knowledge of particular historical commonwealths their generalizations could have no universal validity, he felt.

Harrington of course took exception to this view. This, he said, "is as if a man should tell famous *Hervey,* that he transcribed his *Circulation* of the *bloud,* not out of the *Principles* of Nature, but out of the *Anatomy* of this or that body."[46] Although Harvey did discover the general principle of the circulation of the blood by a study of particular bodies, this principle is nevertheless relevant to the circulatory systems of all animals. Similarly, general political principles, if they could be discovered, would be relevant to all governments. And they, too, would be discovered by a study of particular evidence—in this case, particular governments.

Thus we can see that Harrington's comparison of the study of politics with anatomy was not simply a casual simile. On the contrary, it represented a reasoned belief in the basic likeness of the two disciplines. This resulted, in the first instance, from Harrington's conviction that the subject matter of the two has much in common: the "body politic" (the phrase itself indicates that Harrington was not alone in his belief) and the human body are both extremely complex structures made up of a variety of interrelated parts. Consequently the study of the two should also be similar; Harvey's noteworthy successes in the field of anatomy should serve as an inspiration for the student of

45. Bk. II, Ch. 21.
46. *Oceana,* p. 13.

politics. When Harrington was taken to task by Matthew
Wren for accepting Harvey's method uncritically he replied
that his references to the study of anatomy were to be taken
as "similitudes," and added, "though a Similitude have not
that Proof in it, which may draw a Man, yet it hath such In-
ducement in it as may lead a Man."[47] This presumably can
serve to explain Harrington's frequent use of anatomical
images, such as that in which he compares the Council of
Trade to the Vena Porta[48] or that which likens the two
chambers of the legislature to the two chambers of the
heart. These are not meant to constitute proof of Harrington's argument. Rather they are intended as "induce-
ments," dependent largely it would seem on the prestige
which Harvey had won for the inductive method.

Returning now to Harrington's own method, we may inquire briefly into the nature of the general laws, or principles, which his study enabled him to formulate. Were
they, properly speaking, created by the investigator or discovered by him? On this point Harrington leaves no doubt
—these "laws of nature" exist, and have existed, and will
continue to exist completely independent of the activities
of the political scientist. Thus he speaks of the principle of
political balance as "being as antient in Nature as her self,
and yet as new in Art as my Writing."[49] Consequently the
political scientist is strictly limited in his investigations by
the existence of these eternal principles. If his method is a
proper one, and if the principles he discovers are therefore
true, no one can justly complain of his results, pleasant or
unpleasant though they may be.

This Harrington stated quite explicitly in another of his
many controversies with Matthew Wren. Referring to Harrington's discussion of the principle of balance Wren had

47. *Politicaster, Coll. Works,* p. 595.
48. *Oceana,* p. 110.
49. *Prerogative of Popular Government, Coll. Works,* p. 249.

said that he had "given the world cause to complain of a great disappointment."[50] Harrington answered that this was a ridiculous and meaningless statement. It was, he said, "as if he had told Dr. HARVEY that . . . he had given the world cause to complain of great disappointment in not shewing a Man to be made of Gingerbread, and his Veins to run Malmsy."[51] Like Harvey, Harrington believed that he had simply demonstrated the existence and the content of certain general laws which would continue to operate regardless of anything men could do. Although these laws could not be changed, and therefore it would be foolish to complain about them, it was necessary for men to understand them in order to act intelligently.

Convincing as Harrington's analogy between anatomy and political science may have been, it did raise certain very real problems for the political scientist. Granting the existence of certain immutable general laws of politics, and granting further that these laws may be discovered by a study of empirical evidence, the question still remains where to discover this evidence. It is here that the political scientist and the anatomist must part company. The latter is able to observe, and what is even more important to experiment on, a great number of living animals. This the political scientist cannot do. But nevertheless the political scientist requires as evidence some knowledge of the actual functioning of a considerable number of governments. How is this requirement to be met? Harrington's answer is similar to that given by most empirical students of government: the political scientist must first study the governments which have existed in the past and then investigate the governments of his own time. Said Harrington, "No man can be a Polititian, except he be first an Historian or a Travel-

50. Ibid.
51. Ibid.

ler; for except he can see what Must be, or what May be, he
is no polititian: Now if he have no knowledge in story [i.e.
history] he cannot tell what hath been, and if he hath not
been a Traveller he cannot tell what is; but he that neither
knoweth what hath been, nor what is, can never tell what
must be, or what may be."⁵²

Harrington's early travels on the Continent and his observation of English politics provided him, he felt, with an
adequate knowledge of contemporary governments. He refers in particular to the government of Venice, and to a
lesser extent to those of Switzerland, France, and the Low
Countries. As for knowledge of past governments, this is
to be sought in the writings of historians. From such diverse
works as the Old and New Testaments, Aristotle's *Politics,*
Machiavelli's *Discorsi,* and Selden's *Titles of Honor*
(which are strictly speaking not histories), he gleans many
facts about past governments. It must be remembered, of
course, that the proper histories which were available to
Harrington, such as Raleigh's and Bacon's, were by modern
standards quite unreliable. Interestingly enough, Harrington seems to have been aware of this fact. In using all his
sources, save perhaps the Bible, he maintains a constantly
critical attitude. Although he felt it was possible to derive
accurate knowledge from them, he recognized that none of
them could be accepted at face value. One must compare
the information in them and above all one must apply *reason* to them. Thus if Giannotti and Contarini disagree
about some aspect of Venetian political history one must
first attempt to discover the facts in some third source. But
if, as was so often the case, this proves impossible, one must
simply decide for oneself which account is the more reasonable. In this way Harrington attempted to remedy the de-
ficiencies of his evidence, and in so doing made his method

52. *Oceana,* p. 175.

considerably more artistic, and less scientific, than he was willing to admit.

Even if one grants the weakness of the evidence with which Harrington had to work, it is apparent that a further artistic element is involved in the use of that evidence. What precisely was the method by which the political scientist could derive general principles from the mass of evidence at his disposal? Essentially, Harrington would have said, it was the application of reason to examples, or conversely, the verification of reason by examples. The former consists in an ability to understand the evidence and to generalize from it with accuracy. Harrington certainly did not believe that mere knowledge of past and present governments is sufficient to ensure that a political scientist will reach the proper conclusions; after all, Harvey was by no means the first person to observe the functioning of the circulatory system, but he *was* the first to discover the principle which could explain its functioning. Similarly, Harrington was quite aware that he had discovered no new *facts;* his method virtually precluded this, since his factual data were chiefly garnered from other writers.

He believed, however, that the conclusions he was able to draw from these facts were unique. As he expressed it, "there is a difference between having the sense of a thing, and making a right use of that sense."[53] For instance, Harrington believed that Aristotle, Plutarch, Machiavelli, Selden, Raleigh, and Bacon had all been more or less aware of the facts on which he based his theory of political balance—but none of them was able to discern the principle which explains these facts. Thus it remained for Harrington to "discover" the principle of political balance.[54] And in general we may say that for Harrington sheer knowledge

53. *Art of Lawgiving, Coll. Works,* p. 389.
54. Ibid.

was never sufficient; it must always be augmented by "reason," the ability to see the unity of principle beneath the apparent diversity of evidence.

But surely reason in this sense is an artistic rather than a merely mechanical function even though it can be verified by reference to the empirical evidence. Thus, having laid down the principle that all governments consist of three parts, Harrington, in characteristic phrase, writes, "Whether this be well reason'd . . . will best be shewn by the examples of the ancient Common-wealths taken in their order."[55] It would seem that in this discussion Harrington has had to rely finally upon the ability of the political scientist to extract principles from the evidence at hand. The results of this process can be checked by reference back to this evidence, but this too rests in the last analysis on the assumption that the evidence is properly understood.

This problem is by no means peculiar to Harrington. Indeed, it is fundamental to the very idea of empirical, inductively derived knowledge. Assuming the existence of general laws and the availability of empirical evidence, how is one to derive the former from the latter? At present the manifold successes of the natural sciences might indicate that the task is a simple one. It might appear that a thorough study of the evidence will lead almost inevitably to the formulation of valid generalizations. A moment's reflection, however, should serve to dispel this happy illusion. It is quite apparent that the mass of available evidence, in both natural and political science, is so large and complex as to make generalization tremendously difficult. One is reminded of Aristotle's definition of the imagination as that which "through all the welter of the actual . . . penetrates to the real," perceiving the similarity of apparently dissimilar phenomena and distinguishing between those that seem de-

55. *Oceana,* p. 37.

ceptively similar. It must be said to Harrington's credit that he was at least keenly aware of the problems inherent in the inductive method if not always able to solve them.

A casual reading of almost any of Harrington's works would probably lead one to conclude that his method consisted simply of copying from various governments and political theorists those arrangements and principles which seemed to him valid. What else can one believe when confronted with a sentence such as the following: "The *Censors* [of Oceana] derive their power of removing a *Senator,* from those of *Rome;* the Government of the Ballot, from those of *Venice;* and that of animadversion upon the *Ambitus,* or canvace for Magistracy, from both."[56] It would appear that Harrington is justifying these institutions merely by showing that similar ones had existed elsewhere. But this is not the case. Rather, Harrington's method consisted of what he constantly refers to as a combination of reason and experience. As he once wrote, "that which is against Reason and Experience is impossible."[57] And this reference to a political arrangement as "impossible" brings us to the heart of Harrington's methodology.

The central problem of politics in his day, he felt, was the attempt by ignorant and willful men to impose political systems which were in a very real sense impossible. These arrangements were impossible because they involved some violation of the laws which govern political life. The men who proposed such impossible arrangements did so because they were unaware of the laws of politics, and this in turn resulted from their failure to apply either reason or the lessons of experience. Reason alone, as in the case of Hobbes, is an unrealistic and unreliable guide. But on the other hand, experience can be meaningful only when interpreted

56. Ibid., p. 106.
57. Ibid., p. 89.

by reason.[58] Thus Harrington's ideal became the combination of these two, along lines suggested by Harvey's anatomical investigations.

But if such empirical study can enable one to avoid attempting the impossible, it certainly does not guide one
in choosing among various possible courses of action. This
becomes quite clear in Harrington's writings, although he
seldom admits that it is a real problem. Harrington's scientific study of politics led him to state categorically that
England's present balance of property could support only
a "commonwealth"; any effort to establish a different form
of government was bound to fail. On the other hand Harrington clearly believed that the balance of property can
be changed by political action. In other words, a person
who desired the restoration of the monarchy could conceivably bring this about simply by a redistribution of
property. Presumably the political theorist, at least insofar
as he is a scientist, must be content merely to point out
this fact.

But the interesting thing is that Harrington himself was
not content to stop here. Although basing his theory of
politics on what he believed to be a solid empirical foundation, he then proceeded to make various value judgments
which are clearly not scientifically demonstrable. We will
have occasion in the next chapter to examine in some detail
the relation between these two aspects of Harrington's
thought. For the present it will suffice to note that when
he is working in the realm of values Harrington's approach
is essentially that of the conventional adherent to natural
law theory. His sources are now no longer Aristotle and
Machiavelli and Giannotti, but rather the Bible and Grotius and Richard Hooker. An "equal commonwealth" is

58. See, for instance, the speech of Olphaus Megaletor beginning
on p. 89 of *Oceana,* and Harrington's statement on p. 139 that his
aim is to exclude all the inconveniences of past governments.

no longer simply the form of government that is best suited to a certain distribution of property, rather it is "that onely which is without flaw, and containeth in it the full perfection of Government."[59] A scientific knowledge of the laws of politics is, in short, an indispensable preliminary, but it is only a preliminary to the more important normative enterprise which is the creation of the best form of government.

This last statement may seem inconsistent with the deterministic elements of Harrington's theory noted in the first section of this chapter. Whereas Harrington often speaks as though it were impossible for the political theorist to create any new political order, on occasion he argues that the construction of a well-ordered commonwealth is the supreme expression of human intelligence and power. Is it possible to reconcile these two positions? In any ultimately logical sense it would seem that the answer must be negative. The idea of "the state as a work of art," which clearly motivates the discussion of the creation of the Commonwealth of Oceana, is fundamentally opposed to the belief that the political scientist seeks only to understand the operation of the laws of politics. The difference here is that between the active creator and the passive observer.

In Harrington's case, however, it is probably a mistake to insist on any such clear and logical separation; there is no doubt that he believed firmly in both ideals. And the two, when combined, lead to something which we may characterize as "the state as an architectural feat."[60] When Harrington was appealing to Oliver Cromwell he quite naturally stressed the elements of will, power, and creativity in politics. When he was engaged in controversies with other political theorists he naturally sought to show that

59. *Oceana*, p. 32.
60. Harrington himself once used the term "Political Architecture" (*Art of Lawgiving, Coll. Works*, p. 391).

necessity, as demonstrated by science, was on his side. In fact, this concept of "political architecture" leaves room for neither pure scientific detachment nor sheer artistic creativity. The political theorist must understand the fundamental laws of political life; without such knowledge his efforts would be meaningless. But within the limits imposed by these laws he is free to exercise his creative abilities, presumably in accordance with ethical judgments. In conclusion we may note that by a happy coincidence, the significance of which Harrington never examined too closely, the Commonwealth of Oceana was at the same time the form of government best suited to England's economic condition and the most ethically desirable of polities. In this best of all possible political worlds science and ethics both led to the same conclusions, thus relieving Harrington of the necessity of a logical reconciliation.

CHAPTER 3.

The Principles of Government:
Ancient Prudence

"... being as antient in Nature as her self,
and yet as new in Art as my Writing."
The Prerogative of Popular Government

Empire and Authority

To go mine own way, and yet to follow the Ancients: the Principles of Governments are twofold, *Internal*, or the goods of the *Mind;* and *External*, or the goods of *Fortune.*"[1] With this highly characteristic statement Harrington begins the explication of his theory of politics. Virtually everything he has to say about government can be understood in terms of the twofold classification here laid down, although later commentators have chosen to confine themselves almost solely to one of the two "principles."

The first question this statement raises concerns the meaning of the term "principles of Governments." They are the characteristics or qualities of a government, or a ruler, by virtue of which that government or ruler is able to rule. In other words, these principles of government explain the existence of the political relationship. What are these qualities? On the one hand, Harrington says, they are External, consisting of the "goods of Fortune." These goods of fortune are simply and solely "riches," that is, material wealth. On the other hand, the principles of government are Internal, consisting of the "goods of the Mind." These goods of the mind are various, but the most important among them are wisdom, prudence, and courage. In summary, then, we may say that the phenomenon of government can be explained in terms of the possession by the ruler of a variety of attributes, either internal or external. In other words, we would expect that some governments exist because the rulers possess great wealth, while others result from the presence of exceptionally wise, prudent, or

1. *Oceana,* p. 14. Cf. Aristotle, *Politics,* VII, 1, 2; and Plato, *Laws,* III, 697–98.

courageous rulers. But is the situation in fact so simple? Are there not instances in which these two, goods of the mind and goods of fortune, are in some way related to each other? And, if so, how are they related?

Although both goods of the mind and goods of fortune are "principles of governments," and although both therefore give rise to political power, it is necessary for us to recognize that political power is itself a twofold affair. That sort of power which results from the goods of the mind Harrington calls "authority"; that which results from the goods of fortune is "empire."[2] Thus Harrington writes: "Wherefore *Leviathan,* though he be right where he saith, that *Riches are Power* [i.e. Empire]; is mistaken where he saith that *Prudence, or the reputation of Prudence is power:* for the learning or prudence of a man is no more power [i.e. Empire], then the learning or prudence of a book or Authour, which is properly Authority."[3] It is obvious that the general distinction between empire and authority is not new with Harrington. He himself quotes Livy as saying of Evander, "regebat magis Authoritate quam Imperio."[4] And, as a matter of fact, some such distinction has been current in western political thought at least since the time of the Roman Empire, when the emperor was said to possess "imperium," while censors and senators exercised "auctoritas." Perhaps the most common use of the terms was that made by the Church Fathers to distinguish the power of the Pope from that of the Emperor, or any other secular

---

2. It is rather unfortunate that Harrington chose to use the words "empire" and "power" synonymously, contrasting both with "authority." I have chosen, simply as a matter of convenience, to use the word "power" as a general term to include both "empire" and "authority."

3. *Oceana,* p. 14; see *Leviathan,* I, 10.

4. *Oceana,* p. 14; actually the quotation reads, "Evander . . . auctoritate magis, quam imperio, regebat loca," Livy, I, 7.

ruler.[5] The power of the Pope, "auctoritas," was said to lead men by reason and persuasion, while the power of secular rulers, "potestas," simply compelled them by force to obey. Essentially, then, the traditional distinction is between a power which has certain moral qualities and one which consists solely of physical force.[6] This is clearly the distinction Harrington makes in the introduction to his theory of politics.

Is it true, then, that the basis of Harrington's theory is simply an application of a traditional and commonly accepted principle? And, if this is in fact the case, must we conclude that Harrington's theory is completely lacking in originality? The answer to the first of these questions is, at least in a sense, affirmative. The distinction between empire and authority is both traditional and commonly accepted, and it certainly is also the basis of Harrington's theory of politics. But this does not mean that we must also answer the second question affirmatively. The fact is that Harrington reinterpreted the classic distinction between these two kinds of power in a highly original manner. The originality lies in his making an explicit connection between the goods of the mind and authority on the one hand, and the goods of fortune and empire on the other. We see now that there are two sorts of political power, one moral and the other amoral, one based on wisdom, courage and prudence, the other based on wealth. And with this observation we have arrived at the very heart of Harrington's theory of politics. In order to understand this point more thoroughly it will be necessary for us to consider these two kinds of power

5. On this point Gelasius I was particularly outspoken. "Duo sunt," he wrote, "quibus principaliter hic mundus regitur, *auctoritas* sancta pontificum, et regalis *potestas.*" *Dist.* xcvi, c. 10; italics added.

6. One is reminded of the famous passage from Rousseau: "Force is a physical power, and I fail to see what moral effect it can have." *Social Contract,* I, Ch. 3.

separately. Having done this we will then be in a position
to inquire into their relation.

Harrington begins his discussion of empire, and of the
goods of fortune, by noting that "men are hung upon these,
not of choice as upon the other [i.e. authority], but of
necessity and by the teeth." He explains this by saying that
people must eat and that anyone who feeds another thereby
gains empire over him. Thus, "for as much as he who wanteth bread, is his servant that will feed him: if a man thus
feed an whole people, they are under his Empire."[7] Although this is a completely explicit statement, it seems wise
to avoid interpreting it in a purely literal sense. Unquestionably Harrington intended that it be taken literally—a
starving man *will* serve anyone who feeds him—but he
doubtless also meant for it to have a wider application, that
is, an application in cases somewhat less extreme than sheer
starvation or simple physical sustenance. This becomes
clear as we follow his argument.

In the first place, we learn that empire is of two sorts,
domestic and foreign (or national and provincial). Domestic empire, the variety with which we will be most concerned, is founded on what Harrington calls "Dominion."
This, in turn, is defined as "Propriety reall or personall,
that is to say, in Lands, or in money and goods."[8] In short,
that variety of political power which we call domestic empire will be the possession of those persons who possess property. This, in its simplest form, is Harrington's most famous
contribution to political theory—the theory of the economic foundation of political power. In view of the usual
interpretation of Harrington's theory it is impossible for
one to insist too strongly that this relation between power
and wealth pertains to only *one* of the numerous varieties

7. *Oceana,* p. 14.
8. Ibid.

of political power. It does not apply at all to authority. Furthermore, it does not even apply to foreign empire. Therefore, instead of saying that Harrington taught that political power is a reflection of economic wealth, it is a great deal more accurate to say that he taught that domestic empire is dependent upon the possession of property. Thus his first, and clearest, statement of the principle reads: "such . . . as is the proportion or ballance of dominion or property in Land, such is the nature of the *Empire*."[9]

This statement leads us to a further refinement of Harrington's theory. Not only may we say that empire follows property, we may also explain the existence of various forms of government in these terms. Following the traditional classification, Harrington envisages three possible arrangements:

> If one man be sole Landlord of a Territory, or overballance the people, for example, three parts in four, he is Grand Signior: for so the Turk is call'd from his *Property;* and his *Empire* is absolute *Monarchy*.

> If the Few or a Nobility, or a Nobility with the Clergy be Landlords, or overballance the people unto the like proportion, it makes the *Gothick* ballance . . . and the *Empire* is mixed *Monarchy*. . . .

> And if the whole people be Landlords, or hold the Lands so divided among them, that no one man, or number of men, within the compass of the *Few* or *Aristocracy*, overballance them, the *Empire* (without the interposition of force) is a *Common-wealth*.[10]

It should be emphasized that so far this is all simply an observation of fact on Harrington's part, having nothing whatever to do with considerations of value. An absolute

9. Ibid., pp. 14–15.
10. *Oceana*, p. 15.

monarchy is neither good nor bad because it is based on the great wealth of a single individual, a commonwealth is neither better nor worse because it reflects a widespread distribution of property. The central point is that varying property arrangements will necessarily produce varying political systems.

But here we must note the exception implied above in Harrington's description of a commonwealth. "Without the interposition of force," he wrote. May we take this as an indication that the relation between property arrangements and forms of government is not an absolute one? Is it possible that "force" can impose a government that is not "naturally" suited to the distribution of property? Harrington's answer is at the same time equivocal and revealing. "If force be interposed in any of these three cases," he writes,[11] "it must either frame the Government unto the foundation, or the foundation unto the Government; or holding the Government not according unto the ballance, it is not natural, but violent." The first two cases are, of course, simply a further development of the basic theory, and one of them raises no problems. Surely one must recognize the process of "framing the Government unto the foundation," if the theory is to have any meaning. Although this presumably will not always require force, the intrusion of an element of force does not seem to disturb the theory. If one man possesses three-fourths of the property it is to be expected that he will be able to impose absolute monarchy; otherwise the theory has no meaning. But what of "framing the foundation unto the Government"? In one respect this action is consonant with Harrington's general theory: it does aim at the creation of a situation in which the form of government is appropriate to the balance of property. But in another respect it raises a very real prob-

11. Ibid.

lem. This will become apparent if we stop for a moment to consider why it is that wealth creates empire.

The first indication of the relation between wealth and empire is the statement, already noted, that "if a man . . . feed an whole people, they are under his Empire." This, however, is such an extreme statement, implying as it does an absolute dependence upon one man for physical sustenance, that it has little general significance. Further investigation reveals that what Harrington had in mind here was primarily the ability to support a militia or to hire mercenary soldiers. As for the former, the most interesting passage is one in which Harrington takes issue with Hobbes's assertion that covenants without the sword have no power to oblige any man.[12] This Harrington admits to be perfectly true, but he argues that Hobbes has not carried the argument far enough.

> But as he said of the Law, that without this sword it is but paper; so he might have thought of this sword, that without an hand it is but cold iron. The hand which holdeth this sword is the Militia of a Nation; and the Militia of a Nation, is either an Army in the field, or ready for the field upon occasion. But an Army is a beast that hath a great belly and must be fed; wherefore this will come unto what pastures you have, and what pastures you have will come unto the ballance of propriety, without which the public sword is but a name or meer spit-frog.[13]

In other words, since empire (as distinct from authority, of course) is simply a matter of physical force, the deciding factor *will* be the ability to command military power, but

12. *Leviathan*, II, 18: ". . . covenants being but words and breath, have no force to oblige, contain, constrain, or protect any man, but what it has from the public sword."
13. *Oceana*, p. 16.

this in turn will depend upon possession of wealth. The case with mercenaries is virtually identical. Physical force in this form can be purchased, thus clearly illustrating Harrington's general contention that wealth will produce empire. Actually the case of the mercenary soldier is particularly useful to Harrington because the cash nexus is here unobscured by irrelevant considerations. As he reminds his readers, "Point de Argent, point de Suisse."[14] In both cases then, since empire consists in the ability to make others obey, empire will be an attribute of the person or group possessing a preponderance of wealth.

We may now consider once more Harrington's reference to "framing the foundation unto the Government." This obviously can occur only when the form of government is not suited to the balance of property. In such a case it is apparently possible for the rulers to alter the distribution of property in such a way as to perpetuate their rule. And this obviously can be done only by aggrandizement on the part of the rulers. But if force depends on the prior possession of property, it is difficult to see how this can be accomplished by force. Since Harrington is fond of concrete examples and exact quantitative expression, it will be well for us to visualize such a situation. Let us suppose that a country is ruled by an absolute monarch who possesses only one-fourth of the land of that country, while a nobility owns the remaining three-fourths. Now clearly this country is unsuited to absolute monarchical government and should be ruled by a mixed monarchy, with actual power in the hands of the nobility. And it is equally clear that the nobility should be able to effect this change by "framing the Government unto the foundation." But how is it possible for the king, by force, to alter the balance in such a way that he will possess at least three-fourths of the land? Lack-

14. *Coll. Works,* p. 243. ("no Mony, no Switzers," he translates.)

ing sufficient wealth, the king has not the power to rule absolutely. How, then, can he have the power to deprive the nobility of its property? The only conceivable answer is that some accidental factor must interfere with the natural course of events. Although Harrington says little about this subject, several possibilities can be imagined. It is possible, for instance, that foreign intervention may enable a monarch to seize the wealth, and therefore the power, of his nobility. It is also possible that sheer stupidity or mismanagement on the part of the nobility might lead to the same result. Again, more likely than these, disunity among the nobility, perhaps as a result of the successful use of tactics of *divide et impera* on the part of the monarch, might effectively destroy the power of the nobles. And once these tactics succeed, of course, then the position of the monarch becomes quite firm again; having regained a preponderance of wealth, he should be secure in his power.

But this immediately raises a more fundamental question. If one admits the possibility of a reversal of the general principle by the intrusion of such accidental factors, what validity does the principle retain? Harrington's answer would be this: it is possible, in the short run, that this general principle may not operate with absolute certainty, but over any considerable period of time it is absolutely true that domestic empire will be determined by the distribution of wealth. Indeed, the very process of framing the foundation to fit the government implicitly recognizes this truth. The king who seeks to destroy a too-powerful nobility does so precisely because he realizes, whether explicitly or not, that he must accumulate sufficient wealth vis-à-vis any other individual or group in order to retain his power. The alternative is to attempt "to hold the Government not according unto the ballance." If one man does this, the result is tyranny; if it is done by a few men, the result is oligarchy; if it is done by the people as a whole, the result is anarchy.

Indeed, each of these "unnatural and violent" forms of government is defined by the fact that it is not suited to the particular distribution of property existing at the time. And, as indicated above, none of these forms can hope to endure unless it is successful in altering the balance: "each of which confusions, the ballance standing otherwise, is but of short continuance; because against the nature of the ballance, which not destroyed, destroyeth that which opposeth it."[15]

So far we have been concerned only with cases in which the so-called balance of property in a community is clearly defined; Harrington speaks of a preponderance of three parts out of four.[16] But what, we may inquire, is the result of a situation in which the balance is more nearly equal? In fact Harrington recognizes this possibility and deals with two such situations. In the first place, it is conceivable that the people may possess half the property and the nobility the other half. The result, as in the case where the government does not fit the balance, will be "confusion." But here the confusion will be "of longer continuance, and of greater horror" because no simple solution is available. The very evenness of the balance will make it impossible for anyone to act decisively and therefore "there is no remedy but the one must eat out the other: as the people did the *Nobility* in *Athens,* and the *Nobility* the people in *Rome.*"[17] In other words, the best that can be hoped for in such a case is a gradual alteration of the balance in one direction or the other, leading eventually to a clear preponderance.

The second such situation which Harrington considers is that in which an individual possesses about half the land

15. *Oceana*, p. 15.
16. In his later works Harrington refers to a preponderance of two parts out of three as being equally, or at least sufficiently, clear-cut. See, for example, *A System of Politics, Coll. Works,* p. 498.
17. *Oceana*, p. 15.

and the people the other half. Such an arrangement, he says, existed in the later Roman Empire and made "a very shambles both of the Princes and the people." And he notes that "somewhat of this nature are certain Governments at this day; which are said to subsist by confusion."[18] Oddly enough, in this case Harrington recommends letting well enough alone. Where the government is somehow able to "subsist by confusion" he feels that "to fix the ballance is, to entail misery." The only hopeful possibilities are, again, either a continued muddling along or a gradual alteration of the balance. This is perhaps the only instance in which Harrington is willing to admit the inefficacy of rational management. Under all other circumstances, and so long as stability of government is our only goal, Harrington suggests that the wisest policy is to "fix" the balance by law. "This kind of Law fixing the ballance in Land is called *Agrarian*, and was first introduced by *God himself*, who divided the Land of *Canaan* unto his people by Lots, and is of such virtue, that where ever it hath held, that Government hath not alter'd, except by consent. . . . But without an *Agrarian*, Government whether Monarchical, Aristocraticall, or Popular, hath no long Lease."[19]

One further fact remains to be noted in connection with Harrington's treatment of domestic empire, a fact that for some reason has never been discussed by his commentators. We have spoken of the balance of property, or wealth, as existing in one individual, in a few individuals, or in all the people. Actually the terms which Harrington most often uses are king (or prince), nobility (or aristocracy), and the people, and this terminology is not without significance. It is quite clear that for Harrington the decisive distinction between the various forms of government lies not simply in the *number* of persons who possess a disproportionate

18. Ibid.
19. Ibid., p. 16.

share of wealth. Indeed, if sheer numbers were decisive it would be very difficult to distinguish between an aristocracy and a commonwealth; but more significant is the fact that Harrington never attempted in formulating his theory to supply any general numerical criterion for making such a distinction. And in the light of Harrington's fascination with numbers we can hardly suppose this omission to have been accidental. The fact is that he was more concerned with the *quality* of those who possess wealth than with their number.

It is difficult to arrive at any very precise formulation of Harrington's position here, but some hints are available to us. And of these, the above-mentioned terminology is unquestionably the most significant. A mixed monarchy exists, it will be recalled where "a Nobility, or a Nobility with the Clergy" own a preponderance of property. There can be no doubt that Harrington is here thinking primarily in terms of English history and politics, although of course the principle is a general one. The important fact to note is that Harrington here envisages a nation as being composed not of separate individuals, but rather of great "interests" or classes. And the only truly important distribution, or balance, of property is that among these three interests. Although this view of society pervades all of Harrington's writings, it is clearly expressed only in his last political work, published after his death: "Distribution of shares in Land, as to the three grand Interests, the King, the Nobility, and the People, must be equal or inequal."[20] Therefore the distinction between the three forms of government—absolute monarchy, mixed monarchy, and commonwealth—depends upon whether a king, a group of nobles, or the people possess the requisite amount of property. Leaving absolute monarchy aside, we may say that the

20. *A System of Politics, Coll. Works,* p. 497.

nature of the nobility and of the people are for Harrington the decisive factors in distinguishing between forms of government.

As we have seen, he defines a nobility as "such as live upon their own revenues in plenty, without engagement either unto the tilling of their Lands, or other work for their livelihood," but he also explicitly states that "nobility . . . may be subdivided into . . . such as hold an over-ballance in Dominion or Propriety unto the whole People: or such as hold not an over-ballance."[21] In other words, a nobility is not to be defined simply as a small group holding a preponderant share of land. Wealth is important, but equally important is what Harrington calls "ancient virtue."[22] On the other hand, if a nobility does possess three-fourths of the land of a nation, its individual members, since the class is small, will inevitably be very wealthy. And conversely, a limitation of individual wealth will effectively prevent this small class from accumulating the balance of dominion. The same is true, *mutatis mutandis*, of the people as a whole. Because this class is by definition large, it can jointly possess great wealth without unduly enriching its individual members. But, to conclude this discussion, the important thing for Harrington is the class which holds the balance of wealth. Although a disproportionately large accumulation of wealth by any small group of men will presumably be sufficient to create a mixed monarchy, it is clear that Harrington thinks only in terms of a nobility in the sense of a traditional class of landed aristocrats. This seemingly minor point is of central importance in the subsequent development of his theory.

In our discussion of domestic empire we have spoken rather indiscriminately of "wealth," "riches," "property,"

21. *Oceana,* p. 119. The first definition is taken from Machiavelli, *Discorsi,* I, 55.
22. *Oceana,* p. 119.

and "land." It will be well for us to devote some attention
to Harrington's analysis of the exact form of this wealth.
In his original statement Harrington says categorically that
"as is the proportion or ballance of dominion or property
in *Land,* such is the nature of the Empire."[23] But having
made this assertion, he must have realized that it was possible to discover political situations in which the principle
was either untrue or inapplicable. Of these the most obvious
would be that in which the total amount of land was so
small as to be an insignificant factor in the national economy. Although England in the seventeenth century was
still primarily an agrarian nation, there were fairly clear
signs of the increasing economic significance of commerce
and even manufacture. And still more important at the
time, there were communities in Italy and northern Europe
which not only supported themselves but actually prospered
on an almost purely commercial basis. Certainly it would
have been fatuous to argue that in these trading cities the
location of political power (domestic empire) was dependent on the ownership of land. And it is equally certain that
Harrington did not attempt to do this. In fact the sentence
quoted above is itself modified by the parenthetical phrase:
"except it be in a City that hath little or no Land, and
whose revenue is in Trade." And reading further we discover that what Harrington had in mind was precisely "such
Cities . . . as *Holland* and *Genoa.*"[24] Thus we see that Harrington was willing, in special cases, to broaden his original
statement of the relation between property and domestic
empire in order to include wealth in money and goods. As
he wrote, "the ballance of Treasure may be equal to that
of Land in the cases mentioned." And in so doing Harrington certainly strengthened his general theory, answering in

23. Italics added.
24. *Oceana,* p. 16.

advance those critics who feel that his theory is applicable only to an agrarian society.

But, as is so often the case, this modification did not serve to silence Harrington's critics. Indeed, we are indebted to one of them for stimulating Harrington to a further discussion of this very question. In his *Considerations on Mr. Harrington's . . . Oceana,* Matthew Wren wrote: "The assertion, that Property producing Empire consists only in Land appears too positive."[25] Harrington's immediate reaction to this was one of justified pique: "A Pig of my own Sow; this is no more than I told him."[26] He then proceeded in his *Prerogative of Popular Government* to repeat and expand his views on the relative political importance of money and property in land.

> The balance of Mony may be as good or better than that of Land in three cases. First, where there is no Property of Land as yet introduc'd. . . . Secondly, in Cities of small Territory and great Trade, as *Holland* and *Genoa,* the Land not being able to feed the People, who must live upon Traffic, is overbalanc'd by the means of that Traffic, which is Mony. Thirdly, in a narrow Country . . . if care be not had of Mony in the regulation of the same, it will eat out the balance of Land.[27]

The first of these cases, which Harrington illustrates by the example of "Greece during the time of her antient Imbecillity," is quite obvious; certainly there can be no balance of property in land where there is no property in land at all, and if wealth is to be important it must be wealth in money or goods. The second case is the one which Harrington dealt with in *Oceana* and which we have already noted.

25. P. 14.
26. *Coll. Works,* p. 245.
27. Ibid.

The third case is both new and somewhat more complex.
It seems that Harrington is here envisaging a situation mid-
way between those of England and Genoa, a situation in
which both agriculture and commerce play an important
part in the national economy. This he feels will occur when
there is a significant, but limited, amount of land available—enough, perhaps, to support the population, but not
enough to allow a high standard of living on a purely agrarian basis. Harrington seems to be arguing that in this case
there will be two distinct sources of economic wealth com-
peting for expression through political power. And Harrington's critics were probably correct to the extent at least
that it is true his sympathies in this competition lie on the
side of land. The moral which he draws is that, "In a Commonwealth, whose Territory is very small, the Balance of
the Government being laid upon the Land . . . it will not
be sufficient to forbid Usury [which leads to the accumulation of money], but Mony itself must be forbidden."[28] The
alternative to "forbidding" money is to become like Genoa
or Holland, an alternative which Harrington views rather
unsympathetically. The explanation of his position is to be
found in his belief that property in land is more stable than
that in money, and will therefore provide a more certain
foundation for political power. Thus,

> Tho Riches in general have Wings, and be apt to bate;
> yet those in Land are the most hooded, and ty'd to the
> Perch, wheras those in Mony have the least hold, and
> are the swiftest of flight. . . . Whence [to come to Har-
> rington's central concern] a Bank never paid an Army;
> or paying an Army soon became no Bank. But where
> a Prince or a Nobility has an Estate in Land, the Rev-
> enue wherof will defray this Charge, there their Men

28. Ibid.

are planted, have Toes that are Roots, and Arms that
bring forth what Fruit you please.[29]

Fortunately, England is not faced with any such choice because land is abundantly plentiful: ". . . that such a Territory as *England* or *Spain* cannot be overbalanc'd by Mony,
whether it be a scarce or plentiful Commodity, whether it
be accumulated by Parsimony as in the purse of Henry the
7th, or presented by Fortune, as in the Revenue of the
Indys, is sufficiently demonstrated."[30]

The general point is quite clear. Having originally
framed his theory of the economic base of domestic empire
in terms of his view of the English economy, Harrington
generally confined it to property in land. Finding himself
faced with the increasingly important phenomenon of national economies based solely or primarily on commerce,
he expanded the theory to include also property in money.
And, finally, under the stimulus of Wren's criticism he
enumerated the three situations in which he believed that
money might be *more* important politically than land. Because of his continuing concern for political stability, however, Harrington's sympathies remained on the side of
property in land and an agrarian economy. In any case, the
net result of all this was a theory both broader and stronger
than the original one; broader because it now accounted
for all varieties of wealth, stronger because it was now im-
mune to the sort of criticism which Wren had brought
against it. Like the natural scientists whom he admired so
much, Harrington here attempted to make his theory fit
all the relevant facts which he observed in the world of
politics.

The second variety of empire, provincial empire, constituted a considerable problem for Harrington. It is quite

29. Ibid., p. 243.
30. Ibid., p. 246.

clear that he wished to bring the phenomenon of colonialism within the bounds of his general theory of the basis of
political power, but it was not easy for him to do this without seriously weakening that theory. Previously Harrington
had argued that, on the domestic scene, the locus of political
power (empire) will be determined by the distribution of
wealth; generally speaking, the class which possesses the preponderant share of land will rule. How does it happen then
that England, for instance, should rule areas in America
vastly larger than herself? If the theory were applied as
originally stated, one would expect that England would be
ruled by America. This is the problem Harrington clearly
recognized and sought to solve in his discussion of provincial empire. And it should be emphasized at the outset that
it is in no way a moral problem. Since he is speaking only
of empire, Harrington is here not concerned with the
question of whether the English have a *right* to rule their
American territories; rather he is concerned to find an explanation for the fact that they clearly are *able* to rule them.
As he wrote, ". . . how a Province may be *justly* acquired, ap-
pertaineth to another place; in this I am to shew no more,
then how or upon what kind of ballance it is to be held."[31]

The argument begins with a clear recognition that the
American colonists, or any "provincial" people, might rule
themselves. Indeed, it is here that we encounter Harrington's well-known prediction of the breakdown of colonialism: "For the Colonies in the *Indies,* they are yet babes that
cannot live without sucking the breasts of their mother-
Cities, but such as, I mistake, if when they come of age they
do not wean themselves: which causeth me to wonder at
Princes that delight to be exhausted in that way."[32] When
this comes to pass the problem which now faces Harrington

31. *Oceana,* p. 18; italics added.
32. Ibid., p. 20.

will have disappeared; we will simply have one more instance of national government, of domestic empire.

Meanwhile, however, it is still necessary for Harrington
to fit the fact of colonialism into his theoretical framework.
Having defined "National or Independent Empire" as that
government which is "exercised by them that have the
proper *ballance of Dominion* in the Nation,"[33] he proceeds
to point out that ". . . Provincial or dependent Empire is not
to be exercised by them that have the *ballance of Dominion*
in the Province, because that would bring the Government
from *Provinciall* and *dependent*, to *National* and *Independent.*"[34] In other words, if America were ruled by those
who hold the balance of wealth *in* America, this would no
longer be provincial empire. If one objects that these men
will, after all, still be Englishmen, Harrington replies that
"the richest among the Provincials, though native Subjects,
or Citizens that have been transplanted, are least admitted
to the Government abroad: for men like flowers or roots
being transplanted take after the soyl wherein they grow."[35]
In other words, although these men started as Englishmen,
the British government will discover that they soon become
"Americans" and the empire will change from provincial
to domestic.

The first alternative to such an arrangement is one which
Harrington says is characteristic of absolute monarchy, "as
that of the Turks." In this case natives who emigrate as
colonists are not allowed to own land abroad, and therefore
the question of a provincial balance of wealth can never
arise: "*Absolute Monarchy* . . . neither planteth her people
at home nor abroad, otherwise than as Tenants for life or
at will; wherefore her *National* and her *Provincial* Govern-

33. Ibid., p. 18.
34. Ibid.
35. Ibid., pp. 18–19.

mcnt is all one."[36] Thus absolute monarchy maintains itself at home and preserves its possessions abroad by exactly
the same method, the monopoly of all land. The second
alternative, and one which is more bothersome theoretically, is the case in which colonists *are* allowed to own land
in the colonies. Here again Harrington manages to envisage
a situation in which no real problem arises—a situation in
which there is no possible conflict of interest between the
colonists and the mother country. He cites as an example
of this the early Roman colonization of Italy: ". . . *Rome,*
by planting *Colonies* of her Citizens within the bounds of
Italy, took the best way of propagating herself, and natural-
izing the Country; whereas if she had planted such Colonies
without the bounds of *Italy,* it would have alien'd the Citizens, and given a root unto liberty abroad, that might have
sprung up forraign or savage and hostile to her."[37] The
point seems to be that the contiguity of these "colonies" and
the mother country effectively prevented any division of
interest between them.

But this clearly does not solve the problem of colonies,
such as the English ones in America, which are separated
from the mother country by great distances. And this, after
all, is the real problem which Harrington must solve. He ap-
proaches it somewhat obliquely with a reference to the
rule of the Mamalucs in Egypt. These, according to Harrington,[38] were Circassians who were able to rule Egypt
without possessing any land there. Clearly, this example
embodies Harrington's problem in its most extreme form;
and in fact he proceeds to complicate it still further. "The
Mamaluc's," he wrote, "never durst plant themselves upon
Dominion, which growing naturally up into the National

36. Ibid., p. 18.
37. Ibid., p. 19.
38. Liljegren cites Soranzo's *L'Ottomanno,* I, 32, as the probable
source.

interest must have dissolved the forraign yoke in that Province."[39] In other words, these Circassians not only failed to base their empire on property in land, they also deliberately chose to rule on some other basis.

We have now reached the point at which Harrington can no longer avoid the central issue. He has, perhaps, succeeded in demonstrating that some kinds of provincial rule do not necessarily conflict with his theory of the economic base of political power. This is true either where colonists are forbidden to own land or where the colonies in effect become an integral part of the mother country. But it clearly is not true in other cases, and particularly in cases such as that of the Mamalucs in Egypt. And it is important to note that the cases in which it is not true are, in fact, the characteristically provincial ones. Taking America as typical of the problem, we may ask: how are the "Americans," once they come to own a major portion of land in America, to be prevented from ruling themselves? Or to put it another way: how are the English, once they own only a minor share of land in America, to maintain their provincial rule?

The answer is that provincial empire is essentially different from domestic empire. As Harrington once expressed it, "National Government is an effect of natural Force, or Vigor. Provincial Government is an effect of unnatural force, or Violence."[40] It must be noted once again that this is not meant by Harrington as a value judgment, although the words "vigor" and "violence" may suggest that it is. On the contrary, it is simply an observation of fact. What Harrington is really saying here is that provincial government (empire) is not based on wealth, either in land or in money. What, then, is its basis? Harrington has answered as follows: "*Provinciall ballance* . . . is . . . the *overballance*

39. *Oceana,* p. 19.
40. *A System of Politics, Coll. Works,* p. 496.

of a native Territory to a forraign; for as one Country bal-
lanceth it self by the distribution of propriety according
unto the proportion of the same, so one Country overbal-
lanceth another, by advantage of divers kinds."[41] In other
words, one country comes to rule another because it is in
some way superior to it, just as one class comes to rule do-
mestically because of its superiority in wealth. But what are
these advantages "of divers kinds"? Here we must rely solely
upon the examples which Harrington has given us: ". . .
the Common-wealth of Rome overballanced her provinces
by the *vigor* of a more excellent Government opposed unto
a *crazier,* or by a more *exquisite Militia* opposed unto
one *inferior in Courage or discipline:* the like was that of
the *Mamaluc's* being an *hardy,* unto the *Aegyptians* that
were a *soft people.* And the *ballance* of a *situation* is in this
kind, of wonderfull effect."[42] Clearly then, when we come
to provincial empire we are confronted with a basis of
government which is totally unconnected with economics.
Apparently a hardy people will be able to rule a soft one
regardless of which of the two owns the most land. Indeed,
in a case such as that of the Mamalucs the rulers may own
no land at all.

The difficulty, of course, arises when we try to reconcile
this theory of provincial empire with Harrington's statements concerning domestic empire. If these noneconomic
factors, such as organization, courage, and hardiness, can
play a decisive role in provincial relations, why must we
assume that they have no significance on the domestic political scene? But if they do have such significance, what becomes of Harrington's assertion that "as is the proportion
or ballance of dominion or property of Land, such is the
nature of the Empire"? Apparently Harrington would like
to argue that the two circumstances, domestic and provin-

41. *Oceana,* p. 20.
42. Ibid.

cial, are so different that factors decisive in one are insignificant in the other. But he has nowhere demonstrated the truth of such an argument. On the contrary, even in his discussion of domestic empire he is constantly obliged to admit the importance of noneconomic factors. As we have seen, his mention of "framing the foundation unto the Government" implies some such noneconomic determinant. And we shall see in his discussion of English history that such an implication is not uncommon in Harrington's writings. Surely his admission that Queen Elizabeth was able to delay, if not to reverse, the course of history shows that Harrington was willing to admit the power of personal qualities in political life.

Therefore we must observe that Harrington's theory of the economic base of political power can hardly be defended as an absolute law of politics. And in a way this probably weakens Harrington's general position. But perhaps in a broader sense it strengthens it. Although we must admit that he is not the discoverer of an absolute political law, it can be argued that Harrington's status as an observer of political reality is actually enhanced by this admission. In other words, although Harrington turns out to have been something less of a rationalistic system-builder than one suspected at first, he is now seen to have been a better empirical scientist. Taking one consideration with another, it is to his credit that he was unwilling to sacrifice the facts as he saw them to any procrustean system.

We began our discussion of Harrington's theory of empire with the statement that his sole concern here was with matters of fact, that as yet he did not wish to make value judgments about the various forms of government. On the whole this statement is true, but in concluding this discussion we must note one important exception. There can be little doubt that Harrington approved of governments based on an economic foundation and disapproved of those which were not a reflection of economic balance. This becomes apparent first in Harrington's choice of terms to describe governments of the latter sort; they are, it will be recalled, tyranny, oligarchy, and anarchy. Each of these forms is further described as "unnatural and violent." It can hardly be denied that these are all pejorative words. And we may note further that Harrington also used the words "unnatural and violent" to characterize the one other kind of government which was not based on property, provincial government.

The most extreme indication of Harrington's position, however, occurs in another connection. In a section of his *Art of Lawgiving* devoted to definition of terms, Harrington defines government by divine right in this way: "Wherever, thro Causes unforeseen by Human Providence, the Balance coms to be intirely chang'd, it is the more immediately to be attributed to Divine Providence: And since God cannot will the necessary cause, but he must also will the necessary effect or consequence, what Government soever is in the necessary direction of the Balance, the same is of Divine Right."[43] The religious aspects of this passage will be considered below, but for the present the interesting thing is the special position Harrington assigns to governments which are "in the necessary direction of the Balance," that is, governments which conform to the economic state of the country. The specific use of the term "Divine Right" can in all probability be attributed to Harrington's desire to steal one of the weapons of the advocates of absolute monarchy in the seventeenth century, but the fact remains that he looks with considerably more favor on such governments than on those which are able, by some means, to persist without firm economic underpinnings.

There are several possible explanations of this attitude.

43. *Coll. Works,* p. 388.

In the first place one should not overlook the fact that these "unnatural" governments are, in a very real sense, anomalies in Harrington's system. He unquestionably believed that his theory of the economic foundation of political power was his greatest and most original contribution to man's knowledge of politics, and therefore he had reason to regret any instances which did not conform to the theory. On a somewhat more abstract level, Harrington's prejudice in favor of economically based power was a reflection of his continuing concern with political stability. Circumstances forced him to admit that governments could exist without such a foundation, but he seems never to have believed that such a situation could be permanent. True, Elizabeth had been able to maintain the doomed English monarchy by her extraordinary personal abilities, but this simply postponed its inevitable destruction. Sooner or later the balance of property was bound to make itself felt. And therefore Harrington chose, perhaps irrationally (but very humanly), to align himself with the forces of inevitability. In short, although his honesty forced him to admit that governments could exist by virtue of qualities other than wealth, he was never completely happy about this admission and constantly took the opportunity of expressing his preference for a solid foundation in wealth, and especially in land.

We come now to the second of Harrington's "principles of government," the internal principle based on "the goods of the mind." This principle is, of course, "authority," that variety of political power (using the word in its broadest sense) which possesses moral qualities. Thus we turn from the question of why men *do* obey governments to the question of why they *should* obey them, or more precisely *which* governments they should obey. We may observe at the outset that when a political theorist explicitly contrasts "empire" and "authority," the "goods of fortune" and the "goods of the mind," the odds are that he will in due course choose the latter over the former. And this is certainly true in the case of Harrington. At the very beginning of his discussion of authority Harrington refers to "those principles of power which ballanced upon earthly trash, exclude the heavenly treasures of Virtue, and that influence of it upon Government, which is *Authority*."[44] We will have occasion to return to this reference when we come to consider the relation, in Harrington's system, between empire and authority. At present, however, we must devote our attention to Harrington's theory of authority per se.

"We have wandered the Earth to find out the ballance of power: but to find out that of Authority, we must ascend . . . nearer Heaven, or to the Image of God, which is the Soul of man." In this revealing and uncharacteristically poetic passage Harrington informs his readers that his discussion of the principle of authority will necessarily involve a consideration of human psychology. For it turns out that by "the Soul of man" Harrington understands what a more modern writer might call human personality, or at any rate the basis of human action. He goes on to note that *"the Soul of man . . . is the Mistris of two potent rivalls, the one Reason, the other Passion."*[45] But unlike Hume and the other British psychologists of the following century Harrington does not believe that either of these "rivalls" is the exclusive determinant of human action. Reason, for Harrington, is not necessarily the slave of passion, nor is passion necessarily reason's servant. Rather, as his use of the word "rivalls" indicates, Harrington believes that these two "are in continuall suit."[46] That is, there is within each man a perpetual struggle between reason and passion, the result

44. *Oceana*, pp. 20–21.
45. Ibid., p. 21.
46. Ibid.

of which struggle determines in any particular case whether one's action is reasonable or passionate. Furthermore, the result of the struggle is important because it determines whether one is to act morally or immorally. Thus, ". . . whatever was *passion* in the *contemplation* of a man, being brought forth by his will into action, is *vice* and the *bondage of Sin;* so whatever was *reason* in the *contemplation* of a man, being brought forth by his *will* into *action,* is *virtue* and the *freedome of Soul.*"[47]

It will be noted that Harrington's view of psychology is fairly simple and in no way unusual. The "soul" is characterized by two "motives" (to use Hume's term) either of which may influence the will; the will, in turn, forms the link between contemplation and action. Therefore actions may be said to be indirectly influenced by either reason or passion. The connection between this psychological discussion and the subject of authority becomes evident when we note the varying consequences of passionate and reasonable actions, or "sinful" and "virtuous" actions as Harrington calls them. Thus, ". . . as those *actions* of a man that were *sin,* acquire unto himself *repentance* or *shame,* and affect others with *scorn* or *pity;* so those *actions* of a man that are *virtue,* acquire unto himself *Honour,* and upon others *Authority.*"[48] In other words, we may now define authority as an emotion (or opinion) created in others by one's virtuous actions and consequently giving one a certain power over others. The distinction Harrington makes between honor and authority is central here. The mere opinion of others which results from virtuous action is honor; but authority is necessarily something more than mere opinion. The use of the words "upon others" seems to justify the conclusion that authority is in fact a form of power. But it is, of course, always to be distinguished from

47. Ibid.
48. Ibid.

empire, which is physical force. We may say that authority is the active form of honor, that is, the form which influences the actions of others. If someone obeys me because he honors me, I then may be said to possess authority. And clearly Harrington is right in believing that authority in this sense is a form of power; indeed, he has defined authority so that this will inevitably be the case.

One further fact must be noted before we proceed to consider the political consequences of this psychological theory, rudimentary as it is. Harrington believed, like so many philosophers and political theorists both before and after his time, that the individual is free when he obeys reason. Thus, as we have seen, action in accordance with reason "is virtue and the freedome of Soul." Although the consequence of such a doctrine, distinguishing "true" rational freedom from illusory freedom, has generally been a tendency to stress obedience to some external "reason" rather than simple absence of restraint, the reader is advised to withhold judgment in Harrington's case until after we have noted the application of his psychology to political life.

The immediate connection between Harrington's psychology and his political theory comes with the statement that "Government is no other then the Soul of a Nation or City."[49] What precisely does this mean? One might answer that it means *precisely* nothing, but that its general implication is clear. Harrington, of course, lived in an age when it was common to liken the commonwealth, or body politic,[50] to a human organism; Hobbes's Leviathan is perhaps the most famous contemporaneous instance of this process. In Harrington's case, as with most other writers of the age, this analogy was not carried through in any detailed fashion.

49. Ibid.
50. See above, p. 98.

The commonwealth is a functioning organism composed of a multitude of smaller entities, it acts and its actions may be said to result from either reason or passion. The motivating part of a commonwealth is its government, and this may consequently be likened to the soul which performs the same function in the individual. General as it is, the analogy is useful because it provides a vivid and easily understandable vocabulary for Harrington's discussion of the state.

To continue, then, it follows that a government the actions of which are motivated by reason is by definition a virtuous government. Harrington next adds a statement rather reminiscent of Bodin's discussion of sovereignty: "for as much as the Soul of a City or Nation is the *Soveraign power,* her *virtue* must be *Law.*"[51] In other words, the characteristic manifestation of sovereign power is the making of law, and therefore a virtuous sovereign will make virtuous laws. Finally, to tie the whole discussion together, we are told that "the *Government* whose *Law* is *virtue . . .* is the same whose *Empire* is *Authority.*"[52] That is, government per se (or sovereign power) is simply a matter of force, or empire, but it is possible for a government by acting virtuously to combine empire with authority.

At this point, however, Harrington's combination of psychology and political theory raises a serious problem. He began with the assumption that an individual may act either reasonably or passionately, and, depending upon which he chooses, either virtuously or viciously. Then, by analogy, he stated that a commonwealth could also be characterized by virtue or vice, depending upon whether it is guided by reason or passion. But if an individual can act irrationally, why cannot a commonwealth? The answer, of course, is that a commonwealth can act irrationally, just

51. *Oceana,* p. 21.
52. Ibid.

as an individual can. How, then, is it possible for a common-wealth to be any more reasonable than the individuals who compose it? Harrington is clearly aware of this central difficulty. "The main question," he writes, "seems to be . . . how the debate or result of a Common-wealth is so sure to be according unto reason; seeing they who debate, and they who resolve be but men." Thus, like so many political theorists, Harrington formulates his problem in terms of what one might call the bootstrap difficulty. Given irra-tional men, how is it possible to guarantee that any govern-ment they create and staff will act rationally?

Before we consider Harrington's answer, we may note two possible answers which he did not give. Unlike Plato, he refused to argue that *some* men can be relied on to be-have rationally and should therefore be allowed to rule un-checked by law. And unlike various extreme democratic theorists, he refused to define rationality as simply a char-acteristic of anything a majority decides to do.

This brings us to the central point of this entire discus-sion, namely Harrington's definition of reason and ration-ality. Such a definition is particularly important in view of the fact that Harrington, like Plato now, equates virtue and reason. Any rational action, he tells us, will ipso facto be a virtuous action: "whatever was reason in the contempla-tion of a man, being brought forth by his will into action, is virtue." Thus when we have discovered the meaning of reason we will also have discovered the basis of morality. What, then, is reason? To answer this we must go back for a moment to Harrington's discussion of reason in a com-monwealth. The problem here was to discover how a com-monwealth can be made always to act reasonably despite the fact that the men who compose it are liable to act un-reasonably. At one point Harrington illustrates the problem by paraphrasing a statement of Hobbes's: "And as often as reason is against a man, so often will a man be against reason."[53] Clearly the implication of this statement is that there exists an opposition between reason and interest, and that an individual will always choose the latter over the former. "This is thought to be a shrewd saying," Harrington continues, "but will do no harm."[54] It will do no harm because Harrington's system equates reason and interest, thus (in a sense) removing all possibility of a conflict between them.

But the important thing to note is that at this point it becomes impossible any longer to speak of reason and interest per se as unitary entities: "for be it so, that *reason* is nothing but *interest*, there be divers *interests*, and so divers *reasons*."[55] The amplification of this assertion is sufficiently important to deserve quotation in full:

> As first, there is *Private Reason*, which is the *interest* of a *private man*.

> Secondly, there is *Reason of State*, which is the interest (or errour as was said by *Solomon*) of the *Ruler* or *Rulers*, that is to say, of the *Prince*, of the *Nobility*, or of the *People*.

> Thirdly, there is that *Reason* which is the interest of mankind, or of the whole."[56]

53. Ibid., p. 22; cf. Hobbes, *Leviathan,* Part I, Ch. 15; and also, *English Works of Thomas Hobbes*, ed. Holmesworth, *4* (London, 1840), *Ep. Ded.:* "From the principal parts of Nature, Reason and Passion, have proceeded two kinds of learning, mathematical and dogmatical: the former is free from controversy and dispute, . . . in the other there is nothing undisputable, because it compareth men, & meddleth with their right and profit; in which, as oft as reason is against a man, so oft will a man be against reason."
54. *Oceana*, p. 22.
55. Ibid.
56. Ibid.; the reference to Solomon apparently signifies Ecclesiastes, 10:5, "There is an evil which I have seen under the sun, like an error which proceedeth from a ruler: Folly is set on great heights."

In short, Harrington turns Hobbes's weapon back against
him by insisting that reason *should* be identified with interest. Reason is now to be defined as action in accordance
with some specific interest; but as a consequence we now
find also that there exists a hierarchy of reason. If I act in
such a way as to further my own interest, I am acting reasonably; if a Prince acts in such a way as to further his interest
as a ruler, he is acting reasonably; if anyone acts in such a
way as to further the interest of mankind as a whole, he is
acting reasonably.

Are all these "reasonable" actions equally praiseworthy
and desirable? On the contrary, as one might expect, the
greater the interest served, the better is the action. To illustrate this principle Harrington quotes extensively from
Richard Hooker's *Laws of Ecclesiastical Polity:*

> Now if we see even in those natural agents that want
> sense, that as in themselves they have a Law which di-
> recteth them, in the means whereby they tend to their
> own perfection, so likewise that another Law there is,
> which toucheth them as they are sociable parts united
> into one body, a Law which bindeth them each to
> serve unto others good, and all to prefer the good of the
> whole, before whatsoever their own particular; as
> when stones or heavy things forsake their ordinary
> wont or center, and fly upwards, as if they heard them-
> selves commanded to let go the good they privately
> wish, and to relieve the present distresse of Nature in
> common.[57]

This passage, of course, embodies a twofold argument. In
the first place it assumes the existence, and the superiority,
of an interest common to all mankind. In the second place,
it assumes a *natural* propensity in creatures to serve this

57. (1593 or 1594), I, 3, 5; see also *Prerogative of Popular Government, Coll. Works,* p. 252.

common interest. In short, what we have here is an expression of the classic belief in a law of nature; if this is not clear already Harrington's next statement makes it so: "There is a common right, Law of Nature, or interest of the whole; which is more excellent, and so acknowledged to be by the agents themselves, then the right or interest of the parts onely."[58]

Finally, then, reason in its highest form is seen to be that attribute of man which makes it possible for him to discover the common interest, the Law of Nature. Consequently, we may say that in any action an individual is faced with a variety of choices; he may be directed by passion or by reason in any of its three forms. Only when he acts in accordance with universal reason, however, may his actions be called rational and virtuous in the highest sense. The stones to which Hooker refers act without choice in this manner; animals possess the ability to choose and apparently often act in accordance with an interest (or reason) superior to (i.e. more general than) their own.[59] Mankind, too, is free to choose between actions which aim at the common interest and actions which serve only particular interests. But the example of inferior creatures leads Harrington to believe that man, given the appropriate circumstances, will in general act in accordance with the Law of Nature which his reason reveals to him. "Wretch that he is, shall a Stone upon this occasion fly upwards, and . . . a Man . . . go downwards!"[60]

58. *Oceana*, p. 22.
59. Thus Harrington quotes Grotius: "Wherefore though it may truly be said, that the creatures are naturally carried forth, unto their proper [i.e. individual] utility or profit: that ought not to be taken in too general a sense; seeing divers of them abstain from their own profit, either in regard of those of the same kind, or at the least of their young." *De jure belli ac pacis* (Amsterdam, 1651), *Proleg.*, pp. 2 f.
60. *Prerogative of Popular Government, Coll. Works*, pp. 251–52.

This equation of common interest with common reason, and of both with the Law of Nature, brings us back finally to the realm of politics. In a passage which irresistibly invites comparison with Rousseau, Harrington makes the connection: "*Mankind* then must either be lesse just then the *creature,* or acknowledge also his *common interest* to be *common right.* And if *reason* be nothing else but *interest,* and the *interest of mankind* be the *right interest,* then the *reason of mankind* must be *right reason.* Now compute well, for if the *interest* of *popular Government* come the nearest unto the *interest* of *mankind,* then the *reason* of *popular Government* must come the nearest unto *right reason.*"⁶¹

But this clearly leaves Harrington with the problem of demonstrating that the actions of a "popular government" will in fact accord with the common interest and right reason. The problem, of course, is the classic one of the nature of the thing known as "common interest." Harrington is prepared to recognize that the common interest is not in any meaningful sense identical with the apparent interest of every member of the community; he illustrates this with the usual example: "Upon this acknowledgment of Mankind, a Man that steals is put to death, which certainly is none of his privat Interest; nor is a Man put to death for any other Man's privat Interest: therfore there is a common Interest of Mankind distinct from the parts taken severally."⁶² Therefore it is possible for an individual to find himself in a situation in which his private interest conflicts with the

61. *Oceana,* p. 23; cf. Rousseau: "Every political society is composed of other smaller societies, each of which has its interests. . . . A particular resolution may be advantageous to the smaller community, but pernicious to the greater . . . which irrefragably proves that the most general will is also the most just, and that the voice of the people is in fact the voice of God." *Discourse on Political Economy,* Everyman's ed. (New York, 1947), pp. 237–38.
62. *Prerogative of Popular Government, Coll. Works,* p. 252.

common interest. In such cases, Harrington admits, the individual will generally (if not invariably) prefer his private
interest: "a man doth not look upon *reason* as it is *right* or
wrong in it *self*, but as it makes for him or against him."[63]
This would suggest that for Harrington the general interest
is essentially and systematically distinct from the sum of
private interests, that it is a "general will" rather than a
"will of all." In fact, after a certain amount of vacillation
and ambiguity, he reaches the opposite conclusion: the
common interest *is* the "will of all," the sum of private
interests.[64]

As anyone who reads Harrington's discussion will be
forcefully reminded, however, these terms are distressingly
vague. At the moment all we can say with certainty is that
Harrington wishes to avoid creating a great gulf between
the "interest" of a society and what the mass of the people
in that society actually desire. As we shall see, he does not
go so far as to say that the spontaneous mass-action of the
populace will predictably embody the common interest.
But he does wish to discover the constitutional or institu-

63. *Oceana*, p. 23.
64. This ambiguity, or indeed confusion, is admirably illustrated
by a sentence from *Prerogative of Popular Government* (*Coll. Works*,
p. 253): "the Result of the Many (because every man has an Interest
what to chuse, and that choice which sutes with every man's Interest,
excludes the distinct or privat Interest or Passion of any Man, and
so coms up to the common and public Interest or Reason) is the wisest
Result." The confusing phrase is "which sutes with every man's Interest." It is perfectly clear from the context that Harrington is here
speaking of a vote in the lower chamber of his legislature, a vote in
which a simple majority prevails. Thus, unless the vote should happen
to be unanimous—which we have no reason to suppose—there will
be those who voted against a proposal which they felt to be hostile
to their interest. Whence, then, "every man's Interest"? For reasons
which will become clear below, it is highly unlikely that Harrington
intended to espouse the Rousseauian position which is the only one
that can make sense out of this puzzle.

tional arrangements that will ascertain this interest through consultation with the people, recognizing all the time that when consulted each individual will predictably opt for his private advantage. The fact that he believed this to be possible, short of changing "human nature" by making men unselfish, suggests that in the last analysis his view was utilitarian rather than Rousseauian. It is at this point, of course, that the political or constitutional problem arises. Given human selfishness, how is it possible to ensure that a government will at all times be motivated by a concern for the common interest?

At this point we reach the end of the first part of Harrington's theory of politics, that concerned with empire and authority. It will have been noted that the previous discussion contained singularly few references to authority as such. This is explained largely by the fact that Harrington himself abandoned the use of that word after his preliminary remarks. But this should not be taken to mean that he lost interest in the subject; as he might have said, *mutato nomine,* authority constitutes the subject matter of his discussion of reason and interest. To fill in the missing part of the argument, we may say that authority is an attribute of governments that pursue the common interest. That is, any ruler who governs in accordance with the Law of Nature may be said to exercise authority as well as empire. And this, finally, brings us to the heart of the matter.

In his treatment of empire—power based on force—Harrington shows the basis on which governments are, as a sheer matter of fact, able to rule. In his discussion of authority, on the other hand, he outlines the criteria by which a good government may be distinguished from a bad one. Clearly, at this point there is no particular connection between the two. A government can possess power without authority or authority without power; and it can possess both or even conceivably neither. As Harrington says, "a learned Writer may have authority though he have no power [i.e. empire]; and a foolish Magistrate may have power, though he have otherwise no esteem or authority."[65] His reference to "those principles of power which ballanced upon earthly trash, exclude the heavenly treasures of Virtue" indicates clearly his preference for authority over sheer power. But as a political theorist and a practical man he was fully aware that the simple expression of a preference advances matters very little. If authority is more desirable than empire, it is equally true that empire is more necessary than authority.

One is reminded of Harrington's introductory remark: "To begin with Riches, in regard that men are hung upon these, not of choice as upon the other, but necessity and by the teeth."[66] To put this another way: government *must* possess empire; it *may* also possess authority. Actually, it turns out that the two are more closely related than these statements might indicate. But before we can consider their relation we must go on to discuss Harrington's theory of the nature and function of political institutions. So far he has provided us with an analysis of the necessary foundations of empire and a criterion for distinguishing a good government from a bad one. Being a constructive theorist as well as a mere observer of political phenomena Harrington's immediate problem is to devise a system of government which will successfully embody the requirements of the Law of Nature.

"The Orders of Popular Government"

As we have seen, Harrington wished in his theory of politics to construct a system of government which would always be guided in its conduct by considerations of common

65. *Oceana*, p. 14.
66. Ibid.

interest. The first obstacle to this project was, of course,
man's natural selfishness. Although his reason enables him
to discern the common good, man is more concerned with
whether "it makes for him or against him" as an individual.
This is a particularly bothersome problem because of Harrington's commitment to popular government as that which
comes nearest to embodying right reason.[67] The solution
must be found in the proper *form* of popular government
or, as Harrington expresses it, in appropriate "orders."
Thus,

> unlesse you can shew such *orders* of a *Government,* as
> like those of *God* in *nature* shall be able to constrain
> this or that *creature* to shake off that *inclination* which
> is more peculiar unto it, and take up that which re-
> gards the *common good* or *interest;* all this is to no
> more end, then to perswade every man in a *popular
> Government,* not to carve himself of that which he
> desires most, but to be mannerly at the publick Table,
> and give the best from himself unto decency and the
> *common interest.*[68]

In short, Harrington's political theory has moved from a
consideration of the physical and moral bases of power to
a discussion of institutional arrangements. The problem
now is not why governments are obeyed, or why they should
be obeyed, but rather what form of government best reflects
these physical and moral qualities. Essentially, Harrington
is here attempting to avoid the situation in which, as Rousseau says, "the flaws which make social institutions necessary are the same as make the abuse of them inevitable."[69]
Granting men's selfishness, is it possible to create a system

67. See above, p. 144.
68. *Oceana,* p. 23.
69. *Discourse on the Origin of Inequality,* Everyman's ed. (New
York, 1947), p. 215.

of government which will lead men to act in accord with the common interest?

Rather surprisingly, when Harrington reaches this problem he informs his readers that it is after all remarkably simple to solve. "But that such *orders* may be established as may, nay must, give the upper hand in all cases to the *common right* or *interest,* notwithstanding the nearnesse of that which sticks unto every man in private, and this in a way of equal certainty and facility," he tells us, "is known even unto *girles,* being no other then those that are of common practice with them in divers cases."[70] To illustrate this "common practice" Harrington, in a well-known passage, supposes that two girls jointly possess a cake which they wish to divide in such a way "that each of them . . . may have that which is due." What will happen in this case? The answer, says Harrington, is clear: the girls will agree that one of them is to divide the cake while the other is to choose between the two pieces. The advantage of this common procedure lies in the fact that the girl who divides knows in advance that if she divides unequally she will be left with the smaller piece, "wherefore she divides equally, and so both have right." But this simple technique, Harrington continues, provides us with the answer to all questions of political organization.

> *O the depth of the wisdom of God!* and yet *by the mouthes of babes and sucklings hath he set forth his strength;* that which great *Philosophers* are disputing upon in vain, is brought unto light by two *silly girles,* even the whole *Mystery* of a *Common-wealth:* which lyes only in *dividing and choosing:* nor hath *God* . . . left so much unto *mankind* to dispute upon, as who shall divide, and who choose, but distributed them for ever into two *orders,* whereof the one hath

70. *Oceana,* p. 23.

the naturall right of dividing, and the other of choosing.[71]

We have quoted this passage *in extenso* because it does in
fact reveal Harrington's view of "the whole Mystery of a
Common-wealth." The key to an understanding of politics
lies in a recognition first of the functional distinction between "dividing" and "choosing" and, second, of the corresponding division of mankind into two great classes, each
fitted to perform one of these functions.

But what is the political equivalent of the girls' dividing
and choosing? *"Dividing* and *choosing* in the language of a
Common-wealth," we learn, *"is debating* and *resolving."*[72]
Now we have already noted that for Harrington the characteristic function of government, or of sovereign power, is
legislation.[73] And it is precisely in the legislative process
that these two functions, debating and resolving, become
important. Therefore if we apply the lesson learned from
the two girls to the legislative process, we discover that the
functions of debating and resolving should be separated,
that is, legislative problems should be discussed and proposals written by one body, and a decision should be reached
by another body. If the legislative power is thus divided
and distributed to appropriate organs, Harrington believes,
the passage of unjust laws will become impossible.

All of this depends, of course, on the nature of the debating and the resolving bodies. In the case of the two
girls the division of functions was a matter of indifference;
either could divide or choose so long as neither one did
both. But this is not true in politics. As we have seen, God
himself has distributed mankind into two "orders, whereof
the one hath the naturall right of dividing, and the other of

71. Ibid.
72. Ibid., p. 25.
73. See above, p. 139.

choosing." What are these two orders, and how can we be sure of their existence? Harrington believes that these questions will be answered if we choose at random any group of twenty men and observe their actions: *"twenty men* (if they be not all *ideots,* perhaps if they be) can never come so together, but there will be such difference in them, that about a *third* will be *wiser,* or at least *lesse foolish* then all the rest. . . . Wherefore this can be no other then a *naturall Aristocracy* diffused by *God* throughout the whole body of *mankind."*[74] Furthermore, the remaining two-thirds of our group will naturally recognize the superiority of these natural aristocrats: "these upon acquaintance though it be but small, will be discovered, and (as Stags that have the largest heads) lead the herd; for while the *six* discoursing and arguing one with another shew the eminence of their parts, the *fourteen* discover things that they never thought on . . . wherefore in matters of common concernment, difficulty or danger, they hang upon their lips as *children* upon their *fathers."*[75] And, Harrington continues, the influence thus enjoyed by the natural aristocrats is in fact "authority." Therefore the common "herd" have an obligation, both natural and positive, to be guided by these aristocrats.

Institutionally speaking, this "authority" should be embodied in a senate, an organ concerned with debating and proposing legislation. But the membership of the senate must be such that its power is clearly authority and not empire. Thus, "the *six* then approved of, as in the present case, are the *Senate,* not by *hereditary right,* or in regard of the *greatnesse of their estates* only, which would tend unto such power as might force or *draw the people;* but by *election* for *their excellent parts,* which tendeth unto the advancement of the influence of their *virtue* or *authority* that

74. *Oceana,* p. 24.
75. Ibid.

leads the people."[76] Finally, then, it appears that this senate
of natural aristocrats is not to be a commanding body, but
rather an advising or counseling chamber: "Wherefore the
office of the *Senate,* is not to be *Commanders* but *Counsel-
lors* of the people . . . whence the *Decrees* of the *Senate* are
never *Lawes,* nor so called, but Senatus-Consulta."[77] In this
way Harrington felt he had given institutional embodiment
to the form of power which he calls "authority." A commonwealth which possesses such a consultative senate will make
proper use of the wisdom of its natural aristocracy. But by
withholding from this chamber the right to make laws it
will also avoid the danger of legislation in the interest of a
particular class.

The central principle, then, is that the consultative senate, having divided, shall not choose. Or, using political
terms, that having debated the Senate shall not be empowered to resolve: "if she that divided must have chosen also,
it had been little worse for the other, in case she had not
divided at all, but kept the whole Cake unto herself."[78]
Consequently, Harrington concludes that a legislature consisting of but one chamber will never provide a sufficient
guarantee against arbitrary action. "Nor is there any remedy" for this danger "but to have another *Councill* to
choose."[79] But if the senate was designed to embody the
wisdom of the commonwealth, and to lead it by authority,
it is necessary that the other chamber of the legislature reflect the interests of the people of the commonwealth. Since
the interest of the commonwealth as a whole is most easily
discovered in the entire body of citizens, the ideal solution
would seem to be a continuing popular plebiscite on the
proposals of the senate. This however is impractical, since

76. Ibid.
77. Ibid.
78. Ibid.
79. Ibid., p. 25.

"an whole Nation is too unweildy a body to be assembled."
Therefore the best possible solution is a legislative council
consisting "of such a Representative as may be equall, and
so constituted, as can never contract any other interest then
that of the *whole people*."[80] In other words, the resolving
chamber of the legislature is to be so designed that it will
constitute an accurate sample (in a statistical sense) of the
entire citizenry. Thus for Harrington, as for the nineteenth-
century utilitarians, popular participation or representation in government is not a right, and much less a natural
right, but rather simply a necessary means to a desired end,
namely the expression of the popular interest.

We can now see that the composition of the legislature
in Harrington's best possible commonwealth is a reflection
of two distinct, though related, theories. In the first place,
the bicameral nature of the legislature and the strict division of power between the two chambers is a natural corollary of Harrington's theoretical distinction between dividing and choosing. Politically speaking, debating amounts
to "separating and weighing this reason against that, which
is dividing," and resolving amounts to choosing between alternative proposals. A unification of these functions in the
same hands would, Harrington believes, leave the door
open to arbitrary action simply by allowing one organ of
government an excessive amount of power. But, to come to
the second theoretical consideration, such an institutional
separation of powers would be largely meaningless if the
distinction between the two chambers were purely formal.
If the mere duality of institutions were a sufficient guarantee against arbitrariness, one could elect a single legislature
and merely divide it formally into two chambers. But
clearly this would not serve Harrington's purpose. It is
necessary that the membership of the two chambers be sub-

80. Ibid.

stantially different. The fulfillment of this requirement is greatly facilitated by the natural division of the people into two classes, especially since each class is ideally suited for the performance of one of the two legislative functions. So closely related are these two theories that it is virtually impossible to separate them.

Which is more important for Harrington, the mere separation of debate and resolution or the performance of each of these functions by the appropriate part of the populace? The answer clearly is that the two are equally important and, in fact, inconceivable apart from each other. For instance, we may inquire why the popular chamber cannot be trusted to make laws by itself in view of the fact that it represents the interest of the entire commonwealth? Or, we may ask why the senate should not possess this power since it embodies the wisdom of the commonwealth? The answer to both questions brings us to the heart of Harrington's theory of political institutions and practice: despite the impressive qualifications of each of these bodies, no one institution is to be entrusted with such extensive power. The senate, although wise, may not act in the interest of all the people.[81] On the other hand, the popular chamber, although representative of the national interest, lacks the wisdom requisite for the formulation of legislative alternatives. Therefore only a system which requires the concurrence of these two chambers will guarantee that legislation is sound in terms of both wisdom and common interest.

One final consideration remains in our discussion of the legislative power. As we have already indicated, these polit-

81. Cf. Plato, *Laws*, X, 875a: "although a person knows in the abstract [that both the public and private good . . . are greater when the state and not the individual is first considered], yet if he be possessed of absolute and irresponsible power, he will never remain firm in his principles or persist in regarding the public good as primary in the state, and the private good as secondary." Jowett translation.

ical institutions are intended by Harrington to embody both forms of power—empire and authority. We have seen that authority is in fact reflected by the composition of the senate. But insofar as authority consists in ruling in accordance with the interests of all the people, the popular chamber is also an embodiment of authority. What, then, of empire? Where does it find a place in this legislature? The answer is that it must be embodied in the popular branch of the legislature. But since this is by definition a popularly elected body, it is apparent that wealth, the source of empire, must be possessed by the people as a whole. That is, in order for this system to accord with Harrington's theory of empire, three-fourths of the wealth (or land) of the commonwealth must belong to the people. And we now realize that Harrington has been describing this best form of government without informing his readers of the central fact that it can only exist in the presence of certain economic circumstances. If a single individual, or a nobility, possesses three-fourths of the land of a commonwealth, it is idle to hope that such a popular government can there exist. In other words, such a popular government is morally *desirable* because it is ruled by both wisdom and interest, but it is politically *possible* only if the popular legislature reflects the distribution of wealth in the commonwealth.

Although devoting the greatest attention to the constitution of the legislative power, Harrington realizes that this is only one part of his government. The other is that part which executes the laws, called by Harrington the Magistracy. As the senate is aristocratic in composition and function, and the popular assembly is democratic, so the magistracy is monarchical, and thus a popular commonwealth may be said to enjoy all the advantages of "mixed government" which the ancients described. Specifically, Harrington notes that the executive branch of government may vary considerably in form and composition. But he insists that there is one requirement that must always be met if the commonwealth is not to be dissolved, namely, "that as the *hand* of the *Magistrate* is the *executive power* of the *Law*, so the *head* of the *Magistrate* is answerable unto the *people*, that his *execution* be according unto the Law."[82]

The reason for Harrington's insistence on this point is apparent. The peculiar virtue of popular government lies in the fact that it realizes the interest of the entire commonwealth through the legislative process. In other words, the laws made by the senate and the popular assembly are certain to be an expression of the enlightened will of the people. But the advantages derived from such a system may all be negated by misapplication of these laws. It is therefore necessary to ensure that the executive authorities will be responsible to the people for their actions. But this should not be considered as a further instance of separation of powers among the various parts of the government. On the contrary, we discover that the executive is to be under the control of the popular branch of the legislature. (As we shall see, in the commonwealth of Oceana the magistrates are elected by the Senate from among its own members.) The same is true also of the judicial power, which Harrington does not include as one of the major governmental powers: "Whersoever the power of making Law is, there only is the power of interpreting the Law so made."[83] Therefore the popular, resolving chamber of the legislature possesses effective control over both executive and judicial authorities. Indeed, its power is limited only by the constitution,[84] and by its own inability to initiate or debate legislation.

These three organs—the debating chamber, the resolving chamber, and the magistracy—if they are properly constituted, comprise a commonwealth: "the *Common-wealth*

82. *Oceana*, p. 25.
83. *A System of Politics, Coll. Works*, p. 509.
84. See below, pp. 160 ff.

consisteth of the *Senate proposing, the People resolving, and the Magistracy executing* ... there being no other *Commonwealth* but this in *Art* or *Nature*."[85] This, of course, is simply a matter of definition; by the word commonwealth Harrington understands a government which thus unites wisdom with common interest. But although such a commonwealth is the most desirable form of government, all commonwealths are by no means the same. Thus, "though *Common-wealths* in general be *Governments* of the *Senate proposing, the people resolving, and the Magistracy executing;* yet some are not so good at these *orders* as others, through some impediment or defect in the frame, ballance, or capacity of them, according unto which they are of divers kinds."[86] In the first place, Harrington divides commonwealths into "such as are single" and "such as are by leagues." Since Switzerland and Holland are cited as examples of the latter variety we may conclude that Harrington is here recognizing the phenomenon of federalism. The second division among commonwealths follows Machiavelli's distinction between governments for increase and governments for preservation.[87] Neither of these classifications interests Harrington particularly at this point; it is the third division, "hitherto unseen," with which he is most concerned. This is the division of all commonwealths into those which are "equal" and those which are "unequal," and it is "the main point especially as to domestick peace and *tranquillity*."[88]

It is clear of course that an "equal commonwealth" must be a government composed of a senate debating, the people resolving, and the magistracy executing. To say this is no more than to say that an equal commonwealth is, after all,

85. *Oceana,* p. 25.
86. Ibid., p. 32.
87. *Discorsi,* I, 6.
88. *Oceana,* p. 32.

still a commonwealth. But in addition to this basic structure, "equality" necessitates other institutions. Most important, it necessitates "an equal Agrarian." This is a "perpetuall Law establishing and preserving the ballance of
dominion, by such a distribution, that no one man or number of men within the compasse of the *Few* or *Aristocracy,*
can come to overpower the whole people by their possessions in Lands."[89] This, of course, is no more than an
extension of Harrington's theory of empire. A popular
government can exist only when the people possess the preponderant share of land, and it can persist only so long as
this balance of "dominion" is preserved. The Agrarian Law
which accomplishes this is said to be the "Foundation" of
an equal commonwealth; the "Superstructures" consist of
several procedural devices. The first of these is "equal Rotation," a system of elections and enforced "vacations" from
office designed to prevent "prolongation of Magistracy."[90]
In the long run the purpose of equal rotation in office is
to ensure that each citizen will have an opportunity to become a magistrate, and that magistrates will not develop a
distinct class interest. Another device that contributes to
the "equality" of a commonwealth is the secret ballot. This,
of course, is designed to make all elections in the commonwealth as free as possible. Thus, "The *election* or *suffrage*
of the people is *freest* where it is made or given in such a
manner that it can neither oblige . . . nor disoblige another;
or through fear of an enemy, or bashfulnesse towards a
friend, impair a mans liberty."[91] In summary then, *"An
equal Common-wealth . . . is a Government established
upon an equall Agrarian, arising into the superstructures
or three orders, the Senate debating and proposing, the people resolving, and the Magistracy executing by an equal*

89. Ibid.
90. Ibid.
91. Ibid., p. 33.

Rotation through the suffrage of the people given by the Ballot."[92]

With these additions Harrington has completed his general discussion of the "orders of popular government," and has outlined his solution to the fundamental political problem of uniting in one institutional system both empire and authority. Power in this equal commonwealth will be in the hands of the people, that is the entire citizenry, and the agrarian law ensures its stability. The importance of this power is reflected in the central role assigned to the popular chamber of the legislature, that chamber which embodies the interest of the commonwealth. At the same time the dangers of a unicameral legislature and of an unbridled popular assembly are mitigated by the aristocratic senate, embodying the wisdom of the commonwealth. Finally, rotation and the secret ballot guarantee wide popular participation in government and freedom of elections, while legislative control over the executive branch prevents the possibility of arbitrary administration. Thus in the institutional part of his general theory Harrington sought to meet the challenge which he had expressed in his discussion of "the goods of the Mind": "the *Legislator* that can unite [the goods of the Mind] in his Government with those of fortune, cometh nearest unto the work of God, whose Government consisteth of Heaven and Earth: which was said by *Plato,* though in different words, as, when Princes should be Philosophers, or Philosophers Princes, the world would be happy."[93] In other words, this theoretical outline of an equal commonwealth was intended by Harrington to provide a solution to the fundamental political problem of uniting fact and value, power and morality, empire and authority.

One final subject remains to be discussed before we

92. Ibid.
93. Ibid., p. 20.

leave this consideration of Harrington's theory of "the orders of popular government." Although Harrington himself has little to say about this, it is nevertheless important for us to note that his equal commonwealth is distinguished by the fact that it is a constitutional system of government. This is true regardless of which of the many definitions of constitutionalism we choose. Certainly it is true in Cromwell's sense, that "in every government there must be somewhat fundamental, somewhat like a *Magna Charta,* that should be standing and be unalterable."[94] Indeed, this belief animates Harrington's entire discussion of political organization, as the very phrase "orders of popular government" indicates. In his *Art of Lawgiving* Harrington clearly distinguishes between what he calls "laws" and what he calls "orders." Thus, "Such Constitutions in a Government as regard the Frame or Model of it, are call'd Orders; and such things as are enacted by the Legislative Orders, are called Laws."[95] And this distinction is a centrally important one. If an equal commonwealth is to endure, all its fundamental institutions and procedures must be embodied in "orders," that is, in a written constitution. Thus, "The Mariner trusteth not unto the Sea, but to his Ship. The Spirit of the People is in no wise to be trusted with their Liberty, but by stated Laws or Orders; so the Trust is not in the Spirit of the People, but in the Frame of those Orders."[96] The only alternatives are to place one's trust in a written constitution or in particular individuals: "for where orders are not credited, there Men must be trusted."

But Harrington is at all times unwilling to rely upon the intelligence and good will of men and insists that only "good Orders" are a sufficient safeguard of liberty. Thus he labels the statement, *"Give us good men and they will*

94. Abbott, *Writings and Speeches of Cromwell, 3,* 451.
95. *Coll. Works,* p. 395.
96. *A Discourse upon this Saying, Coll. Works,* p. 602.

make us good Lawes," as "the *Maxime* of a *Demagogue* and
. . . exceeding *fallible."*⁹⁷ On the other hand, *"give us good
orders, and they will make us good men,"* is said to be "the
Maxime of a *Legislator,* and the most *infallible* in the *Poli-
tickes."*⁹⁸ The clear implication of these statements, indeed
the only conclusion that can be drawn from them, is that
the legislature of an equal commonwealth should be power-
less to alter these fundamental "orders." And certainly if
the legislature cannot do this, no other part of the government can. Therefore the equal commonwealth is a constitutional government in the sense of having a written constitution which establishes its institutions, describes their
functions, and limits their powers. We may add also that
the agrarian law, fixing the distribution of property in the
commonwealth, is considered to be a part of the constitution. And finally we may note that Harrington seems not
to have envisaged the possibility of amending the constitution; the orders of his equal commonwealth are literally
"unalterable."

One may summarize the central argument of Harrington's constitutional theory in a few simple propositions:
There exist within a popular commonwealth all the ingredients necessary for good government—notably a natural
aristocracy embodying wisdom, and the mass of the people
comprising the common interest. But these ingredients will
not necessarily or "naturally" combine in the proper fashion; to ensure that they do so is the business of the constitution.

It is impossible to overestimate the importance of this
tendency in Harrington's general theory. The extreme to

97. *Oceana,* p. 56; Liljegren notes Grotius' statement, "Good gov-
ernors bring in good customes," *Politick Maxims* (London, 1654), I,
3, 7.
98. *Oceana,* p. 56; cf. Machiavelli's "the law makes men good" in
Discourses, I, 3.

which he is willing to carry it is best illustrated by a striking
passage in one of his later discourses, where Harrington recounts an experience he had during his travels on the Continent. In Rome at Shrovetide he visited a carnival at which
he witnessed several "Pageants," and one of these entertain-
ments made a particularly strong impression: on the stage
was represented a kitchen "with all the proper Utensils in
Use and Action," but cats, not human cooks, operated these
utensils. "The Cooks were all Cats and Kitlings, set in such
Frames, so ty'd and so ordered that the poor Creatures could
make no Motion to get loose, but the same caused one to
turn the Spit, another to baste the Meat, a third to scim the
Pot, and a fourth to make Green-sauce." Harrington concludes: "If the Frame of your Commonwealth be not such,
as causeth every one to perform his certain Function as
necessarily as this did the Cat to make Green-sauce, it is
not right."[99]

The foundation of Harrington's constitutional system is,
of course, the agrarian law. Since political power must rest
on an economic base, the maintenance of any particular
form of government necessarily requires the fixing of the
appropriate distribution of property. And thus Harrington's system is clearly in the long run a conservative one, as
will be any system based on a conviction that a perfect government can be created in toto by the application of sufficient wisdom at any time. This in itself should not be surprising in view of Harrington's great desire for political
stability. Indeed, he believed that his greatest contribution
to the study of politics consisted in the discovery of the
cause of political instability; unstable governments are, almost without exception, those which do not rest on a solid
economic foundation. Therefore it is clearly in the interest
of any governing class to fix the balance upon which its

99. *A Discourse upon this Saying, Coll. Works,* p. 608.

power is based; apparently the failure to do this can be explained only by sheer stupidity on the part of the rulers.[100] Thus in a sense Harrington's theory offers to any ruler, good or bad, a means of perpetuating his power. It is surely open to question whether Harrington would have preferred good government or stability if faced with a choice between the two. Only because the balance in England was ideally suited to an equal commonwealth was Harrington able to avoid such a choice.

This discussion of the constitutional nature of Harrington's equal commonwealth raises one final point: where do these orders come from? It is quite apparent that Harrington's desire for a written and unchangeable constitution reflects his distrust of unlimited, arbitrary power in the hands of any individual or group. Man can be trusted only when he acts within a strictly defined constitutional framework. But if this is true, what can be said of the men who create that constitutional framework? The passages quoted above have already indicated that Harrington relies on a "Legislator" to do the work of constitution-making. That is, he believes that a constitution must be the creation of a single individual, and that it must be introduced all at once. In both cases Harrington's authority is Machiavelli.[101] But he also believes that any constitution so written must be accepted by the people.[102] Therefore even in the writing and promulgation of the constitution we find a process generally equivalent to the regular legislative process of an equal commonwealth. That is, the "orders" are proposed by the wisest of men and ratified by the people. Of course

100. This is obviously Harrington's explanation of the alteration of the English balance in the 15th century. See below, Ch. 4.
101. This whole subject is discussed at greater length and in more specific detail in Ch. 5, below.
102. This is clearly implied in *Oceana*, p. 206: "the Commonwealth was ratified and established by the whole body of the people."

it is impossible to ensure that any constitution will be thus "constitutionally" introduced, but this clearly seems to have been Harrington's intention. The essential requirement is that the constitution be perfect from the very beginning; anything less will invite tampering and lead to the destruction of the whole system. "If you will have fewer Orders in a Common-wealth you will have more, for where she is not perfect at first, every day, every houre will produce a new Order, the end whereof is to have no Order at all, but to grinde with the clack of some *Demagoge*."[103]

Having said this, however, we must note that Harrington at other times seems to have envisaged a situation in which a new constitution would be imposed upon an unwilling populace. Thus, "Here is the Discouragement; the many through Diversity of Opinions, want of Reach into the Principles of Government, and Unacquaintance with the Good that may by this Means be acquired, are never to be agreed in the Introduction of a new Form: but then there is also this Consolation, that the *many* upon Introduction of a new Form, coming once to feel the Good, and taste the Sweet of it, will never agree to abandon it."[104] Taken in conjunction with Harrington's constant references to Lycurgus (and Machiavelli) this passage seems to indicate his belief that in all probability the popular acceptance envisaged in the *Oceana* is rather too much to be hoped for. As in the classical tradition and in Rousseau, the Legislator, being both wise and omnicompetent, simply imposes upon the people his constitution, knowing that it is in their own best interest. It is vitally important that the constitution should become operative; compared with this the method of its adoption becomes a matter of relatively minor significance.

103. Ibid., p. 204.
104. *Pour enclouer le canon, Coll. Works,* p. 596; it is doubtless significant that this passage was written three years after the *Oceana*.

Religion and Empire

Although Harrington's religious views and proposals
comprise only a subordinate part of his political theory,
they deserve our attention for several reasons. In the first
place, it was his treatment of religion and of religious institutions that raised the greatest storm of controversy during
his own lifetime. One may estimate conservatively that at
least half his writings after the *Oceana* were devoted to disputations over religion. This in turn is a reflection of a
second circumstance that lends interest to Harrington's religious views: he lived in an age when religion and politics
were completely inseparable. It would be folly here to attempt to state categorically that the English Civil Wars
were primarily political, economic, or religious in origin,
but there can be no doubt that religion was crucially important to the participants on all sides. Finally, and perhaps
somewhat less interestingly, it may be noted that one of
the clearest conflicts among modern students of Harrington's thought centers about his religious views. G. P. Gooch
has argued that the tone of Harrington's writings is secular
throughout; J. W. Gough professes himself unable to find
any basis for such a statement, believing that Harrington
is a typical Puritan and Independent.[105] The following
pages are intended simply to outline Harrington's position
on religious questions in order to deal with each of these
three points.[106]

An examination of Harrington's extensive writings on
religious and ecclesiastical matters can leave no doubt of

105. See G. P. Gooch and H. Laski, *English Democratic Ideas in
the 17th Century* (Cambridge, 1954), p. 249, n. 4; and J. W. Gough,
"Harrington and Contemporary Thought," *Political Science Quarterly, 45* (1930), 395–404.

106. Additional discussions will be found in Ch. 5, where the religious institutions of Harrington's proposed commonwealth are outlined, and Ch. 6, which deals with his use of scriptural sources.

the substantial correctness of Gooch's characterization: his
interests, his convictions, and his habits of thought were
all essentially secular. Surely the fact that these writings
on religion are so extensive can no more be taken as evidence of their author's alleged spirituality than can the
fact that Hobbes devoted almost half of his *Leviathan* to the
same subject. All that is demonstrated in both cases is that
a political theorist in seventeenth-century England simply
could not avoid dealing with what was perhaps the most
pressing issue of his age. Much more significant is the spirit
in which this was done—in Harrington's case a spirit utterly
lacking the characteristic zeal and sectarian fervor of the
Puritan.[107] In their place we find a detachment and moder-
ation that are to be explained by the fact that Harrington's
concern, even when treating religious questions, was not
theological or eschatological but rather political. This is
perhaps most easily demonstrable in the case of his well-
known advocacy of religious toleration, or "liberty of conscience."

The arguments used to justify religious toleration are,
as W. K. Jordan has shown,[108] almost infinite in their variety. But surely none of them is more patently political
than the one Harrington chiefly relied upon. Liberty, he

107. We may note in passing one of Gough's least impressive arguments in support of his characterization of Harrington as a Puritan:
he writes that Harrington "invariably makes the practice of the Jewish
commonwealth the first support of every theory he brings forward,
while examples from secular history come second." ("Harrington and
Contemporary Thought," p. 398.) Gough here overlooks the fact that
Harrington almost without exception cites his historical examples in
chronological order and therefore naturally begins with the "Jewish
commonwealth." In fact Harrington once explicitly stated that he
would cite the experience of ancient commonwealths "in their order." *Oceana*, p. 37.

108. *The Development of Religious Toleration in England,* Vol.
3 (Cambridge, Mass., 1938).

argues in effect, is indivisible. The restriction of man's freedom of thought and expression in the area of religion necessarily constitutes a threat to the maintenance of political
freedom as well, and for this reason above all others such
restriction is to be condemned. "Men who have the means
to assert Liberty of Conscience," Harrington tells us in his
System of Politics, "have the means to assert Civil Liberty;
and will do it if they are opprest in their Consciences."[109]
Thus the overriding argument against religious persecution, and against the restriction of religious liberty in general, turns out not to be religious.

A second argument is equally political; indeed, is a re-
production of the classic *politique* position. Any attempt
to impose religious uniformity upon a divided community,
Harrington believes, must be destructive of the social order;
it must, in his word, create "tumult." And, again from the
point of view of politics, it is therefore to be condemned.
The most obvious alternative would seem to be the treatment of religion as a purely personal matter, making the
state the guarantor of religious freedom rather than of
orthodoxy. Up to a point Harrington does in fact advocate
just this. Believing that "Religion not according to a mans
conscience, can as to him be none at all,"[110] he proposes
that all non-Roman Catholic Christians should be free to
worship as they wish and—historically an important addition—should suffer no civil disabilities because of their
choice of religion.[111]

But Harrington was enough of a disciple of Machiavelli
and of "ancient prudence" to be unwilling to settle for this
essentially negative treatment of religion. Despite the pro-

109. *Coll. Works,* p. 506.
110. *Oceana,* p. 37.
111. The exclusions are defended in the conventional way: non-
Christians are unreliable because they cannot be bound by oaths;
Roman Catholics are agents of a foreign conspiracy.

found divisions created by the Reformation and the growth of sectarianism, he recognized the potential power of religion as a unifying social force and therefore advocated the establishment of a national church. Here again the essential secularism of his thought stands out: this church is to be under the direct control of the political authorities of the commonwealth, who are to supervise the formulation of a reasonable and widely acceptable body of doctrine for it. Harrington himself is quite unconcerned about the exact nature of this doctrine and argues, perhaps somewhat cynically, that most men will share his indifference. "There is nothing more certain or demonstrable to common Sense," he writes,[112] "than that the far greater part of Mankind, in matters of Religion, give themselves up to the public Leading." This being the case, it is desirable that public leadership should be provided; since the government is popular, Harrington believes that the great majority of citizens will be content to follow it in matters of religion. But, of course, those who choose not to should in no way be coerced or penalized. Thus here too the keynote of Harrington's religious system is an unwillingness to "force the conscience" of anyone.

Although Gooch is substantially correct in describing the tone of Harrington's writings as *secular,* there is an important sense in which the word is inappropriate, or even irrelevant, in a discussion of Harrington's thought. Historically, the meaning of the word "secular" is to be understood only within the framework of a Christian, dualistic view of the universe. Within this framework a clear distinction is made between the things of this world—the realm of the secular or temporal, of the City of Man—and the things of the next—the realm of the spiritual, of the timeless, of the City of God. The notion of "things which are

112. *Art of Lawgiving, Coll. Works,* p. 448.

Caesar's" is meaningful only insofar as these things are explicitly or implicitly contrasted with those things which are God's. Consequently it is not possible to use the word "secular" without summoning up these dualistic associations, and in doing so one inevitably misrepresents the essence of Harrington's thought. For the fact is that Harrington does not properly belong in this Christian dualistic tradition. As a faithful follower of Machiavelli and an enthusiastic admirer of ancient prudence, he takes his stand with the essentially monistic theorists of classical antiquity. His ideal is the virtuous commonwealth which is both church and state; his national religion is no mere Erastian solution to the problem of religious disorder. Interestingly, his vision of a commonwealth permeated by the politico-religious spirit of civic virtue is most vividly revealed in his discussion of "the empire of the world."

In our discussion of the theory of provincial empire we noted Harrington's explanation of the *fact* of imperialism and observed in passing that this really had nothing at all to do with the question of "how a Province may be justly acquired."[113] We may now look briefly at that part of his theory which might be said to deal with "provincial authority," although this is a term that Harrington never uses. The question here, quite simply, is whether imperialism or provincial government can ever be morally justified, and if so on what terms. It should be said that the relation between this particular question and Harrington's general theoretical system is somewhat tenuous, resting chiefly on the Machiavellian distinction between commonwealths for "preservation" and commonwealths for "increase."[114] What happens is that Harrington creates his own system, culminating in the equal commonwealth, and then claims for it the added virtue of expansiveness. It is difficult to believe

113. *Oceana,* p. 18; see above, pp. 128 ff.
114. *Oceana,* p. 32; cf. Machiavelli, *Discorsi,* I, 6.

that the desirability of "increase" was great enough in Harrington's mind to play any significant role in the shaping of his thought.

Without going into too much detail we may say that Harrington believed that the popular nature of his ideal commonwealth would enable it to win a vast provincial empire, and that the inherent virtues of this commonwealth would give it moral justification for so doing. For the first part of this we may simply note that he defines a commonwealth for increase as one which "taketh in . . . so many [citizens] as are capable of *encrease*."[115] As examples of such a commonwealth he cites Athens and Rome, which are contrasted with Sparta and Venice, two commonwealths for "preservation." The equal commonwealth, largely because of its popular military organization, will prove a more successful imperialist power than any that has existed in the past, even Rome. In the case of England, one must add its recognized naval supremacy, and the fact that each conquest will supply it with further strength for future expansion. Thus,

> if a man shall think, that upon a Province more remote [than Scotland], and divided by Sea, you have not the like hold; he hath not so well considered your wings, as your talons, your shipping being of such nature, as maketh the descent of your Armies almost of equal facility in any Country, so that what you take, you hold, both because your *Militia* being already populous, will bee of great growth in it self, and through your confederates, by whom in taking and holding, you are still more inabled to take and hold.[116]

In short, there can be no doubt of the ability of such a commonwealth to win a vast empire.

115. *Oceana*, p. 32.
116. Ibid., p. 196.

But if the English do not heed Harrington's advice the consequences will be doubly disastrous: "If you lay your Commonwealth upon any other foundation, then the people, you frustrate yourself of proper Arms, and so lose the Empire of the World; nor is this all, but some other Nation will have it."[117] This statement is a reflection of Harrington's general view of European politics in the seventeenth century:[118] all the nations of Europe are "tumbling and tossing upon the bed of sickness" as a result of being governed by the inferior principles of "modern prudence" and the "Gothick ballance." And this general infirmity results in an approximate equality among these nations, for any healthy nation would soon subdue the rest: "If *France, Italy* and *Spain,* were not all sick, all corrupted together, there would bee none of them so, for the sick would not bee able to withstand the sound."[119] And therefore, Harrington argues, the danger to England lies in the possibility that some other nation will be the first to recover her health through the adoption of the principles of ancient prudence: "The first of these Nations (which if you stay her leasure, will in my minde bee *France*) that recovers the health of ancient Prudence, shall assuredly govern the world."[120] Thus in effect Harrington uses these imperialistic arguments, and particularly this appeal to nationalistic and anti-French feeling, in order to support the claims of ancient prudence and his own theory of politics.[121]

In addition to this somewhat opportunist argument, Har-

117. Ibid., p. 197.
118. See Ch. 4.
119. *Oceana,* p. 197.
120. Ibid.
121. Something of the effectiveness of such an appeal is indicated by the existence of strong nationalist sentiment in the England of the Interregnum. See in this connection the unpublished dissertation by George A. Lanyi, "Oliver Cromwell and His Age: A Study in Nationalism," Harvard, 1949.

rington also took the rather extreme view that imperialism was the moral *duty* of an equal commonwealth. In what are perhaps his most poetic passages he summons the people of England to undertake a worldwide crusade, bringing with them the Word of God in the form of a revitalized political system: "to ask whether it bee lawfull for a Commonwealth to aspire unto the Empire of the World, is to ask whether it bee lawfull for her to do her duty; or to put the World into a better condition than it was before."[122] But it must be noted—as many commentators have failed to do—that this crusade was to be completely disinterested and was certainly not to aim at the enrichment of the English. "Do not think that the late appearances of God unto you, have been altogether for your selves; he hath surely seen the affliction of your Bretheren."[123] Thus he warns the English, "if you take [the way] of Athens and Lacedemon; you shall rain snares, but either catch or hold nothing. Lying lips are an abomination unto the Lord, if setting up for liberty you impose yoaks, he will assuredly destroy you." And he leaves no doubt as to what is expected of them: "if you have subdued a Nation that is capable of liberty, you shall make them a present of it."[124] In short, having created for themselves an equal commonwealth after the Harringtonian pattern, it is the privilege and the duty of the English to spread the blessings of liberty and good government throughout the world. "Now if you adde unto the propagation of Civil Liberty, (what is so natural unto this Commonwealth that it cannot bee omitted) the Propagation of the Liberty of Conscience, this Empire, this Patronage of the world, is the Kingdome of Christ."[125]

122. *Oceana*, p. 193.

123. This reference to God should not be taken too literally; Harrington is here quoting from Exodus 3:7 for effect.

124. *Oceana*, p. 195.

125. Ibid., p. 196.

CHAPTER 4

The Principles of Government:
Modern Prudence

"Your *Gothick* Politicians seem unto me rather to have invented some new ammunition, or Gunpowder, in their King and Parliament . . . then Government. For what is become of the Princes (a kind of people) in *Germany?* blown up. Where are the Estates, or the Power of the People in *France?* blown up. Where is that of the people in *Aragon,* and the rest of the *Spanish* kingdoms? blown up. On the other side, where is the King of *Spain's* power in *Holland?* blown up. Where is that of the *Austrian* Princes in *Switz?* blown up, This perpetual peevishnesse and jealousie, under the alternate Empire of the Prince and of the People, is obnoxious unto every Spark. . . . The rest is discourse for Ladies."

The Commonwealth of Oceana

IF HARRINGTON had written nothing but his penetrating account of the nature and origins of the political crisis of his time, he would still deserve an eminent place in western intellectual history. Indeed, fame being as paradoxical as it is, one may wonder whether his reputation might not actually be greater if he had confined himself to this one area, omitting everything in his writings that now seems merely eccentric or old-fashioned. Certainly the historical theories and explanations that Harrington put forward three centuries ago are at the very heart of what is today the liveliest of historiographical controversies; hardly a month passes without the publication of a learned article attacking or defending what is essentially the Harringtonian thesis on the socio-economic origins of the English Civil Wars. And it is equally clear that no one in the seventeenth century, and few in succeeding centuries, possessed Harrington's clarity of vision and power of intellect in dealing with historical phenomena. Impressive as this fact is, it is also rather ironic in the light of Harrington's profoundly pessimistic view of historical development.

In Harrington's theory of modern prudence we find an instance of the belief that human history is a function of imperfection, a consequence of human folly or weakness. Like Machiavelli, he believes that history, in the sense of continuing change through time, can only be a process of decline. What are the sources of this belief? Clearly the first is a conviction that it is possible to create a political system that will, quite literally, be perfect. This being done, such a flawless constitution, because of its perfection and in spite of human infirmities, will enjoy immortality. Thus, "as Man is sinful, but yet the world is perfect, so may the Citizen bee sinful, and yet the Common-wealth be perfect. . . . the Citizen, where the common Wealth is perfect can never commit any such crime, as can render it imperfect, or bring it unto a natural dissolution."[1] As a consequence, "a Commonwealth rightly ordered, may for any internal causes be as immortal, or longlived, as the World." Like so many of his contemporaries, Harrington accepted the fiction that the Venetian constitution had lasted unchanged for a thousand years, and, like them, he regarded Venice, "the immortal commonwealth," as the example of political perfection. Because of her constitution the Venetian state, "at this day with one thousand years upon her back," was thought to be "as young, as fresh, and free from decay, or any appearance of it, as shee was born."[2] We may say then that since by definition it can never improve, and since in fact it will never deteriorate, a perfect commonwealth *has* no history.

This still leaves the possibility of viewing history as the process of achieving such political perfection. Harrington, like Machiavelli, eliminates even this possibility by combining the idea of perfection with the idea of political creation by a Legislator. As we have seen, he quotes Machiavelli to the effect that "the *Legislator* should be one man" and "the *Government* should be made altogether, or at once."[3] It is inconceivable to Harrington that a perfect commonwealth should ever be the product of an evolution through time; it must be created "at once" by one man or it will never exist. Going even further than Machiavelli, Harrington writes: "Think me not vain, for I cannot hold; a Common-wealth that is rightly instituted can never swarve, nor one that is not rightly instituted be secured from swarving by reduction unto her principles."[4] In short, any change or

1. *Oceana,* p. 185.
2. Ibid. See Ch. 6 for a further discussion of Harrington's view of Venice.
3. *Oceana,* p. 58.
4. Ibid., p. 186.

development must inevitably result from imperfection. Any particular change may be relatively good or bad, but qua change it occurs only because of the absence of perfection and can itself never lead to perfection.

Thus it is in his discussion of "modern prudence" that Harrington for the first time considers political questions from an historical point of view. True political principles, "ancient prudence," in a real sense have no history. On the other hand, all of European history since the fall of Rome is the story of the successive decline of political systems, reaching its tragic culmination in the seventeenth century. Harrington's treatment of modern prudence is his most detailed excursion into the realm of political pathology; it is designed chiefly as an illustration of the evils of historical development and a plea for the re-creation of timeless perfection.

Harrington believed that western political history fell naturally into two distinct eras. Indeed the very first sentence of his preliminary discussion of political theory points out that "*Janotti,* the most excellent describer of the Common-wealth of *Venice,* divideth the whole series of Government into two Times or Periods."[5] The first of these, consisting of the classical era of Greek history and the age of the Roman republic, was the time of "ancient prudence." Then government was "an Art whereby a Civil Society of men is instituted and preserved upon the foundation of common right or interest . . . the *Empire* of *Lawes* and not of *Men.*"[6] Clearly for Harrington ancient prudence at least approximates a correct understanding of the nature and purpose of government. Although the ancients were misled in many particulars, and did not enjoy Harrington's thorough comprehension of things political, they nevertheless instinctively tended to establish sound institutions and pur-

5. Ibid., p. 12.
6. Ibid.

sue proper goals. But in the modern world Machiavelli "is the only Politician that hath gone about to retrieve" ancient prudence, and Venice is the only polity that actually embodies its principles.

What can explain the sad fate of ancient prudence? Historically speaking, it was destroyed by "the Arms of Caesar" and replaced by "modern prudence," introduced into the western world "by those inundations of *Huns, Goths, Vandalls, Lombards, Saxons,* which breaking the *Roman Empire,* deformed the whole face of the world, with those ill features of Government, which at this time are becoming far worse in these Western parts."[7] For modern prudence is "an Art whereby some man, or some few men, subject a City or Nation, and rule it according unto his or their private interest . . . the *Empire* of *Men,* and not of *Lawes*,"[8] and therefore a contradiction of all true principles of political morality and natural law.

In discussing the transition from ancient to modern prudence Harrington is faced with a problem which is familiar to the student of political theory as well as to the philosopher and theologian. Essentially this is the problem of the origin of evil, or to be more precise the problem of the flourishing of evil. Like so many of his contemporaries in the centuries following the Renaissance, Harrington held a fairly uncomplicated view of the course of western history. The classical period had been "good" and wise, the Middle Ages had been a time of darkness and reaction, and now it was up to the moderns to remedy the evils of their medieval predecessors and to retrieve the glories of the ancient world. But the question arises, if the classical world had been so good what can account for its decline into the ignorance and barbarism of the Middle Ages? The question becomes particularly urgent if, like Harrington, one be-

7. Ibid.
8. Ibid.

lieves that this medieval ignorance and barbarism are still the characteristic features of the world in which one lives. If the troubles of the seventeenth century are a reflection of mistakes that have persisted since the time of the Roman empire, it becomes doubly important to understand the origin of these mistakes. But, even more significant, if the remedy for these troubles is to be found in a re-establishment of the classical order, it is absolutely essential to explain the original collapse of that order. If ancient prudence is as admirable as we are told it is, and modern prudence as much inferior to it, what can account for the triumph of the latter? "But as there is no appearance in the bulk or constitution of *Moderne Prudence,* that she should ever have been able to come up and Grapple with the *Ancient,* so something of necessity must have interposed, whereby This came to be enervated, and That to receive strength and encouragement."[9]

The decisive factor in the decline of ancient and the rise of modern prudence was, we discover, "the *execrable raign* of the *Roman Emperours,* taking rise from . . . the *Arms* of *Caesar.*"[10] Harrington's account of this development, one of his favorite historical examples, is detailed and remarkably vivid; it will suffice for us to note its general outlines.[11] The basic difficulty was that the Romans "through a negligence committed in their *Agrarian Lawes,* let-in the sink of *Luxury,* and forfeited their inestimable treasure of *Liberty* for themselves and posterity."[12] Specifically, this "negligence"

9. Ibid., p. 39.
10. Ibid.
11. The best of Harrington's discussions occurs in *Oceana,* pp. 39–42; it is interesting to compare this with the series of nine queries which he appends to his translation of Virgil's Eclogues, *An Essay upon Two of Virgil's Eclogues and Two Books of his Aeneis* (London, 1658), especially nos. 3–6.
12. *Oceana,* p. 40.

consisted in the emperors' granting to their soldiers for life lands conquered in war. Originally, Harrington argues, lands were distributed in three ways: "such as were taken from the enemy and distributed unto the people; or such as were taken from the enemy, and under colour of being reserved unto the public use, were by stealth possessed by the *Nobility;* or such as were bought with the *publick Money* to be distributed."[13] But any attempt by law to deprive the nobility of the possessions thus illegally gained "caused *Earthquakes,* nor could ever be obtained by the people; or being obtained, be observed by the *Nobility,* who not onely preserved their prey, but growing vastly rich upon it, bought the people by degrees quite out of those shares that had been conferred upon them."[14] Thus the balance of property in Rome came to be changed radically in the favor of the nobility. This change, the destruction of "the Ballance of the Commonwealth," was perceived by the Gracchi who sought to reverse it by forcible means. But the efforts of these reformers came too late and consequently Harrington believes that they "did ill, seeing it neither could, nor did tend unto any more then to show them by worse effects, that what the Wisdome of their Leaders had discovered was true: for . . . the *Nobility of Rome* under the conduct of *Sylla,* overthrew the people and the *Common-wealth.*"[15]

So far this history is by no means unique; it is simply an instance of the alteration of the balance of dominion, adequately provided for and explained by Harrington's theory. Subsequent developments mark the tragic transition from ancient to modern prudence. In the first place the policy of the emperors led to the creation of "Pretorian Bands," large groups of soldiers dependent upon the favor of the ruler for the possession of their lands, "though these,

13. Ibid.
14. Ibid.
15. Ibid.

according to the incurable flaw already observed in this kind of *Government,* became the most frequent Butchers of their Lords that are to be found in Story."[16] The mere existence of such men posed a constant threat to the rule of the emperors, but in fact the empire was finally overthrown by a much more fundamental weakness. This consisted in the fact that the balance of dominion in the later empire, and particularly after the reign of Augustus, was threefold, property being divided among emperor, nobility, and people. Thus, "this Empire being neither *Hawk* nor *Buzzard,* made a flight accordingly; and having the avarice of the Souldiery on this hand to satisfie upon the people; and the *Senate* and the *people* on the other to be defended from the Souldiery; the *Prince* being perpetually tossed, seldom dy'd any other death than *by* one Horn of this *Dilemma.*"[17]

This basic instability was at first overcome, although with only scant success, by the dependence of the emperors on their pretorian guards, "those Bestiall executioners of their Captains *Tyranny* upon others, and of their own upon him."[18] Eventually, however, Constantine destroyed the power of the pretorians, thus demonstrating "that the Emperours must long before this have found out some other way of support."[19] This "other way" turns out to have been the use of the Goths as mercenary soldiers. But eventually this expedient proved as ruinous as had the earlier use of pretorians, the Goths coming to demand as tribute what they had originally received as payment for services. "And such," Harrington concludes, "was the *transition* of *Ancient* into *Modern prudence;* or that breach which being followed in every part of the *Roman Empire* with inun-

16. Ibid., p. 41.
17. Ibid.
18. Ibid., pp. 41–42.
19. Ibid., p. 42.

dations of *Vandals, Huns, Lombards, Franks, Saxons,* over-
whelmed *ancient Languages, Learning, Prudence, Manners, Cities.*"[20]

This, then, was the origin of modern prudence. The specific political form which it assumed in western Europe
Harrington characterizes as "the Gothick ballance," which
is virtually identical with what a modern observer would
call feudalism. As his starting-point Harrington cites the
definition of the word *"feudum"* given by John Calvin:[21]
"Feudum, saith *Calvine* the *Lawyer,* is a *Gothick* word of
divers significations; for it is taken either for *War,* or for a
*possession of conquered Lands, distributed by the Victor
unto such of his Captains and Souldiers as had merited in
his wars, upon condition to acknowledge him to be their
perpetuall Lord, and themselves to be his Subjects."* Harrington then proceeds to distinguish three kinds or orders
of these "feudatory principalities": *Regalia,* involving "the
right to coyn Mony, create Magistrates, take Tole, Customs,
Confiscations and the like"; *baronies,* created by these feudatory princes with the consent of the king; and *vavasors,*
conferred upon private men by barons.[22] The Gothic balance, then, is characterized by these typical feudal arrangements. Having cited Calvin's definition, Harrington concludes his general discussion of modern prudence with this
statement: *"And this is the Gothick Ballance, by which all
the Kingdoms this day in Christendome were at first erect-
ed;* for which cause if I had time, I should open in this
place the *Empire* of *Germany,* and *the Kingdomes of
France, Spain and Poland;* but so much as hath been said

20. Ibid.
21. Ibid. As Liljegren notes, the reference is not to the reformer
but to Jean Calvinus, professor at Heidelberg. See his *Lexicon Juri-
dicum* (Geneva, 1645), p. 368: "Feudum vocabulum est Gotthicum."
22. *Oceana,* p. 42; see Calvin, *Lexicon,* p. 369, "Unde tres Feu-
dorum gradus facti sunt."

being sufficient for the discovery of the principles of *Modern Prudence in general* . . . the remainder of my Discourse . . . is more particular."[23] The remainder of the discourse, to which we must now turn, is a more detailed discussion of the political history of England.

"The Gothick Ballance"

As we have noted, Harrington's discussion in the *Oceana* of English political history (thinly disguised by fictitious names assigned to persons and places) serves several purposes. First, it provides us with a working example of Harrington's analytic method. Having discussed his general theory of politics we may now observe the manner in which he applies this theory to particular historical materials. Secondly, this discussion illustrates the precise nature of modern prudence. Finally, and perhaps most important of all, a consideration of Harrington's treatment of English history will give us added insight into his view of the age in which he lived. It should already be apparent that Harrington considered England's political problems to be a reflection, or rather a culmination, of a long historical process. It is this more than anything else that explains the truly extraordinary objectivity and detachment of his account of the English Civil Wars. More, perhaps, than any of his contemporaries, Harrington refused to consider these wars as a conflict between good men and evil men. Rather, he believed that they were the almost inevitable outcome of a succession of earlier events.

Harrington divides his discussion of English history into three parts: a general account of the British constitution, an explanation of the Civil Wars, and a description of the events leading to the creation of the commonwealth. Of these the last two are particularly interesting, but the first

23. *Oceana,* p. 43.

is important as an example of a "Gothick" monarchy. Harrington passes rapidly over the Roman period of British history because its provincial character places it somewhat apart from the developments with which he is primarily concerned. He observes in passing that "if we have given over running up and down naked and with dappled hides, learn't to write and read, to be instructed with good Arts, for all these we are beholding to the *Romans* either *immediately,* or *mediately.*"²⁴

The first domestic government of England was that of the Teutons (Saxons), who introduced "the form of the late Monarchy," that is, the Gothic balance. This is characterized by the creation of "three sorts of Feuds," in other words three varieties of feudal tenure: Ealdormen, Kingsthanes, and Middle-thanes. On the basis of this distinction Harrington is able to describe "the ballance of the Teuton Monarchy," as dominated by the vast wealth of the earls (Ealdormen), who "were not onely called *Reguli* or little Kings, but were such indeed."²⁵ The power, or empire, of the earls is evident in the fact that they controlled both county courts and "the high Court of the Kingdom." This latter, of course, is what has come to be known as Parliament. All the feudal tenants, Earls, Kings-thanes, Bishops, Abbots, and Middle-thanes "had in the High Court or *Parliament* of the *Kingdome* a more publick jurisdiction, consisting, *first,* of *Deliberative power* for advising upon, and assenting unto new *Lawes. Secondly,* of giving Counsel in matters of *State;* and *thirdly,* of Judicature upon *Suits,* and *Complaints.*"²⁶ And although he is willing to admit that this Parliament was dominated by the power of the earls, at the expense of the king, lesser nobles, and burgesses, Harrington insists on the fact that the commons were at this

24. Ibid.
25. Ibid., p. 44.
26. Ibid., p. 45.

time a regular part of Parliament, qualified by election in borough or shire, and sitting as a separate house. He concludes, "the *Parliament* of the *Teutons* consisted of the *King,* the *Lords Spiritual and Temporal,* and the *Commons* of the *Nation,* notwithstanding the style of divers *Acts* of *Parliament,* which runs as that of *Magna Charta* in the *Kings* name only, seeing the same was neverthelesse enacted by the *King, Peers,* and *Commons* of the *Land,* as is testified in those words by a subsequent *Act.*"27

This in brief outline is Harrington's picture of the English monarchy created by the Saxons and left relatively unchanged by the Danes; it lasted in this form, he tells us, for about 220 years.28 In form and in theory this was a government by estates—by king, lords spiritual and temporal, and commons. In practice it was a government dominated by the overwhelming wealth and consequent power of great nobles known as earls or ealdormen.

The first significant change in this system, Harrington argues, was occasioned by the Norman conquest. Having successfully invaded and conquered England, William "used it as conquered, distributing the *Earldomes, Thane-Lands, Bishopricks and Prelacies* of the whole *Realm* amongst his [Normans]."29 The immediate result of this, aside from certain changes in feudal terminology, was an

27. Ibid. The first Act of Parliament referred to is 25 Edw. I. 3, *Confirmatio Cartarum,* which begins simply, "Edward par la grace de dieu, Roy Dengleterre Seignur Dirland . . ."; the second, 25 Edw. 3. Cap. I, reads, "Nostre Seignur le Roi, a son parlement tenuz a Westminster . . . par assent de Prelatz, Countz, Barons & autres grants, & tote la Comunalte de son roialme, au dit parelement somons, ad ordene & establi les choses souzescriptes."

28. Thus, figuring backward from the Norman conquest it becomes apparent that Harrington believed the Anglo-Saxon monarchy to have reached its full development somewhere around the middle of the 9th century. This is not very different from modern estimates.

29. *Oceana,* pp. 45–46.

alteration of the balance of property in England. Harrington here performs various complex and somewhat dubious mathematical operations on figures given by Coke and Bracton and arrives at the following conclusion: "the *Ballance* and *Foundation* of this Government was in the 60,000 *Knights fees,* and these being possest by the 250 *Lords,* it was a *Government* of the *Few,* or of the *Nobility;* wherein the *people* might also assemble, but could have no more than a meer name."[30] Consequently, it is plain, according to Harrington's theory, that actual power must have rested with the nobility, although it was perhaps exercised by the king through their sufferance. At first the Norman monarchs were actually able to rule as "absolute Princes," despite the fact that this was contrary to "the nature of their foundation," simply because their Norman nobles considered themselves to be foreigners and soldiers rather than citizens. Thus, the Normans "while they were but forraigne Plants, having no security against the Natives, but in growing up by their Princes side" failed to demand the political power to which their possessions entitled them. Eventually, however, and inevitably, these nobles began to identify themselves with England, considered their position to be the same as that of the English barons and "grew as fierce in the Vindication of the Auncient rights and liberties of the same, as if they had beene alwaies Natives." And the fruits of this, "the Kings being as obstinate on the one side for their absolute power, as these on the other for their immunities," were the so-called Barons' Wars of the early thirteenth century. The unfortunate John sought to overcome the resistance of his barons by calling to his "councills" only such men as would support him, regardless of whether their possessions entitled them to be considered barons. Thus, John "seeing the effects of such *Dominion,* began first . . .

30. Ibid., pp. 46–47. The clergy possessed a third of the land and were therefore also considerably more important than the commons.

to call such by *Writs* as were otherwise no *Barons,* by which meanes striving to avoid the consequence of the *Ballance,* in coming unwillingly to set the *Government streight,* he was the first that set it *awry.*"[31]

At this point the stage is finally set for the struggle between the monarchy and the nobility that was eventually to lead to the destruction of both. The essential problem was that the balance of power clearly rested with the nobility while the monarchs were unwilling to abandon their dream of absolute rule; the people were left completely out of the picture. John, by devising the scheme of creating a nobility solely dependent on the king, virtually guaranteed that the issue would be raised in violent form. And it is this fundamental dualism, this inevitable conflict between a landed nobility and a would-be absolute monarch, that Harrington finds to be the first characteristic of modern prudence and the Gothic balance. Thus in a rather bitter passage he observes, "By which meanes this *Government* being indeed the *Master-piece* of *Moderne Prudence* hath beene cry'd up to the *Skyes,* as the only invention whereby at once to maintaine the soveraignty of a *Prince,* and the liberty of the *people:* whereas indeed it hath beene no other than a wrestling match, wherein the *Nobility,* as they have been stronger have thrown the *King;* or the *King* if he have been stronger, hath thrown the *Nobility.*"[32]

As the words quoted at the beginning of this chapter indicate, this was Harrington's view of the fundamental flaw in all modern governments. The political disturbances that beset Europe during the seventeenth century, and notably the Thirty Years' War, the English Civil Wars, and the wars of the Fronde, resulted from the breakdown of this uneasy balance between kings and their estates. Indeed, the very fact that the outcome of this universal struggle varied

31. *Oceana,* p. 47.
32. Ibid., pp. 47–48.

188 An Immortal Commonwealth

from country to country indicated the evenness of the balance. But whatever the result of the "wrestling match," the cause was in all cases the same; any attempt to distribute power among the estates (king, nobles, clergy, and commons) must lead to violence, as must an attempt on the part of any of the estates to rule without sufficient economic power. As English history demonstrates, with the Thirty Years' War as a terrible corroboration, the seventeenth century was the time of decision. The medieval order that had lasted for so many centuries, and was characterized by "the Gothick ballance," was now doomed to destruction. A further consideration of English history reveals its fate.

Dissolution of the English Monarchy

The reign of Richard II gave striking proof of the instability of this Gothic balance. Reviving the device originated by John, Richard foolishly created a number of barons by letters patent. These, Harrington observes, "were hands in the *Kings Purse,* and had no *shoulders* for his *Throne.*" Indeed, "Of these when the house of *Peers* came once to be full . . . there was nothing more empty."[33] But in the meantime the barons created by Richard constituted no threat to the throne of England since this had "other supports." The older barons, however, looked with great disfavor on Richard's proceedings and, still possessing the balance of dominion, were successful in deposing him. And this was in many ways the beginning of the end of the English monarchy. The barons, having deposed Richard, "got the trick of it, and never gave over setting up, and pulling down of their *Kings* according to their various interests, and that faction of the *White and Red* into which they had been thenceforth divided."[34] The quasi-anarchy of the Wars of

33. Ibid., p. 48.
34. Ibid.

the Roses lasted until finally Henry VII "was more by their favor than his right advanced unto the *Crown*."[35] With the beginning of the Tudor period began also the final dissolution of the monarchy.

Henry VII's essential difficulty was that he was clever enough to see the weakness of his position but not clever enough to understand it fully or find a remedy for it. "Through his naturall subtilty" Henry reflected upon the "greatnesse of [the barons'] power, and the inconstancy of their favour" and concluded that "a *Throne* supported by a *Nobility* is not so hard to be ascended, as kept warm."[36] He therefore devoted his energies to the weakening of the position of his barons, believing that this was the surest way to enhance his own power. This he did by various means, of which Harrington cites three in particular: statutes "for *Population*, . . . against *Retainers*, . . . and for *Aliena-tions*."[37] The first of these, the Statute of Population, provided that "all houses of *husbandry* that were used with twenty Acres of ground and upwards were to be maintained, and kept up for ever with a competent proportion of Land laid to them, and in no wise . . . to be severed."[38] Harrington, with his sure eye for economic and social developments, notes that this Act did "in effect *amortize* a great part of the Lands unto the hold and possession of the *Yeomanry*, or *middle people* . . . upon which the *Lords* had so little power that from henceforth they may be computed to have been disarmed."[39] And as the Statute of Population deprived the nobility of its infantry and created an independent yeoman

35. Ibid.
36. Ibid.
37. Ibid.
38. Ibid., pp. 48–49; see 4 Hen. VII c. 19, *An Acte agaynst pullyng doun of Tounes,* also cited as *An Acte for kepyng up of houses for husbandrye.*
39. *Oceana,* pp. 48–49.

class, so the Statute of Retainers destroyed the cavalry of the noble party.[40] The picture is completed by the Statute of Alienations: "Henceforth the Country-lives, and great tables of the *Nobility,* which no longer nourished veins that would bleed for them, were fruitlesse and loathsome till they changed the *Air,* and of *Princes* became *Courtiers,* where their *Revenues* . . . were found narrow, whence followed *wracking of Rents,* and at length sale of *Lands;* the riddance through the Statute of *Alienations* being rendred far more quick and facile, than formerly it had been."[41]

It is interesting to note that in this case the primary cause of the economic change is an alteration of manners. Partly as a result of the two previous Statutes, the nobility of England became dissatisfied with its earlier simple country life and began moving to the royal court. This proved expensive and eventually necessitated the sale of land, which was facilitated by the new Statute of Alienations. As a result of all three laws the balance of property in England was fundamentally altered. Harrington argued that the possession of the bulk of the land of England by less than 300 people would create a monarchical balance, by between 300 and 5000 people an aristocracy, and by more than 5000 people a commonwealth.[42] The transformation during the reign of Henry VII was clearly from an aristocratic balance to one appropriate to a commonwealth.

Before continuing our account of the dissolution of the monarchy we may look briefly at several features of this transformation. In the first place, Harrington's account helps to explain the paradox raised by his reference to altering the foundation to fit the form of government.[43] Al-

40. See 19 Hen. VII c. 14, *De retentionibus illicitis.*
41. *Oceana,* p. 49: see 4 Hen. VII c. 4, *An Acte for the passing and transmutation of lands without Fyne.*
42. *Art of Lawgiving, Coll. Works,* p. 392.
43. See above, pp. 116 ff.

though Henry VII was unwittingly altering the foundation in the wrong direction, his method is nevertheless instructive. The important fact is that he did not *compel* the nobility to limit their possessions or sell their land. Rather, he simply created conditions which tended to bring about this result. In this connection the Statute of Alienations is most instructive, since it did no more than make convenient the sale of land, but actually was as effective as if it had made this sale compulsory. A second interesting point, and one which Harrington unfortunately never discusses in detail, is the fact that this alteration seems to be qualitative as well as quantitative. That is, the character, as well as the number, of those owning land changes. The alteration of the balance occurred only after the nobility had become effete and alienated from its former simple rural existence. Possession was transferred to the yeomanry or "middle people," who lived "not in a servile or indigent fashion" but rather "in a free and plentifull manner."[44] Harrington obviously looks with considerable favor on this qualitative change.[45]

The years between the time of Henry VII and the accession of James I further contributed to the undermining of the English monarchy. Henry VIII, by dissolving the monasteries, continued the process of diffusing the ownership of land, thus accelerating the development begun by his father. As Harrington says, this "brought with the declining

44. *Oceana,* p. 49.

45. See Richard Koebner, "Oceana," in *Englische Philologie, 68* (Leipzig, 1934), 364-68, and Christian Wershofen, *James Harrington und sein wunschbild vom germanischen staate* (Bonn, 1935), passim, for a somewhat extreme statement of this view. Apparently it was fashionable in Germany in the mid-30's to interpret Harrington as an advocate of a sort of sturdy peasant community. And it is certainly true that Harrington, like Machiavelli, was an admirer of the rural virtues. But both of these accounts, and particularly Wershofen's, overemphasize this element in Harrington and fail to relate it sufficiently to his general theory.

estate of the *Nobility* so vast a prey unto the Industry of the
people, that the *Ballance* of the *Common-wealth* was too
apparently in the *Popular party*."⁴⁶ In other words, the
work of the first two Tudors had succeeded in destroying
the effective power of the English nobility only to put in its
place the even more dangerous power of the people. A popular balance, Harrington argues, is more dangerous because
it attacks not only individual monarchs but also the very
institution of monarchy. Thus he describes the results of
the policies of Henry VII and his son in these words: "while
to establish his own safety, he by mixing water with their
Wine, first began to open those *Sluces* that have since over-
whelmed not the *King* onely, but the *Throne:* For whereas
a *Nobility* striketh not at the *Throne* without which they
cannot subsist, but at some *King* that they do not like; *Popular power* striketh through the *King* at the *Throne,* as that
which is incompatible with it."⁴⁷

By the time of Elizabeth the balance had been completely
altered and England was no longer capable of supporting
monarchical government. The brilliantly successful reign
of the great queen was possible only because, first, Elizabeth
realized that her power depended on winning the favor of
her people and thus was prepared to deal firmly with the nobility, and, second, she was an extraordinarily skillful monarch. Harrington's description of Elizabeth's rule is perhaps
the most felicitous of all his writings: the popular balance,
he notes, was too obvious "to be unseen by the wise Councel
of Queen [Elizabeth], who converting her reign through the
perpetuall Love-tricks that passed between her and her people into a kind of *Romanze;* wholly neglected the *Nobility*."⁴⁸ Harrington has here captured, in a skillful phrase,
the intensely personal quality of Elizabeth's rule. But he

46. *Oceana*, p. 49.
47. Ibid., p. 48.
48. Ibid., p. 49.

recognizes that such devices as she used could at best serve merely to postpone the inevitable transfer of political power to the people of England.

The final development in this process begins with the accession of James I, and it, too, is a combination of personal and impersonal elements. The first two Tudor monarchs had set the stage for the overthrow of the monarchy, Elizabeth had managed to survive by her skill, and it only remained for James and especially Charles, by their extraordinary ineptitude, to set off the inevitable conflagration. Here again Harrington's description is so apt that any paraphrase would be inferior to a quotation:

> And by these degrees came the House of *Commons* to raise that head, which since hath been so high and formidable unto their *Princes;* that they have looked pale upon those assemblies. Nor was there any thing now wanting unto the destruction of the *Throne,* but that the *people* not apt to see their own strength, should be put to feel it; when a *Prince,* as stiffe in disputes as the nerve of *Monarchy* was grown slack, received that unhappy encouragement from his *Clergy,* which became his utter Ruine, while trusting more unto their Logick, than the rough *Philosophy* of his *Parliament,* it came unto an irreparable breach; for the house of *Peers* which alone had stood in this Gap, now sinking down between the *King* and the *Commons,* shewed that *Crassus* was dead. . . . But a *Monarchy* divested of her *Nobility,* hath no refuge under Heaven, but an Army. *Wherefore the dissolution of this Government caused the War, not the War the dissolution of this Government.*[49]

In short, the fundamental cause of the war was the attempt of the Stuarts to exercise a power which the balance of prop-

49. Ibid., pp. 49–50.

erty denied them; lacking an economic foundation their
only recourse was to force. But, as Harrington's theory has
taught us, it was highly improbable that their military efforts should succeed. And indeed the chief result of the
armed conflict of the 1640's was to demonstrate to the people of England how great their strength was and to make
it impossible that they should in the future submit to
monarchical government. One gathers that the wisest course
for the Stuarts to pursue, short of abdication, would have
been one of submission to the will of the people while maintaining the forms of monarchy. The attempt to assert a royal
power that did not in fact exist was fatal both to Charles I
and to the English monarchy.

The immediate significance of this is, of course, quite apparent, but its broader implications are more interesting.
Harrington here denies the argument that the people of
England, the House of Commons, and the Independents,
were responsible for a deliberate revolt against the established order of things, the British constitution. On the contrary, if there is any responsibility for the Civil Wars it
must rest with the Stuarts. But, in a broader sense, even
they must not be judged too harshly. A later appraisal of
Charles I is interesting in this connection: "And this happen'd in the [reign of the] next King, who too secure in that
undoubted right wherby he was advanc'd to a Throne
which had no foundation, dar'd to put this to an unseason-
able trial; on whom therefore fell the Tower in *Silo*. Nor
may we think that they upon whom this Tower fell, were
Sinners above all men; but that we, unless we repent, and
look better to the true foundations, must likewise perish."[50]
Unquestionably Charles was a foolish man, but Harrington,
perhaps because of his friendship, is unwilling to condemn
him on moral grounds. Indeed, he explicitly admits that

50. *Art of Lawgiving, Coll. Works*, p. 391.

Charles had an "undoubted right" to the throne of England.

In this connection we may note Harrington's one brief discussion of the problem of allegiance to the monarchy. If this was in fact a legitimate government—as Harrington admits it was—must we not also admit that the Civil Wars constituted a violation of the people's obligation to obey? Harrington's general answer, as we have seen, is that the government had been dissolved prior to the Civil Wars. But in a more abstract vein he goes so far as to say that a change of the balance is sufficient to "absolve" any previous right, law, or oath of allegiance. Thus he argues, "if the right of *Kings* were as immediately derived from the breath of *God*, as the life of man; yet this excludeth not *death and dissolution*. But, that the *dissolution* of the late *Monarchy was as natural as the death of a man*, hath already been shewn . . . [Therefore] the *Oath* of *Allegiance*, as all other *Monarchical Lawes*, imply an impossibility, and are therefore void."[51] Harrington has here carried his original theory one step further. At first the question of the balance of property was a purely practical one: whoever possessed a predominant amount of land would be able to rule. But now we see that the balance also determines the matter of obligation to obey. Since an unfavorable balance makes monarchy "impossible"—and this is surely an extreme version of Harrington's original position—there is no obligation to obey a monarch in these circumstances. And this would seem to be the reasoning behind Harrington's statement, noted above, that government according to the balance is of "Divine Right."[52] One is reluctantly forced to conclude that when faced with practical problems Harrington tends to abandon his distinction between empire and authority, physical power and moral right, and to attribute

51. *Oceana,* pp. 54–55.
52. See above, p. 134, for a discussion of the paradoxical implications of this statement.

certain moral qualities to mere physical power. But it may
be added that he does this only when he is attempting to
find moral as well as practical justification for the English
Civil Wars.

The Interregnum

A much more convincing moral justification of the Civil
Wars would exist, of course, if these wars were to lead to
the creation of a superior political order in England. If this
were to happen, Harrington could then conveniently return
to his twofold system of analysis, defending the new commonwealth on both counts. As far as empire is concerned
it would have the inestimable advantage of resting on an
appropriate economic base; and its dedication to the common interest would give it authority far exceeding that of
the Stuart monarchy. But Harrington was quick to recognize the difference between the mere destruction of the old
order and the substitution of something better. Although
his theory proved the inevitability of the former, it by no
means guaranteed the achievement of the latter. And indeed
the events between the destruction of the monarchy in 1649
and the publication of the *Oceana* in 1656 demonstrated
the difficulties attending the hoped-for creation of an "equal
commonwealth" in England, while the following four years
were even more discouraging.

Harrington did consider this, however, a time of transition from the outmoded monarchy to the inevitable commonwealth. And he sought to speed the transition. Thus,
"the *Ballance* being in the *people,* the *Common-wealth*
(though they do not see it) is already in the Nature of them:
. . . there wanteth nothing else but *time* (which is slow and
dangerous) or *art* (which would be more quick and secure)
for bringing those native *Arms* (wherewithall they are
found already) . . . unto such maturity as may fix them upon

their own strength and *Bottom.*"[53] The most interesting
aspect of this passage is the contrast between time and art,
between the slow and apparently uncertain working of
political laws and deliberate human intervention. The art
that is involved here, Harrington tells us, is *"Prudence,"*
namely "the skill of raising such *Superstructures* of *Government,* as are natural to the known *Foundations.*"[54] And
this, of course, is very different from the intervention of
Henry VII or Elizabeth or Charles I, all of whom sought to
struggle against "the known Foundations."

But once we admit the possibility and the efficacy of deliberate human action the problem of determinism and inevitability again confronts us. We have already noted the
fundamental ambiguity of Harrington's atttitude toward
this problem, an ambiguity that undoubtedly reflects very
practical considerations. If Harrington is addressing himself to an audience which doubts the possibility of his desired equal commonwealth, he stresses the inevitability of
such political arrangements. If, on the other hand, he is
attempting to gain active support for his proposals, he emphasizes the necessity of working for the good cause.[55] The
greatest confusion, of course, stems from the fact that he
seldom confines himself at any given moment to either of
these techniques, but seeks always to combine both in one
argument. It is nevertheless possible to abstract from Harrington's writings a fairly consistent theory of the relation
between time and art in the particular instance of seventeenth-century England.

At this point we must revert briefly to Harrington's distinction between a commonwealth and an equal commonwealth.[56] It will be recalled that for Harrington *"Common-*

53. *Oceana,* p. 53.
54. Ibid.
55. The analogy to the Marxists is striking.
56. See above, pp. 156 ff.

wealths in generall be *Governments* of the *Senate proposing, the people resolving, and the Magistracy executing,"*[57]
while an equal commonwealth requires the addition of an
agrarian law, rotation in office, and voting by ballot.[58] In
terms of this distinction we may now say that in 1656 there
were four conceivable solutions for England's political
problems: 1) a government might be established completely
at variance with the balance of property, 2) a government
might be established which was "popular" in the sense of
placing power in the hands of the people without being a
"commonwealth," 3) a commonwealth might be established
without an equal agrarian law and without a balloting
system, and 4) an "equal commonwealth" might be established. This way of stating the situation will enable us to
arrive at a more precise understanding of that element of
Harrington's thought which we have been referring to
rather loosely as "inevitability."

   In what sense can one say that any of these four possibilities was inevitable in seventeenth-century England? The
answer is that we must speak of stability or longevity rather
than inevitability. The first possibility, a monarchy or aristocracy (or more precisely, a tyranny or oligarchy), will be
doomed to failure because it is not in accord with the balance. What, then, of a popular government that is not a
commonwealth? This, too, will fail because its constitution
places too much power in the hands of the people and provides no limitation on their activities. A commonwealth,
even without an agrarian law and a balloting system, will
have a better chance of success simply because it does remedy some of the defects of the previous form. But it, too, will
inevitably lack stability. The absence of an agrarian law
will leave the possibility of an alteration of the balance on
which the government is based; the absence of rotation and

57. *Oceana,* p. 32.
58. Ibid., p. 33.

balloting will leave the possibility of the growth of a privileged political class. Therefore only an equal commonwealth provides sufficient guarantees for the maintenance of popular government in the common interest.

But it should now be apparent that the major difference between a tyrannical government and an unequal commonwealth, from this point of view, is one of degree. Given the economic state of England in 1656, both are likely to fail, but the chances of failure are somewhat less in the case of a commonwealth. "In the present case of *England,* Commonwealthsmen may fail thro want of Art, but Royalists must fail thro want of Matter; the former may miss thro impotence, the latter must thro impossibility."[59] Thus, instead of saying that an equal commonwealth was inevitable in England in 1656, it is more accurate to say that such a system of government is the only one sure to succeed. And we are now in a position to appreciate better Harrington's alternation between calm assurance that time would inevitably prove his theory correct and rather impassioned pleas for support. The advantages of an equal commonwealth would, in the long run, be apparent to all simply because no other form of government could endure. But the actual creation of such a system required deliberate action.

This, then, is the position in which Harrington found himself toward the middle of the seventeenth century. And there can be no doubt that his view of "modern prudence" was to a large extent determined by precisely these theoretical considerations. Specifically, he wished to support an equal commonwealth against each of the other three imaginable political arrangements noted above. His discussion of the dissolution of the English monarchy was, he felt, sufficient proof of the impossibility of a government resting on any but a popular foundation. To this may be added

59. *Ways and Means, Coll. Works,* p. 540.

the argument that a monarchical or aristocratic government, even if it were possible, would be morally less desirable than a popular one.[60] In short, Harrington's entire
discussion of domestic empire may be considered to be an
argument against the restoration of monarchy in England.

But his opposition to any popular government not fitting
his definition of a commonwealth was equally strong. The
best example of this is to be found in his discussion of the
Agreement of the People, which in a marginal note he
refers to as illustrating "the Anarchy of the Levellers."[61]
Harrington objects to the system of government proposed
in the *Agreement* for several reasons, and of these one is
obviously crucial. In the first place, the establishment of a
representative body composed of only four hundred men
seems to him impossible. "The Many," he writes, "cannot
be otherwise represented in a State of Liberty, than by so
many . . . as may within the compass of that number and
nature imbrace the interest of the whole People."[62] Furthermore, this difficulty is merely aggravated by limiting
the sessions of the representative body to eight months out
of each two years. And this limitation, in turn, raises the
question of who is to exercise sovereign power in England
during the interval between meetings of the representative
body. The proposed Council of State, Harrington feels, is
"so much worse, as this Council consists of fewer. Thus far
this Commonwealth is Oligarchy."[63]

The major objection, however, arises from the provision

60. See *Oceana,* p. 54.
61. *Art of Lawgiving, Coll. Works,* p. 430; despite Harrington's
mention of the Levellers, it is obvious from his discussion that the
document in question is the *Agreement of the People* of Jan. 15, 1649,
and not the more extreme Leveller version of Oct. 1647. See S. R.
Gardiner, *Constitutional Documents of the Puritan Revolution* (3rd
ed., Oxford, 1927), pp. 359–71, for the text.
62. *Art of Lawgiving, Coll. Works,* p. 430.
63. Ibid.

of the Agreement which declares that "these Representatives have Soverain Power, save that in som things the People may resist them by Arms."[64] With keen perception Harrington observes that this provision "first is a flat contradiction, and next is downright Anarchy."[65] It is, as he sees clearly, an attempt to evade the issue of sovereignty. On the surface, it would seem that sovereign power is to be divided between the Representatives on the one hand and the people on the other. Thus the Representatives shall have "the highest and final judgment, concerning all natural or civil things," but six particulars are enumerated with which they cannot interfere. But Harrington, like Bodin a century earlier, insists that the concept of a limited or divided sovereignty is simply a contradiction in terms. "Where the Soverain Power is not as intire and absolute as in Monarchy it self," he writes, "there can be no Government at all."[66] The problem with the *Agreement* is that, as Gardiner observes, "the English Council of the Army either did not understand [that it was useless to attempt to bind a nation in perpetuity], or distrusted the nation too far to make provision for what they knew must come in time."[67] Thus when Harrington says that this is "no Government at all" he means that the proposed system provides no machinery by which the people can express their ultimate power. And therefore this system is not only "a flat contradiction," but also "downright Anarchy." For in fact it must be recognized

64. Ibid. The statement is Harrington's. He refers probably to the section of the *Agreement* which states, "That the Representatives have, and shall be understood to have, the supreme trust in order to the preservation and government of the whole . . . Provided that . . . these six particulars next following are . . . to be excepted and reserved from our Representatives." Gardiner, *Constitutional Documents,* p. 368.

65. *Art of Lawgiving, Coll. Works,* p. 430.

66. Ibid., pp. 430–31.

67. Gardiner, *Constitutional Documents,* p. li.

that sovereignty here does reside ultimately with the people, who can resist their representatives. For Harrington, as indeed for most political theorists, an uncontrolled and uninstitutionalized exercise of power by the mass of the people amounts to anarchy.

The contrast between the *Agreement of the People* and his own proposals is made quite explicit by Harrington:

> It is not the limitation of Soverain Power that is the cause of a Commonwealth, but such a libration, or poize of Orders, that there can be in the same no number of men having the interest, that can have the power; nor any number of men having the power, that can have the interest, to invade or disturb the Government. As the Orders of Commonwealths are more approaching to, or remote from this Maxim (of which this of the Levellers has nothing) so are they more quiet or turbulent.[68]

Thus the basic weakness of the *Agreement* is its attempt to divide the sovereign power between the representative assembly and the people. If the attempt should succeed, the result will be mere confusion; if the people should retain sovereignty, the result will be anarchy. Finally, Harrington notes that the religious provisions of the *Agreement* are satisfactory insofar as they contemplate liberty of conscience, but not particularly useful because they say nothing of the means by which this is to be achieved. In general we may say that he rejects this proposed system primarily because it envisages popular government—in fact, popular sovereignty—without providing adequate checks against the abuse of this power by the people.

Toward the end of his career, in May of 1659, Harrington wrote that only three things could possibly stand in the way

68. *Art of Lawgiving, Coll. Works,* p. 431.

of the establishment of a commonwealth in England, and
only two further things could then prevent the establishment of an *equal* commonwealth. The first three are a monarchy imposed by foreign invasion, a tyranny, and an oligarchy. The other two are "a Senate for Life" and "an Optimacy."[69] It is interesting, in the first place, to note that by
this time Harrington considered both a monarchy imposed
by a foreign power and a tyranny "only possible, and not a
whit probable."[70] Even more significantly, he ignores completely the possibility of a government along the lines suggested by the *Agreement of the People*. Furthermore, the
three remaining possibilities—oligarchy, a senate for life,
and an optimacy—are all very much alike. Specifically, they
all involve the placing of political power in the hands of a
small and privileged group.

What can explain this apparent shift of emphasis in Harrington's thought from fear of monarchy or anarchy to fear
of oligarchy? The answer quite clearly is that Harrington
had been greatly impressed by the political experiments of
Oliver Cromwell during the period of the Protectorate and
believed that the greatest danger facing England was the
possibility of government by an un-elected council which
either dispensed with Parliament or was able to control
parliamentary elections. Compared with this the danger
of the introduction of monarchy, tyranny, or anarchy was
slight. Thus,

> The Power at which such a Council doth naturally
> drive, is to call Parliaments, and to govern in the In-
> tervals. But the Success of such a Council, will be, that

69. *Pour enclouer le canon, Coll. Works,* pp. 597–98. In an "Optimacy," he explains, the people are divided into classes according to
wealth, and the wealthier classes "may give the suffrage of the whole
people . . ." Ibid., pp. 599–600.
70. Ibid.

> if in calling Parliaments, it do not pack them, it will
> be forthwith ruined; and if it do pack them, then the
> case of such a Council, and a Parliament, will be no
> otherwise different from the Case of a single Person
> and a Parliament, than that more Masters . . . will be
> a Burthen by so much more heavy.[71]

In these words Harrington has isolated the fundamental
political problem that faced England during the Interregnum. Despite all of Cromwell's attempts to constitutionalize
his power, the suspicion and hostility between the Lord
Protector and the Army Council on the one hand and the
people's representatives on the other were too profound
to admit of any cooperative solution. As the *Agreement of
the People* illustrated one side of this dilemma, so Cromwell's policies reveal the other. And it is here that Harrington discovers the cause of England's political instability:
"A Councill without a *Ballance* is not a *Common-wealth,*
but an *Oligarchy;* & every *Oligarchy,* except she be put to
the defence of her wickedness, or power, against some outward danger, is factious: Wherfore the errours of the *people* being from their *Governours* . . . if the *people of Oceana* have beene factious, the cause is apparent: *But what
remedy?*"[72] With this question we may turn from our consideration of modern prudence and its weaknesses to an
examination of Harrington's proposed solution.

71. Ibid., p. 598.
72. *Oceana,* p. 58.

CHAPTER 5.

The Commonwealth of Oceana

"I think I have omitted nothing, but the Props and Scaffolds which are not of use but in building. And how much is here? Shew me another Commonwealth in this compass. How many things? Shew me another intire Government consisting but of thirty Orders. If you go to suit there lye unto some of your Courts two hundred original Writs; If you stir your hand, there go more nerves and bones unto the motion; If you play, you have more Cards in the pack; nay you could not sit with your ease in that chair, if it consisted not of more parts, will you not allow unto your Legislator, what you can afford your Upholster; unto the Throne, what is necessary to a Chair?"

The Commonwealth of Oceana

J AMES HARRINGTON'S *Commonwealth of Oceana,* one of the multitude of "aierie modells" of government produced in England during the Interregnum, is perhaps the most detailed political system created by a single individual since Plato's *Laws.* Lacking the almost unbridled imagination that characterized the utopian socialists of the nineteenth century, and lacking also the literary flair of Plato and More, Harrington presented his readers with a prosaic and excessively intricate description of a governmental structure ideally suited, he felt, to seventeenth-century England.

The reaction of his readers was what might be expected—they generally refused to take the whole thing seriously. With a political instinct superior to that of the "expert" Harrington, they realized that the adoption of any political system sprung full-blown from the brow of a political theorist was a consummation hardly to be expected in England, if indeed it was even devoutly to be wished. The mirth that greeted Harrington's magnum opus was unquestionably a blow to its author, but perhaps worse from his point of view was the reaction of others, who were willing to take the work seriously but rather as a compendium of political devices than as a finished and coherent political system. That this should have happened was perhaps a form of poetic justice to Harrington, the most eclectic of political theorists. And it was perhaps predictable in view of the alleged English distaste for abstract systems and preference for piecemeal, pragmatic solutions. But in any case it represented a serious challenge to Harrington because it resulted, he felt, from a total misunderstanding of the nature of his theory. The great virtue of the system of government presented in the *Oceana,* Harrington believed, lay not in the cleverness of any particular institutions or arrangements which it contained, but rather in the fact that it was a *system* constructed in terms of true political principles. For Harrington the importance of *Oceana* was twofold: first, it was a complete model, a whole much greater than the sum of its parts, and second it was a model that rested firmly on a sound theoretical base. Consequently, the practice of lifting various parts of the system from their institutional and theoretical context seemed to Harrington inexcusable. For example, voting by ballot, one of the most widely admired of Harrington's proposed devices, is a good thing, but only if suffrage is properly arranged and the purpose of elections is strictly defined. The same is true of all other parts of the system—for Harrington this was quite clearly intended as an all-or-nothing proposition.

The practice of treating the *Oceana* as a sort of political cafeteria, from which attractive items might be selected, results primarily from a failure to understand the connection between Harrington's general theory of politics and his specific political proposals. It is apparently based on the assumption that the proposed constitution of the commonwealth of Oceana was simply a child of Harrington's free imagination. In fact it was nothing of the sort. Rather, it was an elaborate attempt to translate abstract political principles into a workable governmental system. Every institution, device, and arrangement in the commonwealth is dictated by some theoretical consideration—nothing is incidental, nothing is gratuitous. And indeed it is this which makes the *Commonwealth of Oceana* such an uncommonly interesting document. In writing it, Harrington set himself a staggeringly difficult task. Unwilling to settle for either an abstract treatise on political theory or simply a cleverly improvised institutional solution to England's problems, he sought to combine theory and practice, ideas and institutions, in a way unseen since the time of Plato. That he succeeded to a considerable extent is surely a tribute to his abilities as both political theorist and political practitioner. That he failed to gain effective support for his system qua system is, perhaps, a reflection on his overly hopeful nature, but the modern reader, recognizing the impossibility of his goal, will not condemn him too strongly for this reason. Even in failure Harrington taught posterity a valuable lesson about the relation between political theory and political practice.

In the previous chapter we noted and discussed the most significant principles of Harrington's theory of politics. In the present chapter we will examine the institutions of the commonwealth of Oceana and attempt to point out their relation to these principles. In so doing we will find ourselves faced with one of the problems that troubled Harrington greatly in the writing of the book—that is, the problem of describing a system of government in detail without making too great demands on the patience of the reader. The peculiar form of the *Commonwealth of Oceana* —a mélange of theoretical exposition, mock-historical narrative and institutional description—undoubtedly reflects Harrington's concern with this problem. He almost certainly feared that the mass of detailed information he had to communicate, if set down in a straightforward fashion, would make his book intolerably dull, and it is revealing that in his later works he eliminated much of this detail, paring his proposals down to what he considered a basic minimum. In the *Oceana* itself Harrington sought to enliven his description by the inclusion of a succession of speeches by fictitious Oceanic statesmen, and by the invention of an imaginary history of the commonwealth after the adoption of its new constitution. It must be admitted that neither of these devices served its purpose very successfully; the book is still dull and overly burdened with detail. Unfortunately these are weaknesses which simply cannot be avoided if one is to do what Harrington set out to do in the

Oceana. In our description of the commonwealth we will have the advantage of being able to select, but even this cannot completely eliminate the problem. Perhaps the best we can do is to warn the reader at the outset that this chapter will be considerably burdened with matters of detail and ask for his indulgence.

General Description

Fortunately it is unnecessary to give any detailed physical description of Oceana; it will suffice to say that in this respect it is identical with England. Furthermore, the history of Oceana until the adoption of its new constitution (circa 1657 A.D.) is identical with the history of England.[1] Only in cases where the seventeenth-century Oceanic view of history or geography differs from the modern one will further comment be necessary.

As far as historical background is concerned, then, we

1. See Ch. 4. The following is a list of the principal names used by Harrington in the *Oceana* in referring to places and persons in England:

Adoxus—King John	Morpheus—James I
Alma—St. James's Palace	Mt. Celia—Windsor
Convallium—Hampton Court	Neustrians—Normans
Coraunus—Henry VIII	Olphaus Megaletor—Oliver Cromwell
Dicotome—Richard II	Panopea—Ireland
Emporium—London	Pantheon—Westminster Hall
Halcionia—The Thames	Panurgus—Henry VII
Halo—Whitehall	Parthenia—Queen Elizabeth
Hemisua—The Trent	Scandians—Danes
Hiera—Westminster	Turbo—William the Conqueror
Leviathan—Hobbes	Verulamius—Francis Bacon
Marpesia—Scotland	

It will be noted that there is little difficulty in identifying Harrington's pseudonyms, some of which are rather enlightening. Liljegren in his notes to the *Oceana* has done a magnificent job of tracing the derivations of these and other names.

need only note that the traditional government of Oceana
—by king, lords, and commons—was overthrown in the
'forties of the seventeenth century by civil war. Although
religious and political factors were involved in these wars,
Harrington believed that their major cause was economic.
A change in the distribution of landed property between
the reigns of Panurgus (Henry VII) and Morpheus (James
I) necessitated a corresponding change in the form of government. When this change became impossible through
peaceful means, civil war resulted. After the overthrow of
the monarchy, actual physical power in Oceana was in the
hands of the victorious parliamentary army, commanded by
Olphaus Megalctor (Cromwell). Basically, however, power
was concentrated in the class of small landowners, and it
was inevitable that they should play a major role in future
Oceanic politics.

The parliament of Oceana, a somewhat modified vestige
of the old constitution, was apparently unable to recognize
this fact or to devise a system of government able to rule
successfully. Consequently, Megaletor went to the army and
asked for power to create a new constitution. Recognizing
his mastery of political theory and trusting his motives, the
army proceeded to depose the parliament and, by universal
suffrage, made Megaletor Lord Archon of Oceana. By this
act he became "sole legislator" of the commonwealth.[2] The
army then appointed a council of fifty men to assist him in
his labors, providing however that he should still be sole
director of the work. A committee of twelve was appointed
to receive suggestions from the population at large, and
this committee was prudently provided with an armed
guard of about three hundred soldiers "lest the heat of the
dispute might break the peace."[3] After several months of
research in history and the history of political theory by the

2. *Oceana*, p. 59.
3. Ibid., p. 60.

Legislator and Council, the constitution was completed and, following considerable debate in the Council, was "ratified and established by the whole body of the people."[4] Whereupon, Harrington informs us (following the Psalmist), "The Sea roared, and the Clouds clapt their hands."[5]

Several points here are especially worthy of our attention. First of all, the new commonwealth was to be governed by a written constitution; as we have already noted, Harrington believed strongly in the necessity of permanent political institutions—"good orders," as he called them.[6] In the second place, the constitution was to be written by the Legislator. Like Plato with Dionysius, and Rousseau with his godlike Legislator, Harrington falls back on the device of the superman. But it would be wrong to let the familiarity and weakness of his solution blind us to its real virtues. This extraordinary power was given to Megaletor only after the failure of both monarchy and parliament to rule Oceana successfully. We should further note that this power was *given* to him by the army; it was not seized by a *coup de main*. And again we should note that although he did possess full power to write a constitution, he made use of fifty colleagues and welcomed popular advice. Presumably, throughout the process of writing the constitution the army retained sufficient power to stop him.

The main consideration, from Harrington's point of view, is that a constitution, like any work of art, must be

4. Ibid., p. 206.
5. Ibid., p. 205.
6. Ibid., p. 56; by "orders" Harrington always means fundamental constitutional provisions; what we would call the "articles" of the constitution of Oceana are known as Orders. As he wrote in *The Art of Lawgiving (Coll. Works,* p. 395), "Such Constitutions in a Government as regard the Frame or Model of it, are call'd Orders; and such things as are enacted by the Legislative Orders, are called Laws." See also above, p. 160.

the creation of a single individual. As he wrote, "whereas a Book or a Building hath not been known to attaine to perfection, if it have not had a sole Author, or Architect: a Common-wealth, as to the Fabrick of it, is of the like nature."[7] The provision for popular participation turns out, therefore, to have been little more than a very shrewd gesture on Megaletor's part: "This was that which made the people (who were neither safely to be admitted unto, nor conveniently excluded from the framing of their Commonwealth) verily believe when it came forth, that it was no other than that whereof they themselves had been the makers."[8] And the advisory council of fifty served partly as a research organization for Megaletor and partly as a sounding board for Harrington, but contributed nothing to the actual writing of the constitution. Admittedly all of this depends upon the presence (and the discovery) of the requisite superman who is to create the constitution; and admittedly it is all fraught with danger. But in Harrington's defense we may say that Oliver Cromwell, though not omniscient, in fact came close to being as public-spirited as Olphaus Megaletor. Moreover, Harrington was himself aware of the dangers implicit in this sort of procedure. As he argued:

> a wise *Legislator,* and one whose mind is firmly set, not upon *private* but the *publick* interest, not upon his *posterity* but upon his *Country,* may justly endeavour to get the soveraigne *power* into his own hands; nor shall any man that is master of reason blame such extraordinary meanes as in that case shall be necessary, the end proving no other than the constitution of a well ordered *Common-wealth.* The reason of this is demonstrable; for the ordinary meanes not failing, the

7. *Oceana,* p. 59.
8. Ibid., p. 60.

> *Common-wealth* hath no need of a *Legislator;* but the *ordinary* meanes failing, there is no recourse to be had but to such as are *extraordinary.*[9]

Finally, it is relevant to note that the completed constitution was submitted to the people of Oceana for ratification, which it of course received. Therefore if one objects to the method of introduction of the constitution of Oceana it cannot be on the ground that it was forced upon an unwilling populace, but rather it must be because the constitution was the creation of that political deus ex machina, the Legislator.

Before proceeding to the constitution itself we should look briefly at the social and economic state of Oceana in the seventeenth century, for the government was deliberately designed to suit, and indeed to perpetuate, these conditions. According to modern estimates the population of England in the seventeenth century was approximately four-and-a-half million, less than a third the population of France and considerably smaller than those of Spain and Austria. To this may be added the combined populations of Scotland and Ireland, a total of about two million.[10] Harrington estimated that the adult male population of Oceana alone amounted to one million, which would presumably give a grand total in the neighborhood of three-and-a-half million. The reader will do well to keep this figure in mind, since the constitution of Oceana is based on it rather than on twentieth-century estimates.[11] Although Marpesia (Scotland) is said by Harrington to be inhabited by "a populous and hardy people," and to have become by the seventeenth century "an inexhaustible Magazeen" of soldiers for the

9. Ibid., pp. 58–59.
10. See Friedrich, *Age of the Baroque,* pp. 3–5, for a discussion of the available figures and their reliability.
11. See *Oceana,* p. 155.

armies of Oceana, Panopea (Ireland) was considered by
him to be "the soft mother of a slothful and pusillanimous
people," constituting a perpetual problem for the government of Oceana.[12] Therefore it might be argued that the
advantages derived from the former were at least balanced
by the liabilities of the latter, leaving Oceana proper in its
previous position as a "middle power" in European political
life.

According to Harrington, whose views are more important to us than the actual facts, Oceana in the seventeenth
century was a predominantly agricultural society of small
landowners. He once estimated that ninety per cent of the
land of Oceana was owned by the "people," by which he
meant the small proprietors and the gentry as distinguished
from the nobility.[13] Again, Harrington stated that there
were no more than three hundred families in all of Oceana
with property worth more than two thousand pounds annually, whereas the total amount of land was worth some

12. The characterizations of Ireland and Scotland are to be found
in *Oceana,* pp. 10–11. The state of Ireland was so bad that Harrington
seriously suggested that it be repopulated with Jews imported for the
purpose. The passage is striking enough to deserve quotation: the
rehabilitation of Ireland, Harrington says, "in my opinion . . . might
have best been done by planting it with Jewes, allowing them their
own Rites and Lawes, for that would have brought them suddainly
from all parts of the World, and in sufficient numbers . . . having a
fruitfull Country and good Ports too, they would be good at both
[Merchandize and Agriculture]." It is interesting to speculate on the
relation between this view and the evangelical belief that the signal
for the establishment of Christ's kingdom on earth would be the con-
version of the Jews, an event which many predicted would occur
precisely in 1656. See Louise F. Brown, *Baptists and Fifth Monarchy
Men* (Washington, 1912), pp. 15–24.

13. *Oceana,* p. 119; it will be recalled that Harrington, following
Machiavelli, defined "nobility" as "such as live upon their own revenues in plenty, without ingagement either to the tilling of their
lands, or other work for their livelihood."

ten million pounds annually.[14] Therefore we may conclude
that the characteristic economic establishment of the time
was the small farm, supporting one family in comfort but
certainly not giving rise to luxurious living. Although trade,
and especially foreign trade, was becoming increasingly important in the economy of Oceana—a fact which Harrington recognized—manufacture was still of only minor significance.

It will not be necessary for us to describe the remaining
features of Oceana because they, too, parallel those of seventeenth-century England. Oceana was beset by the same
religious conflicts, the same foreign and colonial problems,
and the same intellectual disturbances. It now remains for
us to examine the governmental system which Olphaus
Megaletor devised for Oceana.

Elections

In Oceana the electoral system, comprising as it does an
intricately contrived succession of gatherings and ballotings
at various times and places, is by all odds the most complex
feature of the government. Harrington described this system at the greatest length in his first book, only to eliminate
it almost immediately from his later writings. Even after
he had ceased to burden his readers with involved electoral
details, however, Harrington continued to insist on their
importance, and argued that in practice the electoral system
would be a great deal simpler than it sounded. Thus in his
Seven Models of Popular Government he wrote, "The use
of the Ballot, being as full of prolixity and abstruseness in
writing, as of dispatch and facility in practice, is presum'd
throut all Elections and Results in this Model."[15] As Harrington realized, the method and arrangement of elections

14. Ibid., pp. 92–93, and 155.
15. *Coll. Works,* p. 537.

are the foundations on which all the political institutions of Oceana rest. They determine which of the populace shall have a voice in the political affairs of the commonwealth, the extent of that voice, and the means by which it can make itself heard. In any republican polity the electoral system is the vital link between the people and their government, determining first who the "people" are, and second what part they shall play in political life. For this reason alone the electoral system of Oceana would deserve our attention, but in addition that system embodies many devices and procedures which are of considerable practical and theoretical interest in themselves.

The basis of the entire system is to be found in certain divisions of the population of Oceana which were instituted as a preliminary to the creation of the commonwealth, at the very time the Council of Legislators was meeting in Emporium (London). First there was the division according to what Harrington terms "quality," into freemen or citizens on the one hand and servants on the other. The criterion here is simply economic self-sufficiency; any person who can support himself is entitled to be a citizen of the commonwealth.[16] One gathers from Harrington's discussion, although this is nowhere made explicit, that this first division has only slight political significance, because virtually every inhabitant of Oceana is a citizen, and the few who are not may become citizens simply by improving their economic condition.[17] The second of these preliminary divisions, politically a much more important one, was made within the body of citizens according to age: those citizens between the ages of eighteen and thirty are called "Youth," while those

---

16. We may note in passing two exceptions: any man who has prodigally wasted his patrimony is to be ineligible either to vote or to hold office, and the same is true of those who refuse military service.

17. *Oceana*, p. 64.

above the age of thirty are "Elders."[18] The third division, again within the body of citizens, was made according to economic status: those citizens with an annual income in land, goods, or money of one hundred pounds or more are to constitute the Horse class, while those with a smaller income comprise the Foot class.[19] The fourth and last of these preliminary divisions was geographical: the country as a whole was divided into ten thousand Parishes (the basic governmental unit), one thousand Hundreds, and fifty Tribes. The method by which this division was made was a purely mechanical one: the country was divided into approximately equal northern and southern districts along the River Hemisua (Trent), a thousand surveyors were sent into the field to determine the location of the Parishes, these were then organized geographically into groups of ten known as Hundreds, and the Hundreds were similarly joined into groups of twenty known as Tribes. It is assumed throughout Harrington's discussion that the Parishes, and therefore also the Hundreds and Tribes, will be of approximately equal size and population. Harrington seems to have contemplated, at least once, the possibility that their populations would vary substantially, however, when he made provision for different voting procedures in the Parishes depending upon whether the number of electors was below fifty, between fifty and a thousand, or above a thousand.[20]

In justifying these arrangements Harrington first tells us that, "In the Institution or building of a Common-wealth, the first Work (as that of builders) can be no other then fitting and distributing the Materials. The materials of a

18. Ibid.
19. These terms, as we shall have occasion to note, refer to the military organization of Oceana.
20. *Oceana,* p. 66.

Common-wealth are the people."[21] One sees here, among other things, an indication of Harrington's passion for orderliness and organization. It is difficult to avoid concluding that he derived real satisfaction and comfort simply from this sort of mechanical manipulation, especially in cases where mathematical expression was possible. The division into citizens and servants Harrington has called "not constitutive, but naturally inherent in the Balance."[22] By this he means, of course, that those persons who are not economically independent will in the nature of things never be politically significant, regardless of what the law says. And this, it is clear, is a reflection of Harrington's view of the relation between economics and politics; since political power is a reflection of economic power, it is to be expected that those without the latter will also lack the former. This view is expressed in words reminiscent of Aristotle: "this Order needeth no proof, in regard of the nature of servitude, which is inconsistent with Freedom or Participation of *Government* in a *Common-wealth.*"[23]

The division into Youth and Elders, which Harrington admits to be "constitutive" as well as "personal,"[24] is defended by him on purely military grounds at first. The Youth, we are told, are best fitted to serve as the marching army of the commonwealth, while the elders are best left as a standing army. The political implications of this classification will be discussed below. The same is true of the division into Horse and Foot, the criterion being the ability to afford the equipment appropriate to the rank of cavalry soldier. As for the territorial divisions, Harrington notes that they are to the commonwealth as stairs are to a house, "not that Stairs in themselves are desirable, but that

21. Ibid., p. 64.
22. *Art of Lawgiving, Coll. Works,* p. 436.
23. *Oceana,* p. 64.
24. *Art of Lawgiving, Coll. Works,* p. 437.

without them there is no getting into the Chambers."²⁵ He
admits that the precise figures which he quotes may be in-
exact for Oceana, but excuses this by noting that "for the
carrying on of discourse it is requisit to pitch upon some
certainty."²⁶

Actual voting in Oceana takes place according to an
elaborate system of indirect elections, made more complex
by the fact that at most levels two sorts of officers are chosen,
those who serve locally and those who go on to participate in
elections at a higher level. The situation is not improved by
the existence of almost incomprehensibly involved electoral
procedures designed to make elections orderly and to prevent the possibility of fraud. The following outline of elections in Oceana omits most of the superfluous details and
repetitions, although it is still necessarily rather complicated.

The first elections take place in each of the ten thousand
Parishes at nine o'clock on the morning of the first Monday
in January of each year, at which time the entire body of
Elders assembles in the Parish church. The purpose of
these elections is to choose the Deputies of the various Parishes, who amount in number to one-fifth the total number
of Elders. Briefly the manner of election is as follows: one
Elder is chosen by lot from among the assembly to serve
as "proposer"; the proposer stands before the assembly and
suggests candidates for election as Deputies; as each candidate is suggested, the Elders vote on his name by casting a
simple affirmative or negative ballot; this process continues
until the requisite number of Deputies has been chosen.
After the election has been made, a list of those elected is
drawn up in order of choice, with the exception that all
Deputies belonging to the Horse class (if there should be
any) are placed at the head of the list. The significance of
this exception becomes apparent when we note that the

25. Ibid., p. 438.
26. Ibid.

five Deputies whose names appear first on the list become Parish officials in addition to their regular duties as Deputies; those whose names are first and second on the list become Overseers of the Parish, the third becomes Constable, and the fourth and fifth become Church Wardens.[27] All the Elders so elected, including these five, serve for one year as Deputies of the Parish and are ineligible for re-election for a period of two years following the expiration of their term.

The second group of elections in Oceana takes place on the first Monday in February of each year at a place known as the Rendezvous of the Hundred. The election in each of the Hundreds is attended by the Deputies of the ten Parishes within the Hundred, who serve as electors in the choice of seven officials. Four of these seven—a Justice of the Peace, a juryman, a Captain of the Hundred, and an Ensign—must belong to the Horse class; the remaining three—a second juryman, a Coroner, and a High Constable —must be chosen from among the Foot class. The manner of election is more complicated here than in the Parishes, partly because the body of electors is approximately twice as large, but in essence the procedure is the same. Nominators are again chosen by lot, this time one for each office to be filled. Each nominator chooses three candidates for a particular office, subject to the approval of the electors. Then, a sufficient number of suitable candidates having been chosen, the three candidates for each office are voted on separately, again in terms of a simple affirmative or negative ballot, with the entire body of Deputies participating equally and in secrecy. The candidate for each office who receives the largest *majority* is elected to that office.[28]

27. For the functions of all these officials, see below, pp. 262 ff.
28. Since the candidates are voted on separately it is possible, and apparently Harrington believed it was probable, that more than one candidate for any one office might receive a majority of affirmative votes.

The third elections take place on the first Monday in March of each year at the Rendezvous of each of the fifty Tribes of Oceana. The electors here are still the Deputies of each of the two hundred Parishes which comprise the Tribe. The procedure here is so complex as to make any description almost impossible, but again the basic pattern remains unchanged. Nominators are chosen by lot from among the approximately two thousand Deputies present,[29] election is secret, and suffrage is equal. Those receiving the greatest majorities are elected to six Tribal offices: a Lord High Sheriff, a Lord Lieutenant, a Lord Custos Rotulorum (Keeper of the Rolls), a Conductor, and two Censors.[30]

The final elections take place on the following day, the first Tuesday after the first Monday in March, also at the Rendezvous of the Tribe. Here again the electors are the Deputies of the Parishes, but the men now elected are no longer local officials. Rather they are sent by the Tribe to the national legislature in Emporium (London). At this time each Tribe elects nine men, five of whom must belong to the Horse class and four to the Foot class. Two of these nine, both Horse men, become the Tribe's representatives in the upper chamber of the Oceanic legislature; the remaining seven, three Horse and four Foot, represent the Tribe in the lower chamber. Since these elections are held annually in each of the fifty Tribes of Oceana it will be seen that each year 100 members of the upper chamber and 350 members of the lower chamber are elected, and since these men serve for three years the total membership of the two chambers amounts to 300 and 1050 respectively. The terms of the members are so arranged that each year one-third of

29. Harrington cites the figure of 2200 Deputies for the Tribe of Nubia, of which 700 are Horse and 1500 Foot. See *Oceana,* p. 77.
30. The functions of all these officials will be discussed below; see pp. 263 ff.

each chamber is replaced, a procedure which Harrington calls rotation.

It seems hardly necessary to devote a great deal of time to an elaboration of the major points of interest in the Oceanic electoral system. Although the system is complex the principles it embodies are apparent. The most significant feature, the sweeping restriction of suffrage, is so obvious that it might be overlooked unless attention were drawn to it. In the first place it will be noted that women are completely excluded from political participation, a provision which is surely not unusual in the seventeenth century, but which nevertheless does result in the disfranchisement of approximately half the population of Oceana. Furthermore, we have seen that all persons who are not self-supporting are also not entitled to be citizens of the commonwealth. Somewhat more startling, and certainly more significant, is the restriction of suffrage to the class of Elders. Since life expectancy in the seventeenth century was considerably less than it is at present we may assume that this restriction resulted in the elimination from all political activity of, at the very least, half the *citizen* population of Oceana.[31] Fi-

31. Information on mortality and life expectancy in 17th-century England is unfortunately meager. In 1662, however, John Graunt published a book entitled *Natural and Political Observations Upon the Bills of Mortality*, based upon records of births and deaths in London. Although modern statisticians have discovered numerous weaknesses in the data used by Graunt and in his use of them, we may note that his figures indicate an approximate life expectancy at birth of 18 years. Graunt's work also suggests that approximately one-fifth of the population of England in the mid-17th century would have been over 30 years of age. On the basis of these figures, the electoral restrictions of Oceana would have eliminated nine-tenths of the population (including, of course, women and infants). For an account of Graunt's tables see Louis I. Dublin and Alfred J. Lotka, *Length of Life* (New York, 1936), p. 40. I am indebted for the interpretation of these figures to J. E. Hoskins of the Actuarial Department of the Travelers' Insurance Company, Hartford. It should also be noted

nally, it should be noted that even this highly limited group of Elders—presumably a group amounting to considerably less than one-fourth of the total population—is allowed to vote as a whole only once, in the Parish elections. After these first elections the effective political class in Oceana, the class which elects all officials and all members of the legislature, consists of only one-fifth of the total number of Elders, and therefore presumably of less than one-twentieth of the total population. It should be noted, however, that the proportion of voters to the total population is still in all probability substantially higher in Oceana than it was in seventeenth-century England.

After this initial sweeping restriction, elections in Oceana are carried on both freely and equally. The element of chance, choice by lot, which the Greeks considered to be an expression of the purest democracy, determines the selection of nominators at all levels. Each elector has one vote, which he casts secretly, and a simple majority is sufficient for election. The secrecy of the ballot Harrington defends in the usual manner, arguing that it will prevent the influencing of votes by either intimidation or bribery. "Men are naturally subject to all kinds of Passion," he points out, "some you have that are not able to withstand the brow of an Enemy; And, others that make nothing of this, are lesse of proof against that of a Friend; So that if your Suffrage be barefaced, I dare say you shall not have one fair cast in twenty. But whatever a mans fortune be at the [ballot] box, he neither knoweth whom to thank, nor whom to Challenge."[32] And it might be noted in passing that the combination of chance in the choice of nominators and

---

that the use of 30 years as the dividing point is reminiscent of classical political thought; see Zera Fink, *The Classical Republicans* (Evanston, 1945), p. 43.

32. *Oceana,* p. 102.

secrecy in the casting of votes makes almost impossible anything resembling party discipline.

Here, however, another nondemocratic element enters the picture. Although the members of the electorate are chosen on a fairly democratic, albeit limited, basis, the only requirements being citizenship and age, and although they vote freely and equally, they are nevertheless limited in their choice of candidates by the fact that certain offices and legislative positions can be filled only by members of the economically superior Horse class, while others are open only to members of the Foot class. This is clearly an application of the theory of elective aristocracy which holds that the mass of the people are capable of choosing worthy officials to govern them, but incapable in the mass of governing themselves. To some extent it is felt in Oceana that the members of the Foot class are competent to serve as electors for all local offices and for the legislative assembly, but should not themselves be eligible to fill several of these offices. It is quite clear, however, that this is not the whole explanation; it cannot account for the fact that there are some offices which are open *only* to members of the Foot class. If we assume simply that the Horse class is supposed to be superior to the Foot this latter phenomenon will be incomprehensible. In fact the situation is more complex, and also politically more interesting. The only possible explanation is that this restriction of certain offices to members of certain classes is designed to ensure representation of both rich and poor among the body of magistrates and legislators.

This brings us finally to a somewhat more general view of the Oceanic electoral system. Practically speaking, the purpose of these elections is simply to choose men to fill certain offices. But if this were the sole purpose the system would be needlessly complex. Actually, certain theoretical considerations intrude themselves at this point. The purpose of the elections is not merely to choose men, but rather to

choose a particular kind of men, namely, men who will
represent the "interests" of the people of Oceana. Since, as
we have seen, Harrington's view of political life is economically oriented, this means primarily the choice of men who
will represent the major economic groups in Oceana. This is
all complicated, however, by the fact that Harrington did
believe in a real connection between economic and intellectual status. In the preliminary section of the *Oceana* he refers to "a *naturall Aristocracy* diffused by *God* throughout
the whole body of *mankind*."[33] Therefore the electoral
system, as set out in the *Oceana,* really performs simultaneously two distinct functions. In the first place, by requiring
that certain magistrates, the entire upper chamber of the
legislature, and nearly half of the lower chamber, be chosen
from among the Horse class the constitution ensures the
presence in the government of a considerable number of
natural aristocrats. In the second place, the constitution also
requires the election of many members of the Foot class,
obviously in the name of representation of interests. This
latter goal is also presumably served by the territorial division of Oceana, guaranteeing that each part of the country
will be represented in the legislature. We will return to this
subject when we discuss the nature and functioning of the
Oceanic legislature.[34]

The Agrarian Law

Apart from those constitutional provisions which establish and regulate the various governmental institutions of
Oceana, the most important of the fundamental laws of the
commonwealth is unquestionably the so-called Agrarian
Law. Harrington makes this quite plain in the *Oceana,*

33. Ibid., p. 24.
34. See below, pp. 234 ff.

where he writes: "The Center or Basis of every Government, is no other then the Fundamentall Lawes of the same. *Fundamentall Lawes* are such as state what it is that a man may call his own, that is to say, Proprietie; and what the meanes be whereby a man may enjoy his own. . . . *Wherefore* the Fundamentall Lawes of *Oceana,* or the Center of this *Common-wealth* are the *Agrarian* and the *Ballot.*"[35] This law, which is an integral part of the Constitution of Oceana, is designed to provide a stable and appropriate economic base for the government, in accordance with Harrington's theory of the relation of economics and politics.[36]

In form the Agrarian Law is quite simple. Its essential aim is to provide that, in the future, landed estates in Oceana shall not exceed a given value—two thousand pounds annual income—while recognizing the inadvisability of enforcing such a limitation immediately. Since the purpose of the law is to ensure that in the course of a few generations such a division and limitation of estates will be achieved, its terms relate to the inheritance of land. It deals in the first instance with estates so large that even an equal division among the heirs of the owner would not bring the worth of the various parts below an annual value of two thousand pounds. In the case of such estates the law requires equal division among the sons of the owner upon his death. In the case of smaller estates, or a larger number of sons, the division may be unequal provided only that the eldest son receives land with an annual value not exceeding two thousand pounds.[37] The third provision of the Agrarian Law

35. *Oceana,* p. 85.
36. See above, Ch. 3.
37. This provision applies equally, of course, to the portion received by any one son, but it was assumed that the eldest son would invariably receive the largest inheritance, and therefore a limitation on the size of his estate was ipso facto a limitation on those of his brothers.

states that, with the exception of lawful inheritance as envisaged in the first provision, no man "shall receive, enjoy,
. . . acquire or purchase unto himself" land amounting to
more than two thousand pounds per year. The law further
provides that no woman, unless she be a lawful heir under
the earlier provisions, shall possess land, goods, or money
worth more than fifteen hundred pounds annually when she
is given in marriage. On the other hand, all heirs and wid-
ows are allowed to receive full inheritance in cases where
no division is possible (due to the absence of siblings), on
the understanding that such division will be made in accordance with law as soon as possible. Finally, the law provides that the same regulations shall apply to Marpesia
(Scotland) and Panopea (Ireland), except that in the former
the general standard shall be set at five hundred rather than
two thousand pounds. Anyone who is lawfully convicted of
possessing more than the allowed amount of property must
forfeit the surplus for the use of the state.[38]

In view of the importance of this Agrarian Law, as well
as its highly original character, it will be worthwhile for us
to consider the arguments used by Harrington in its defense.
Before this, however, we may note a few pertinent statistics.
In the first place, it is possible for us to discover from another passage in the *Oceana* that income from land in Oceana in the seventeenth century amounted to approximately
five per cent annually.[39] Therefore we can determine that
the effect of the Agrarian Law was to limit estates to a value
of some forty thousand pounds, certainly a considerable
sum. Furthermore Harrington tells us that if the entire land
of Oceana were divided into estates each worth this amount,
there would be a total of five thousand such estates. And
therefore we know also that the total value of land in the

38. For the text of the law see *Oceana*, pp. 85–86.
39. On p. 219 Harrington tells us that the state owned property
worth £8,000,000, which brought in an annual income of £400,000.

commonwealth was approximately two hundred million pounds, bringing an annual income in the neighborhood of ten million pounds.[40]

Keeping these figures in mind, we may now proceed to consider the debate concerning the Agrarian Law which occurred in the Council of Legislators. When the law was first introduced into the Council, it was greeted by the protests of one Philautus de Garbo, who had four brothers and was, by the system of primogeniture, sole heir to his father's estate of ten thousand pounds.[41] Philautus de Garbo[42] argued that the Agrarian Law was unsound for six reasons:

(1) It was unnecessary. To prove this, Philautus, in good Harringtonian fashion, simply pointed out that no such law had existed in Venice and that Aristotle had criticized Phaleas for attempting to introduce a similar law in Athens.[43]

(2) It was dangerous to the commonwealth. The danger of an Agrarian Law, he contended, was demonstrated conclusively by Machiavelli in his discussion of the destruction of the Roman Empire,[44] and was equally evident in the history of Sparta.

(3) It did not serve its avowed purpose. The purpose of the Agrarian Law, Philautus noted, was to prevent the establishment of a monarchy in Oceana. That it was not sufficient to achieve this end, he said, was evident from the fact

40. See *Oceana*, pp. 92 and 155.

41. For the sake of convenience, the value of estates will be described in terms of the annual income they produce; thus an estate of £10,000 is an estate which annually brings its owner that sum.

42. As Liljegren has pointed out, his name is derived from the Greek word meaning "selfish" and the Italian word meaning "polite." *Oceana*, p. 297.

43. Aristotle, *Politics*, II, 7.

44. Machiavelli, *Discorsi*, I, 37.

that the people of Israel voluntarily submitted to monarchical government despite the fact that they possessed an Agrarian Law.

(4) It was destructive of families. In support of this assertion Philautus had little concrete evidence to offer. "This also is so apparent," he said, "that it needeth pity rather then proof." Instead he limited himself to a brief statement of the debt of Oceana to her great and noble families, which he supposed would be destroyed by the proposed law.

(5) It was destructive of industry. Philautus' argument here is the familiar one that limitation of wealth in any guise would undermine ambition and industry. "But take heed," he warned, "how you admit of such assaults and sallyes upon mens Estates as may slacken the Nerve of labour, and give others also reason to believe that their sweat is in vain." The proof of this assertion he found in the history of Sparta.

(6) It was impossible to enforce in Oceana. Here Philautus argued that the complexity of land tenure in Oceana would simply make the introduction of any such law impracticable. Such a law might, he conceded, be introduced sucessfully in a land "without any consideration of the former Proprietor. . . . But in this Nation no such Division can be introduced, the lands being already in the hands of Proprietors . . . [and] being also of Tenures in nature so different." Thus the polite but selfish Philautus concluded that "that which is against Reason and Experience is impossible."[45]

In response to this challenge the Lord Archon, Olphaus Megaletor, Harrington's spokesman throughout the proceedings, delivered a lengthy address, which he began by

45. For Philautus' speech, see *Oceana,* pp. 86–89.

saying that Philautus had considerably oversimplified the subject. The primary purpose of the Agrarian Law, we learn, is to prevent the existence of a landed aristocracy in Oceana. Starting with the usual Harringtonian premise that a popular government can exist only where the ownership of land is widely diffused, the Archon insists that it is necessary to fix this particular arrangement by law lest the balance of property, and consequently also the government, be overthrown. Indeed, he recognizes the existence of a natural tendency for the balance of property to change in the absence of any law to prevent its doing so, "each being else apt to change into some other."[46] And in view of the necessity of an Agrarian Law the Archon is unimpressed by the claim that it is dangerous. "And if a Cure be necessary," he argues, "it excuseth not the Patient, his disease being otherwise desparate, that it is dangerous."[47] Similarly, the Archon is not impressed by the example of Israel which Philautus cited. True, the people of Israel did choose voluntarily to submit to a monarchical government despite the fact that they were governed by an Agrarian Law, but it is precisely the voluntary nature of this act, one might almost say its gratuitous character, that most impresses the Archon. "For the Monarchy neither grew upon them, nor could by reason of the Agrarian possibly have invaded them, if they had not pull'd it upon themselves by the election of a King."[48] As a result, Megaletor considers this whole episode to have been "beside the Course of Nature" and therefore of no interest as a precedent; the Israelites were simply "given up by God unto infatuation." Assuming, then, that an Agrarian Law is necessary to the maintenance of popular government, that it is not impossibly dangerous, and that it

46. Ibid., p. 91.
47. Ibid.
48. Ibid., p. 92.

will in fact lead to the desired effect, what is to be said of the alleged ill consequences mentioned by Philautus?

The argument concerning the supposed destruction of families is of particular interest as an indication of the essentially conservative nature of this apparently radical feature of the Oceanic constitution. According to the Archon the effect of the Agrarian Law would actually be to fix the existing balance of property in Oceana rather than to introduce any substantial alteration. "For we do not now argue for that which we would have," he declares, "but for that which we are already possessed of."[49] In fact, Megaletor argues that there are presently (1656) no more than three hundred families in Oceana owning more than two thousand pounds in land. And for this reason he is unmoved by the plea that the proposed Agrarian Law would destroy the families of Oceana; "with what brow can the Interest of so few be ballanced with that of the whole Nation?"[50] Indeed the abolition of primogeniture and the substitution of a modified form of gavelkind, as envisaged by the Agrarian Law, would actually be in the best interest of even these few wealthy families. "And truly, when I consider that our Countrymen are none of the worst natur'd, I must confesse I marvell much how it comes to passe, that we should use our Children as we do our Puppies; take one, lay it in the lap, feed it with every good bit, and drown five! Nay worse; for as much as the Puppies are once drown'd, whereas the Children are left perpetually drowning. Really, my Lords, it is a flinty Custome!"[51] The explanation of such a flinty custom is, of course, the desire of many fathers to prevent the division of their fortunes; and the Archon's attack on the custom, aside from its incidental humanitarian motive,

49. Ibid., p. 93.
50. Ibid.
51. Ibid., p. 94.

is aimed against precisely the sort of accumulation of wealth which primogeniture encourages.

So far this desired distribution of wealth has been defended solely on political and humanitarian grounds. The Archon now proceeds to point out that it will also have beneficial economic effects: "The Land through which the River *Nilus* [Nile] wanders in one stream, is barren, but where he parts into Seven, he multiplies his fertile shores, by distributing, yet keeping and improving such a Propriety and Nutrition, as is a prudent *Agrarian* unto a well ordered *Common-wealth*."[52] Or again, "is a Political body rendered any fitter for Industry, by having one Gowty, and another withered Leg, than a naturall: It tendeth not unto the improvement of Merchandize that there be some who have no need of their Trading, and others that are not able to follow it."[53] The ideal here is clearly that of "distributing, yet keeping," of maintaining private property while insuring that ownership will be widely diffused throughout the community. If this is done by law, the political result will be a stable popular government, the economic result will be an increase of wealth.

Like so many theorists from Aristotle to the present, Harrington is disturbed by the existence of extremes of wealth and poverty and prefers a more equal distribution of small holdings. But his justification of this preference is not a moral one; rather he argues that it will be economically more efficient and productive, as well as politically desirable. Similarly, the Lord Archon does not believe that this limitation of wealth will result in a decline of industry on the part of those affected; or, at least, he does not believe that this is a necessary result. In the first place, he argues, it will still be possible for wealthy men to give their money to charitable causes. Furthermore, those who have

52. Ibid.
53. Ibid.

earned as much money as the law allows will then be free to devote their skills and energies to the service of the commonwealth: "if a man shall think, that there may be an Industry lesse greasie, or more noble, and so cast his thoughts upon the *Common-wealth,* he will have Leisure for her."[54] Finally, the Archon denies Philautus' assertion that the institution of an Agrarian Law would be impossible in Oceana. Admitting the difficulties raised by the complex system of land tenure, he cites the Domesday survey as an illustration of what can be accomplished despite this complexity.

Thus in the Agrarian Law of the commonwealth of Oceana Harrington has sought to institutionalize his theory of the economic basis of politics. The two essential features of the law are its permanent constitutional nature and the fact that it is designed to perpetuate the existing distribution of landed property in the commonwealth. Since a popular commonwealth was the form of government Harrington desired, and since the balance of property in Oceana suited this form of government, it was necessary only to fix that balance. If the balance had been different, two alternatives would have presented themselves: it would have been possible to frame a government to fit the existing balance, and it would have been possible to change the balance to fit the desired form of government. In either case, however, the new government would have had to include in its constitution an Agrarian Law, for the essential purpose of an Agrarian Law is neither necessarily popular nor monarchical, but rather conservative. In view of Harrington's search for political stability this should not surprise us.

The Legislature

If the Agrarian Law can be called the foundation on which the political structure of Oceana rests, the legislature

54. Ibid., p. 95.

is unquestionably the most important part of that structure. In addition to the law-making power which is of course associated with a legislative body, the parliament of Oceana possesses the authority to choose the members of the executive branch of the government, to supervise their activities, and to serve as the supreme judicial organ of the commonwealth. In a very real sense it is correct to say that the legislature *is* the national government of Oceana since all political power derives directly from it. Furthermore, it is in the functioning of the legislature that we see most clearly the application of Harrington's theory of representative government.

As we have noted, the legislature of the commonwealth consists of two chambers, known as the Senate and the Prerogative (or Prerogative Tribe). The Senate is composed of 300 members, known as Knights, all necessarily belonging to the Horse class; the Prerogative is composed of 1050 members, known as Deputies, of whom 450 must be Horse men and 600 Foot men. We have also seen that these legislators are elected by the Deputies of the various Parishes of Oceana, meeting at the Tribal level, and that each Tribe is represented in the legislature by six Knights and twenty-one Deputies. Finally, we have had occasion to note the existence of what Harrington describes as "rotation" in the legislature, whereby as a result of annual elections and three-year terms one-third of each chamber is replaced each year.

This device of rotation was a particular favorite of Harrington's and gave its name to his famous Rota Club. He defended it as an ideal compromise between the need for experienced public officials and the danger of what he called "prolongation of Magistracy."[55] Each year one-third of the legislature will retire and be replaced by new members, but

55. *Prerogative of Popular Government, Coll. Works*, p. 303.

THE MANNER AND USE OF THE BALLOT*

Key

A —the Lord Strategus

B —the Orator

C —three Commissioners of the Seal

D —three Commissioners of the Treasury (one serves temporarily as
        E)

E —Censor (temporary)

F —Middle Urn

G —Benches on either side of the Chamber

H —Benches on either side of the Chamber

I —Censors' chairs; unoccupied during balloting

K —Censors (permanent)

L —Outward Urns

M—Clerks or Secretaries of the House

N —Clerks' tables and bowls

O —Seats on the floor of the Chamber (actually wool-sacks)

P —Two Tribunes of the Horse

Q—Two Tribunes of the Foot

R —Judges

S —Senators, coming from their seats (H) to the side Urns (L)

T —Senators, drawing at the side Urn (L)

V —Senator, having drawn successfully at the side Urn, going to mid-
        dle Urn

W—Senator, having drawn successfully, already drawing at middle
        Urn (F)

X —Senators, unsuccessful at the side Urn, return to their seats

a —Senator, unsuccessful at the middle Urn, throws blank into bowl
        (b)

c —Senator, successful at the middle Urn

d —Bench for Senators successful at the middle Urn

e —Senators successful at the middle Urn, now Electors

f —Ballotins or Pages

g —Portable ballot boxes

h —Counting bowls (identical with N)

*Originally published by Harrington as a broadside, reprinted by
Toland in his various editions of Harrington's *Collected Works,* to
illustrate the balloting in the Senate of Oceana.

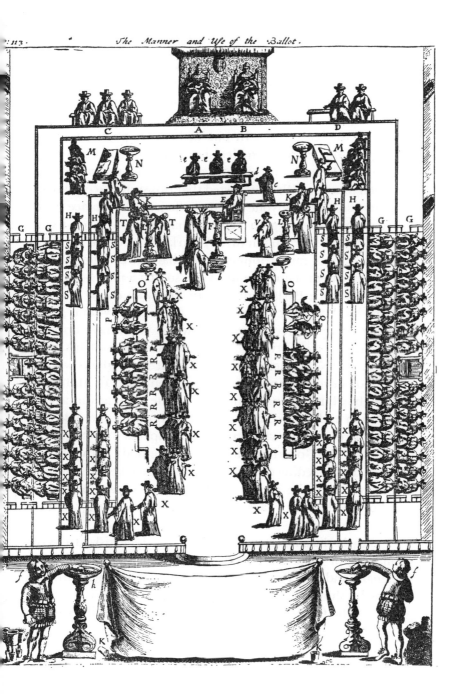

this will leave a majority of experienced men to carry on
the work at hand. An element of continuity is preserved at
all times since there is never a complete change of membership, nor, most dangerous of all, an interval between meetings of the legislature. In one of his rare poetic moments
Harrington described the legislature as being like an orange
tree that bears buds, blooms, and fruit at the same time.
When Matthew Wren objected that this system would make
it impossible for anyone to gain sufficient experience in the
legislature, Harrington replied that it is superior to the
former British Parliament: "A Parlament in the late Government was rarely longer liv'd than three months, nor
more frequent than once in a year; so that a man having bin
twelve years a Parlament-man in England, could not have
born his Magistracy above three years. . . . Wheras a Parlament-man in Oceana may in twelve years have born his
Magistracy six, notwithstanding the necessity of his Vacations. . . . Nevertheless the Parlament of England was seldom or never without men of sufficient skill or ability."[56]
Finally, Harrington felt that one of the great advantages of
rotation and enforced "vacations" was that it increased the
number of citizens who actively participated in government,
causing "the Government to take in the Body of the People,
by parts succeeding others."[57] This, he believed, is infinitely
preferable to the growth of a group of career politicians
who, by that very fact, will become increasingly remote
from the people.

Clearly the characteristic business of the legislature is the
making of laws, and in this process the functions of the
Senate and the Prerogative are quite different. This can
best be shown by following briefly the typical career of a
law in the Oceanic legislature. The process begins with an

56. Ibid., p. 321.
57. Ibid., p. 303.

original proposal by one of the magistrates.[58] The proposal having been made, it is debated by the appropriate Council and the most interesting opinions expressed during this debate are recorded by the secretary of the Council.[59] This having been done, any magistrate or censor may convene the Senate, which then listens to these opinions and debates them further. In this debate the members of the appropriate Council are given first opportunity to speak, followed by the Knights in order of seniority. Finally, each opinion is voted on by the entire Senate according to an involved procedure: employees of the Senate walk through the chamber carrying ballot boxes, one for affirmative votes on each proposal, one for negative votes, and one for votes of "no opinion." Each Senator casts his ballot in one of these boxes. If none of the proposals receives a majority of affirmative votes, that which received the smallest number is eliminated and the procedure is repeated. This continues until one proposal receives a majority, or no proposal remains. If a majority of the Knights vote "no opinion," which may happen as early as the first vote, the entire issue is temporarily removed from the purview of the Senate. In this case the appropriate Council may reconsider the issue and return with new proposals, but this need not necessarily be done. If, on the other hand, one of the proposals does achieve an affirmative majority, that is a number of affirmative votes equal to more than half the number of Knights voting, it then becomes a Decree of the Senate. If this Decree is administrative in nature it is immediately binding. As Harrington says, "[if] it is either in matter of State, or Government according to Law enacted already . . . then it is good without going any further."[60]

58. See below, pp. 248 ff., for a discussion of the magistracy of Oceana.
59. See below, pp. 249 ff., for a discussion of the Councils.
60. *Oceana*, p. 117.

If, on the other hand, the decree passed by the Senate "is in matter of Law to be enacted, repealed, or amended . . . especially if it be for a War, or for a Levy of Men or Money," it is invalid until it receives the approval of the second chamber, the Prerogative Tribe.[61] In order to obtain this approval the Senate appoints two officials, known as Proposers, from among the body of magistrates, and causes the Decree to be published. At a time at least six weeks later, a meeting of the Prerogative is called to vote on the Decree, and during the intervening six-week period the Censors and Tribunes of the commonwealth are charged with the responsibility of insuring that "there be no laying of heads together, Conventicles, or Canvassing to carry on, or oppose any thing; but that all may be done in a free and open way."[62] At the meeting of the Prerogative Tribe the two Senatorial Proposers "rehearse the whole Matter, and expound it to the People," after which the vote is taken. The first vote is upon the general purpose of the Decree, the alternatives being affirmative, negative, and "no opinion." If a majority of Deputies vote that they have "no opinion," the Proposers cease their work and the matter is returned to the Senate for further debate. If the majority vote in the negative the whole matter is immediately dropped. If the majority of Deputies vote in the affirmative the Proposers then proceed to present the Senate's Decree to the Prerogative Tribe clause by clause, with only affirmative and negative votes allowed. Each clause which receives a majority of affirmative votes is thereby enacted into law.

This, then, is an outline of the law-making process in the commonwealth of Oceana. In addition to the general picture a few points are of particular interest. In the first place there is the central fact, the one which Harrington stressed

61. Ibid.
62. Ibid., p. 142.

above all others, that the Prerogative Tribe never engages
in debate, but simply votes on measures proposed to it by
the Senate. This is, of course, no accident. Harrington informs us that those elected to the Prerogative must immediately take an oath, "That they will neither introduce, cause,
nor to their power suffer debate to be introduced into any
popular Assembly of this Government."[63] Furthermore it
should be noted that the violation of this oath is one crime
in Oceana for which the mandatory penalty is death.[64]

What can explain this aversion to debate in the lower
chamber of the legislature? According to Harrington, the
writing of laws, which is the most important part of the
governmental process, is a task for experts. It requires native intelligence, knowledge of political theory and practice,
and above all calm and dispassionate discussion. As Harrington said, reminding his readers of the distinction he
had made between dividing and choosing,[65] "to debate, is
to discern or put a difference between things that being
alike are not the same, or it is separating and weighing this
reason against that, and that reason against this, which is
dividing."[66] This indispensable function of debating, or
dividing, should necessarily be performed by the wisest and
most virtuous members of the community, meeting together
in a body small enough to permit calm and fruitful discussion. This body is the Senate of Oceana, composed of men
chosen "not by hereditary right, or in regard of the greatnesse of their estates onely . . . but by election for their excellent parts."[67] The Prerogative, on the other hand, is
made up simply of representatives of the people. Unlike a
Knight in the Senate, an individual member of the Prerog-

63. Ibid., p. 127.
64. Ibid., p. 109.
65. See above, Ch. 3.
66. *Oceana*, p. 24.
67. Ibid.

ative is not expected to be particularly intelligent; rather, his duty is simply to reflect the wishes of his constituents.

It must be admitted that such a clear-cut distinction between the two chambers seems highly improbable when we recall that the only necessary difference between them is that the Senate is composed solely of Horse men, while the Prerogative is composed of both Horse and Foot men, in the proportion of three to four. Since the members of both chambers are elected at the same time, in the same manner, and by the same electors, the mere fact that some fifty-nine per cent of the Prerogative belong to a slightly lower economic class seems hardly to deserve the importance which Harrington attributes to it. There is one further difference between the two chambers, namely the fact that the Senate is less than one-third the size of the Prerogative. Although this does figure in Harrington's calculations it again does not seem important enough to justify the sharp line which he draws between the two houses of the parliament. Despite these apparent weaknesses in Harrington's argument, we shall never understand his position unless we simply accept his view that the Senate does embody the natural aristocracy of Oceana while the Prerogative serves to represent the people as a whole.

In defense of Harrington's scheme two things may be said. In the first place, the Oceanic Senate, because it is elected rather than hereditary, seems somewhat more likely to contain natural aristocrats than did the ancient House of Lords of England. And in the second place, Harrington firmly believed that the common people would recognize and respect the natural aristocrats among them.[68]

As we have seen, the legislation proposed by the Senate must be published and made available to the Prerogative for a period of six weeks. What is supposed to occur during

68. See above, pp. 150–52.

the required waiting period? The answer is almost surely that the individual members of the Prerogative are to consult their constituents about the proposed law and give it thought themselves. Since the individual Deputy is forbidden by law from consulting his legislative colleagues he will presumably have recourse to his constituents, say in the Tribe of Nubia. Having discovered the opinion of the people of Nubia on the proposed law, he will then return to the Prerogative to vote. Now the important thing is that nothing shall happen to interfere with his casting of his vote in the way desired by his constituents. If we ask what *could* possibly interfere, the answer will be, debate in the Prerogative. It is for this reason that Harrington has imposed a penalty of death on any man who introduces debate in the Prerogative. If each Deputy votes in accordance with the interest of his constituents, the result will necessarily be the national interest, Harrington argues. Thus, "the Result of the Many (because every man has an Interest what to chuse, and that which sutes with every man's Interest, excludes the distinct or privat Interest of any man, and so coms up to the common and public Interest or Reason) is the wisest Result."[69]

The rationale of the entire law-making process in the commonwealth of Oceana is perhaps best expressed in the following passage from *The Art of Lawgiving:*

> A Council (especially if of a loose Election) having not only the Debate, but the Result also, is capable of being influenc'd from without, and of being sway'd by Interest within. There may be a form'd, a prejudic'd Party, that will hasten or outbaul you from the Debate to the Question, and then precipitat you upon the Result: Wheras if it had no power of Result, there could remain to the same no more than Debate only,

69. *Prerogative of Popular Government, Coll. Works,* p. 253.

without any Bias, or cause of diverting such Debate from Maturity; in which Maturity of unbias'd Debate lys the final cause of the Senate, and the whole Light that can be given to a People. But when this is don, if your resolving Assembly be not such as can imbibe or contract no other Interest than that only of the whole People, all again is lost: for the Result of all Assemblys gos principally upon that which they conceive to be their own Interest. But how an Assembly upon Rotation, consisting of one thousand, where the vote is six to four in the lower sort, should be capable of any other Interest than that only of the whole People by which they are orderly elected, has never yet bin, nor, I believe, ever will be shewn. In like distribution therefore of Debate and Result, consists the highest Mystery of Popular Government.[70]

In short, legislation requires two distinct elements, wisdom in debate and the representation of interests in arriving at a final decision. Either of these alone will be dangerous to the commonwealth: wisdom alone may run counter to the interests of the people, interest alone may prove shortsighted. The existence of a natural aristocracy makes it possible to create a body of wise men who will debate legislation; it would be a grave error, however, to allow this body to pass laws by its own authority since its particular interest might run counter to that of the people as a whole. Therefore the Senate of Oceana acts in a purely initiatory and advisory capacity. On the other hand, a popular assembly with the right to debate proposed legislation would inevitably distort the very reflection of interests which is its raison d'être. Therefore the Prerogative Tribe, which has the final say on proposed laws, is forbidden to do more than vote.

70. *Art of Lawgiving, Coll. Works,* p. 447.

Actually more time-consuming, although somewhat less important, than their legislative functions are certain other activities of the two chambers of the Oceanic parliament. The first of these is the judicial function of the Prerogative Tribe. It is provided in the Constitution that the Prerogative shall be the supreme judicial body of the commonwealth, having original jurisdiction in some cases and appellate jurisdiction in others. It is to try, in the first instance, all cases involving what Harrington calls "Crimes against the Majesty of the People," that is, high treason, theft of public funds, or misuse of public funds. In addition, any person may appeal to the Prerogative from the judgment of any court in the commonwealth, with the exception of courts martial and the Council of War, provided only that the appellant must deposit the sum of one hundred pounds which is to be forfeited if his appeal is unsuccessful.

The judicial procedure of the Prerogative is complicated, but also so unusual as to make at least a brief description worthwhile. All cases are tried before the entire Prerogative, 1050 men. Each party to the case, or his counsel, is allowed an hour and a half in which to present his arguments, exclusive of time spent in reading documents and examining witnesses. This presentation having been concluded, the entire house votes "guilty," "not guilty," or "no opinion." If a majority votes "no opinion" the arguments are resumed for an additional three hours; if there have been two re-arguments (a total of nine hours) the "no opinion" vote is not allowed in the third balloting. If a majority votes that the accused is innocent, the trial is concluded. If a majority votes that the accused is guilty, a further vote must be taken on the penalty to be imposed. Here there are six possible alternatives, although Harrington recognizes that some of them may be inappropriate in particular cases:

1—Whether he shall have a writt of ease.
2—Whether he shall be fined so much, or so much.
3—Whether he shall be Confiscated.
4—Whether he shall be rendered incapable of Magistracy.
5—Whether he shall be banished.
6—Whether he shall be put to Death.[71]

These alternatives, or at least three of them, are voted on, affirmatively or negatively, by the Prerogative. Whichever penalty receives a majority of affirmative votes is the sentence of the court.[72] As in the case of legislation, this function, which presumably occupies the major part of the meeting time of the Prerogative Tribe, is to be performed without any discussion or consultation; the vote is to be taken immediately upon the conclusion of the arguments. It may be said with no exaggeration that the members of the Prerogative can sit together in the same assembly for three years without ever learning each other's opinions.

In defense of the judicial power of the popular assembly, Harrington argues that "the Power of a Magistracy not accomptable unto the People from whom it was received becoming of private use, the Common-wealth loses her Liberty."[73] This power is therefore viewed as a positive check on the activities of all magistrates in the commonwealth, not simply as a convenient manner of deciding legal disputes. Having shown that a similar right of final appeal to a popular assembly has existed in all commonwealths, Harrington claims that without this right "there can be no such thing as Popular Government."[74]

71. *Oceana*, p. 144.
72. It is not clear whether only one of these six penalties can be imposed in any one case, or a combination of several of them.
73. *Oceana*, p. 146.
74. Ibid.

The only other occupation of the Prerogative results from the fact that its major duties will presumably be insufficient to occupy its time fully. The twenty-third Order of the Constitution provides: "whereas by the Constitution of this Common-wealth it may appear that neither the Propositions of the Senate nor the Judicature of the people, will be so frequent as to hold the Prerogative in continual imployment; the Senate . . . shall duly (if they have no greater affairs to divert them) cause an oration to be made unto the Prerogative by some Knight or Magistrate of the Senate."[75]

The final function of the legislature, choice of the Magistrates and Councils of Occana, is performed by the Senate alone. In the description of this procedure it will be necessary to remember that, with the system of rotation, the Senate is at all times composed of three classes of Knights: those who are serving the third year of their term, those who are serving their second year, and those who have been newly elected. These three classes are known as the first, second, and third Regions of the Senate. The election of Magistrates is the first business of the Senate when it convenes early in April. Each year six Magistrates are elected, four of whom serve one-year terms while the remaining two serve three-year terms. The four annual Magistrates, so called, may be chosen from any Region of the Senate, but the triennial Magistrates must, of course, be chosen from the third Region lest their senatorial term expire before their magistracy.

The method of election, which Harrington has explained in great detail, is, he claims, "a thing as difficult in discourse or writing, as facil in practice."[76] For our present purposes it is enough to say that the voting is by secret ballot and that a simple majority suffices. The annual Magistrates elected

75. Ibid., p. 144.
76. Ibid., p. 113. See illustration on p. 237.

at this time are the Lord Strategus, the Lord Orator, and the first and second Censors. The triennial Magistrates are the third Commissioner of the Seal and the third Commissioner of the Treasury.[77] On the same day, the first Monday in April, the Senate also elects the members of the three great Councils of the commonwealth: the Council of State, the Council of Religion, and the Council of Trade.[78] Each year, from the third Region, five Knights are elected to the Council of State, four to the Council of Religion, and an additional four to the Council of Trade. These elections, too, are by secret ballot and a simple majority suffices for election to any Council. The Senate is also responsible for the election of ambassadors, emergency election of extraordinary magistrates and ambassadors, and the institution of a dictator in time of crisis.[79]

The Executive

The executive authority of the commonwealth, insofar as it is proper to speak of executive authority at all in Oceana, is exercised by the Magistrates and Councils chosen by the Senate from among its own members. It is therefore immediately apparent that the constitution of Oceana is of the so-called parliamentary variety, lacking any popularly elected national executive to formulate policy or preside over what can be called, in the narrow sense, a government (or administration). Actually the constitution of Oceana creates a much more extreme form of parliamentary government than exists, for instance, in Britain today, to say nothing of the seventeenth century.

Perhaps the closest approach to a single supreme execu-

77. See below, pp. 253 ff., for a discussion of the nature of the various magistracies of Oceana.
78. A fourth, the Council of War, is chosen by the Council of State.
79. All of these will be discussed immediately below.

tive in Oceana is the Lord Strategus, the foremost of the magistrates. But the Lord Strategus serves simply as president of the Senate and leader of Oceana's armies in time of war. Apart from this he has no administrative duties, no power of appointing or removing magistrates or Council members, and no authority over, or responsibility for, the actions of other executive officials. Similarly, the Lord Orator, who ranks second among the magistrates, is responsible simply for keeping order in the Senate.[80] The last of the annual magistrates, the two Censors, perform an odd variety of functions none of which can be said to have any direct political significance. Specifically, the Censors are ex officio chancellors of the two great universities of Oceana, joint presidents of the Council of Religion, and guardians of governmental probity, having the power to remove magistrates or members of the Senate for misbehavior. The six Commissioners, all triennial magistrates, are primarily judicial rather than executive officials. The three Commissioners of the Seal serve as judges in Chancery, while the three Commissioners of the Treasury are judges in Exchequer. Each of these ten magistrates has the right under the constitution to propose legislation to the Senate.

After the Magistrates, the second and most important part of the Oceanic executive is made up of the four great Councils. These Councils, it will be recalled, are composed of members of the Senate and are elected by that body. By the familiar device of annual elections and three-year terms of office, it is guaranteed that each Council will be composed of members of each of the three Regions of the Senate in equal numbers; and thus the phenomenon of rotation characterizes the Councils as well as their parent body. Since the Councils are the actual locus of administrative authority in the commonwealth, and since their activity will indicate

80. He is likened to the Speaker of the British Parliament, and in a later work is called by this title. *Seven Models, Coll. Works,* p. 533.

clearly the scope of the government as a whole, it will be worthwhile for us to consider their functions in some detail.

The Council of State, which is composed of fifteen Knights, is entrusted, in the first place, with the foreign affairs of the commonwealth. It is to carry on all correspondence with foreign governments, to receive all foreign ambassadors, and to issue instructions to the ambassadors of Oceana. Further, it is to serve as the liaison between the government of Oceana and those of its provinces. In addition, as the most important of all the Councils of Oceana, the Council of State is to consider all laws that are to be enacted, amended, or repealed by the legislature; generally it is expected that the great bulk of legislation will be introduced in the Senate by this Council. Finally, the Council of State has a special responsibility to oversee all legislation involving taxation, levies of men, the declaration of war and peace, and the making of leagues and associations by the commonwealth.

The Council of War is, in most respects, simply an adjunct of the Council of State. It is the one Council not elected by the Senate as a whole; rather it is chosen by the Council of State from among its own members. Consisting of nine members, its primary function is to carry on diplomatic negotiations and to manage the operations of Oceana's intelligence services and military forces. Its raison d'être is the need for secrecy in these matters; Harrington explicitly notes that "all such affaires [which] otherwise appertayning unto the Council of State are, for the good of the Common-wealth, to be carried with greater secrecy, [shall] be managed by the Council of Warr."[81] For this reason the Council of War is the only one of the Councils that is allowed to carry on its activities without the knowledge of the Senate, although the Constitution does provide

81. *Oceana,* p. 109.

that it should communicate with the Senate at "such times as it may be had without detriment unto the business."[82] In view of this extraordinary freedom of action, it was perhaps to be expected that the Constitution should go on to limit the Council of War to the extent that "they shall have no power to engage the Commonwealth in a Warr, without the consent of the Senate and the People."[83] This provision, of course, reflects the age-old problem of ensuring legislative control over foreign policy, and especially over that part of foreign policy which requires secrecy. The Council of War also has supreme authority over all the storehouses, armories, arsenals, and magazines of the commonwealth, and it is given the responsibility of enforcing the constitutional prohibition of debate in the Prerogative Tribe; it is to try anyone accused of this crime and to execute those convicted, subject to no appeal.

The Council of Religion, consisting of twelve Knights, has power over all matters relating to religion in the commonwealth. In a rather broad definition the constitution provides that this is to include "Religion, Christian Charity, and a pious life," as well as "Liberty of Conscience."[84] Specifically, this Council has control of all appointments to the two great universities, it is to supervise the conduct and employment of the clergy of the established church, and it is to preside over national convocations. As the protector of liberty of conscience in Oceana the Council of Religion has the responsibility of preventing any coercion in matters of religion. Finally, more as a matter of convenience than of rational apportionment of work, it is the business of the Council to receive all petitions addressed to the Senate, to examine and debate them, and to introduce such as seem proper and useful.

82. Ibid.
83. Ibid.
84. Ibid.

Rather significantly, the constitution of Oceana has very little to say concerning the powers and responsibilities of the Council of Trade. We are told simply that, "The Council of Trade being the Vena Porta of this Nation[85] shall hereafter receive Instructions more at large: for the present, their experience attaining unto a right Understanding of those Trades and Mysteries that feed the veins of this Common-wealth, and a true distinction of them from those that suck or exhaust the same; they shall acquaint the Senate with the Conveniences and Inconveniences, to the end that encouragement may be applyd to the one, and remedy to the other."[86] In view of the brevity of this description it is not possible to say much more than that the existence of the Council of Trade is an indication of the currency of mercantilist ideas in Oceana in the seventeenth century. The economy of Oceana is viewed as a single entity which can be enriched or impoverished by trade, and it is thought to be the duty of the government, by encouragement and remedies, to regulate the national economy—the wealth of the nation. Finally, from the constitutional viewpoint it is interesting to note the provision that the Council "shall hereafter receive Instructions more at large." This would seem to indicate that the Councils are to be controlled by some other organ of government, presumably the Senate which elects them.

As a matter of fact, the function of these great national Councils is the most ambiguously formulated part of the constitution of Oceana. If one inquires whether the Councils are executive or legislative it is not really possible to give any definitive reply. When the Lord Archon came to discuss the institution of the Councils he spoke of them as being distinctly legislative, very much like committees of the British Parliament or the American Congress: "Your

85. The Harveian reference is interesting.
86. *Oceana,* p. 110.

Councils . . . are proper and native Springs and Sources you
see, which . . . derive the full stream of businesse into the
Senate, so pure, and so far from the possibility of being
troubled or steined . . . with any kind of private interest or
partiality."[87] On the other hand, it is quite apparent that
each of the Councils exercises powers which are unquestionably executive in nature. Surely the regulation of trade,
the management of the army, and the supervision of the
national religion are all of this sort. Perhaps the most convincing proof that the Councils are to act in an executive
capacity is the fact that there is no other organ of government empowered to do this.

We have still not located what might be considered a
unified executive authority. The closest approximation to
such an authority is the so-called Signory, which is composed of the three Commissioners of the Seal, the three
Commissioners of the Treasury, and the Lord Strategus.
This seven-man council which, as Harrington notes,[88] is
intended to be a replica of the Venetian executive, has authority to "take into their consideration all matters of State,
or of Government."[89] The exact meaning of this sweeping
grant of power is far from clear, but it most certainly does
include the right to propose measures for consideration by
any of the Councils of Oceana. Furthermore, in order "that
the Councils may be held unto their duty," the Signory
has the right to superintend their activities and to circum-
vent them by proposing measures directly to the Senate.[90]
Finally, any individual member of the Signory has the right
to propose both to the Councils and to the Senate of Oceana.

Why, then, can we not call this a unified executive authority? The answer is that it evidently remains nothing

87. Ibid., p. 112.
88. Ibid., p. 106.
89. Ibid., p. 115.
90. Ibid., pp. 115–16.

more than a group of seven individuals, and there seem to be several reasons for this. In the first place, the members of the Signory are chosen individually by the Senate, unlike the modern British cabinet, for instance, which is chosen by one responsible Prime Minister. Secondly, the members of the Signory are elected at different times; each year two of the six Commissioners and the Lord Strategus are elected and join the four previously elected Commissioners. Thirdly, there is an absence in Oceana of any system of political parties which might, despite all these obstacles, serve to unite the members of the Signory in pursuit of a common program of action. Fourthly, the Signory operates on a principle which is the exact opposite of collective responsibility: each member, far from being bound by the decisions of his colleagues, is completely free to perform as an individual all the executive functions of the group as a whole. Finally, and perhaps most important, the Signory has no control over the administrative authorities of Oceana and is empowered only to propose to the Senate.

In his later writings Harrington increased the power of the Signory to the extent of providing that its members should have "session and suffrage" in all the Councils of Oceana.[91] Assuming the seven members of the Signory voted as a bloc in the various Councils their power would appear to be substantially enhanced; it will be recalled that the Council of State has fifteen members, the Councils of Religion and Trade twelve, and the Council of War only nine. But here two difficulties arise: in the first place, even decisive control over the Councils would not constitute true executive authority, and in the second place the assumption of unanimity among the members of the Signory is clearly unrealistic. This brings us back to our original observation that the Signory does not constitute a true national execu-

91. *Art of Lawgiving, Coll. Works,* p. 442.

tive largely because it is nothing more than a group of seven independent individuals, united simply by the accident of senatorial election.

In the light of all this we must conclude that in the normal course of events the government of Oceana lacks any individual or institution with real powers of executive leadership. This means that the legislature itself represents the only element of unity or continuity in the constitution; apart from general legislative control there is no apparent means of coordinating, for instance, economic and foreign policy. The complete lack of an independent executive in Oceana, and the extreme form of legislative supremacy envisioned by the constitution, are almost unquestionably a reflection of Harrington's fear of usurpation of power by the executive, which in turn probably resulted from his observation of the first two Stuart monarchs and Oliver Cromwell, and is further reflected in his insistence that the legislature meet continuously.

The curious position of the executive authorities in Oceana is quite conveniently emphasized by the constitutional provision for emergency powers. Here, and particularly in the institution of the dictatorship, we find that element of unified leadership which is so conspicuously absent from the rest of the constitution. Harrington recognized, and expressed rather succinctly, the need for and the dangers of speedy action in time of crisis: "But whereas it is incident unto Common-wealths upon Emergences requiring extraordinary speed, or secrecie, either through their natural delayes, or unnatural haste to incur equal danger, while holding unto the slow pace of their Orders, they come not in time to defend themselves from some suddain blow; or breaking them for the greater speed, they but haste unto their own Destruction."[92] In order to meet this

92. *Oceana,* pp. 111–12.

need while avoiding these dangers, provision was made in the constitution for the establishment of a dictatorship. The procedure is simple: at any time the Senate may elect nine Knights to be added to the Council of War for a term of three months. The augmented Council of War becomes for these three months the Dictator of Oceana, having the power to levy men and money, to make war and peace, and to enact laws. All of this is, of course, designed to meet the need for quick, decisive, and perhaps secret action. Further provisions are designed to avoid, or at least to minimize, the dangers inherent in the establishment of such a power. The laws enacted by the Dictator can at any time be repealed by the legislature, which continues to sit, following its regular procedure. Furthermore, these laws are in any case valid only for a period of one year unless they receive the explicit confirmation of the legislature. Finally, the constitution provides that "the Dictator shall have no power to do any thing that tendeth not unto his proper end and institution; but all unto the Preservation of the Commonwealth as it is established; And, for the suddain restitution of the same unto the natural channel and common course of Government."[93] Although no institution or procedure is provided to determine when the Dictator is acting unconstitutionally, it may be assumed that this function is performed by the legislature itself which, as we have seen, continues to meet during the period of emergency.

The essential justification of the dictatorship in Oceana, according to Harrington, is the fact that it is part of the constitution of the commonwealth. Recognizing that such extraordinary powers will be necessary in time of emergency, Harrington insists that they must be provided for by the constitution. Otherwise the people will be forced to ignore the constitution, thus setting a dangerous precedent.

93. Ibid., p. 112.

As he says, citing Machiavelli's opinion, "And indeed a Common-wealth is like a Grey-hound, which having once coasted, will never again run fair, but grow sloathful; and when she comes to make a common practice of taking nearer ways then her orders, she is dissolved; for the being of a Common-wealth consists in her Orders."[94] Aside from its interest as an illustration of Harrington's emphasis on constitutional forms, the institution of the dictatorship serves also as a reminder of the slowness and ponderousness of the regular governmental process in Oceana.

It will perhaps seem strange to the modern reader that we have now reached the end of our discussion of the regular executive authorities of the national government of Oceana. This impression will certainly be heightened when we note the final constitutional provision concerning the executive, namely that each Council shall have two secretaries, two doorkeepers and two messengers, and shall have the power to employ more help in case of emergency. These twenty-four employees, six for each of the four Councils, evidently constitute the entire permanent civil service of the commonwealth! Living in an age when even the least totalitarian of states require the services of hundreds of thousands of employees we must inevitably look with wonder on this provision of the Oceanic constitution. A more relevant, though hardly less startling, comparison can be made between the constitution of Oceana and those of nations contemporary with it. By the time of the Tudors a century earlier, the number of royal, or governmental, officials in Britain had grown to considerable proportions. But it was precisely during the seventeenth century that government bureaucracy on a vast scale became a charac-

94. Ibid., p. 114; the verb "coast" is defined by the *New English Dictionary* as "To run from the straight course so as to cut off the chased animal when it doubles." Cf. Machiavelli, *Discorsi*, I, 34.

teristic feature of the national state, fostered by the Stuarts and Cromwell in England, and reaching its height in the France of Louis XIV. For this reason it is doubly surprising to find in the constitution of Oceana no recognition of, or provision for, this phenomenon. Surely no one who had lived in seventeenth-century England and had visited the France of Richelieu, as Harrington had done, could have been unaware of the increasing importance of an ever expanding executive establishment. And the paradox certainly cannot be explained away by arguing that the government of Oceana performed so few functitons that it was able to dispense with an elaborate bureaucracy.

The mercantilist policies, interest in which is clearly indicated by the existence of the Council of Trade, will unquestionably require enforcement by public officials. Who is to do this? Who are to be the customs inspectors, the statisticians, the planners, the engineers, the bureaucrats of all sorts? The answer seems to lie in the very vagueness with which the whole subject is treated in the constitution of Oceana. Since we can assume with almost absolute certainty that such officials will be needed to carry on the work contemplated in the constitution, we can then also assume that there are parts of the national government of Oceana which are simply not mentioned in the constitution. As a general rule, it appears that the constitution is confined to discussion of political institutions of two sorts: those concerned with the formation of public policy, and those which are strikingly new, at least in the sense of not having existed in the government of seventeenth-century England. And it is clear that a national bureaucracy fits neither of these descriptions: it does not overtly create public policy, and it had certainly been a feature of English government in the past. Therefore its omission from the constitution should not lead us to believe that it is also absent from the government of Oceana.

A second example proving the necessity of some considerable body of public officials in Oceana is the complex electoral system; surely this, too, would require administration. The answer here is explicit and equally instructive: elections are supervised by officials at levels of government below the national. Thus Parish elections are managed by Parish officials, Hundred elections by Hundred officials, and Tribe elections by Tribal officials. This in itself is neither startling nor particularly important. But it takes on added interest when we realize that this same pattern of what a modern observer might call "decentralization" is applied to numerous other governmental functions in Oceana. This is true of the administration of justice, the management of military affairs, religious government, and, perhaps most interesting of all, taxation. As might be expected, taxes are levied in the first instance by the national legislature. But the collection of taxes is completely decentralized. The parliament demands a certain sum from each Phylarch, the governing body of the Tribe. The Phylarch then taxes the various Hundreds within the Tribe, which in turn pass the demand on to the Parishes. The money is collected locally by the various Parishes, is passed on to the Hundred and the Tribe, and so proceeds up to the national government. This, then, would seem to be a second explanation of the striking absence of a national bureaucracy in the formal constitution of Oceana. The functions which had generally been performed at the national level are, at least to a considerable degree, performed locally and by locally elected officials.[95]

Two final aspects of the central government of Oceana remain to be discussed here: the appointment of ambassa-

95. This process is particularly interesting in the matter of church government, where it becomes a doctrinal as well as a practical issue. See below, pp. 271 ff.

dors and the payment of public officials. The commonwealth employs only four regular ambassadors, each of
whom serves for eight years. Following a system of rotation,
each ambassador resides for two years at the court of France,
two years at the court of Spain, two years in Venice, and two
years in Constantinople, in that order. Upon completion of
his service in Constantinople an ambassador returns to
Oceana, where he is expected to spend his remaining years
instructing his countrymen in the ways of the world. Every
other year, therefore, it is necessary for the Senate to elect
a new ambassador. This is done by the suffrage of the entire
chamber, the constitution providing that no member of the
Senate or Prerogative Tribe can be chosen since this would
either interfere with his term in the legislature or lead to
an accumulation of magistracy, both of which are considered undesirable. Furthermore, no man over the age of
thirty-five is eligible for election to an ambassadorial post
because it is thought unlikely that an older man will outlive
his eight-year term by many years.

Extraordinary ambassadors may be elected by the Senate
with the advice of the Council of State. Actually, this is
done by a procedure known as the "scrutiny" of the Council of State. This means that the Council nominates one
candidate for the position, the Senate nominates four more,
and one of the five is elected by the Senate. Harrington believed that in this case the Senate would almost invariably
choose the candidate proposed by the Council, thus gaining
the advantage of its superior knowledge. He explains this
by saying that the very fact that the Senate *can* reject the
Council's candidate will keep it from feeling coerced and
lead it to accept willingly the Council's advice. Thereby the
power of the legislature is maintained but the effect of expert leadership is also secured. As Harrington says, "The
cause why the great Council, in Venice scarce ever elects any
other then the Name that is brought in by Scrutiny, is very

probable to be; that they may.''[96] This mode of election by "scrutiny" is the procedure followed in choosing all extraordinary officials in Oceana, the choice of the participating Council being determined by the nature of the office to be filled.

With respect to the payment of various government officials and employees, the most significant fact is certainly that the members of the legislature are paid regular salaries, Knights receiving £500 yearly, Horse Deputies £104 and Foot Deputies £78. The total cost of all government salaries amounts to something less than 300,000 pounds annually, a sum which Harrington thought modest in the light of the advantages gained: "the beauty they [the salaries] will adde unto the Common-wealth will be exceeding great, and the people delight in the beauty of their Common-wealth, the encouragement they will give unto the study of the publick very profitable, the accomodation they will afford unto your Magistrates, very honourable and easie.''[97] But even more important, this provision for salaries will make it possible for poor men to devote themselves to the service of the commonwealth without great personal loss: "On the other side, if a poor man (as such an one may save a City) give his sweat unto the publick, with what conscience can you suffer his Family in the mean time to sterve. But he that layes his hand unto this plough, shall not lose by taking it off from his own: and a Commonwealth that will mend this, shall be penny-wise.''[98] The entire system of government of Oceana is predicated on the assumption of widespread public spirit and devoted service and here, finally, the constitution provides a reward for these virtues.[99]

96. *Oceana*, p. 108. Liljegren (p. 308) is certainly incorrect in believing this sentence to be incomplete.
97. Ibid., p. 157.
98. Ibid.
99. See Appendix II for a list of government salaries in Oceana.

Local Authorities

Our previous discussion has indicated that many of the functions usually associated with national government were in Oceana performed by local authorities. It will become apparent as we proceed that relatively little is known about local government in the commonwealth, and this fact is perhaps of some interest in itself. Our major source of information about Oceana is, of course, the constitution of the commonwealth. The fact that the constitution says so little about local government is due primarily to the fact, already noted, that that document strongly emphasizes institutions which create national policy and institutions which are noteworthy because of their novelty. But perhaps the most significant fact about the local authorities in Oceana is precisely their lack of novelty; in almost every instance one is struck by the continuity at the local level between the institutions of Oceana and those of the pre-Civil War British government.

At the lowest level of government in Oceana we find the Parish officials. This group consists of two Overseers, a Constable, and two Church Wardens, all of whom serve one-year terms. It is the duty of the Overseers to supervise all elections in the Parish, to keep records of the results of these elections, and, apparently, to do nothing more. The constitution tells us nothing concerning the duties of either Constable or Church Wardens, but we may assume that the former is entrusted with keeping the peace in the Parish, while the latter in all probability are in charge of church property and perhaps are also guardians of the poor of the Parish, according to pre-Oceanic English usage. We do know, as noted above, that someone in the Parish must collect the taxes levied upon it by the Hundred, but there is no indication in the constitution of which official performs this function. It seems likely that it is done by one or both of the Overseers.

At the next highest level, that of the Hundreds, there are seven officials: a Justice of the Peace, two jurymen, a Captain, an Ensign, a High Constable and a Crowner (Coroner). Unfortunately nothing is known of the local functions of any of these officials save that the jurymen and the High Constable supervise Hundred elections, while the Captain and the Ensign are military officials. We can only suppose, as we did in the case of the Parish officials, that the titles of these various officers are a sufficient indication of their duties, relying again upon the analogy of English usage. In addition to their local functions, as we shall see, the jurymen, the Justices of the Peace, and the High Constables are ex officio members of the judicial body known as the "Prerogative Troop,"[100] while the jurymen and Justices of the Peace also serve on the "Phylarch," or governing body of the Tribe.[101]

At the Tribal level six more officials are chosen: a Lord High Sheriff, a Lord Lieutenant, a Lord Custos Rotulorum, a Conductor, and two Censors. These six magistrates join with the Hundred officials noted above to form the Prerogative Troop and the Phylarch of the Tribe, and they are known collectively as the "Prime Magnitude" of the Tribe. The Lord High Sheriff, we are told explicitly, is above all else to perform "his more ancient Offices,"[102] namely the keeping of peace in the Tribe and the maintenance of liaison with the central government. In addition to this he is to supervise Tribal elections and to serve as chief Magistrate of the Phylarch. The Lord Lieutenant also has several duties in connection with balloting at the Tribal level, but his chief tasks are to serve as commander of the musters of

100. Not to be confused with the national legislative Prerogative Tribe.

101. In each Tribe there are, of course, 40 jurymen, 20 Justices of the Peace, and 20 Constables.

102. *Oceana*, p. 78.

the Youth of the Tribe[103] and as second Magistrate of the Phylarch. The Lord Custos Rotulorum, as his title implies, is in charge of the muster rolls of the Tribe, which he must deliver annually to the central government in Emporium (London); he also serves as third Magistrate of the Phylarch. The Censors, in cooperation with the Overseers of the various Parishes, are entrusted with the enforcement of the electoral laws of the commonwealth and have also the responsibility of ensuring that clergymen of the national church do not meddle in politics. The Conductor is simply an electoral official.

As we have noted, the two chief organs of government at the Tribal level are the Prerogative Troop and the Phylarch. The Prerogative Troop, which is composed of the six Magistrates of the Prime Magnitude plus the jurymen, Justices of the Peace, and Constables of the various Parishes, is primarily a judicial body. Although its exact functions are never clearly defined, we are told "that this Troop [shall] bring in and assist the Justices of Assize, hold the Quarter Sessions in their several Capacities, and perform their other Functions as formerly."[104] Perhaps more revealing is Harrington's statement that as a result of the work of the Prerogative Troop "the Commonwealth at its introduction may imbrace the Law as it stands, that is, unreformed."[105] In the light of this it would appear that the major function of the Prerogative Troop as a body—quite apart from the duties of its individual members—is to ensure the enforcement of the laws of Oceana at the local level.

The chief governmental body at the Tribal level is the Phylarch, the composition of which is identical with that of the Prerogative Troop save that the Constables of the

103. See below, p. 269.
104. *Art of Lawgiving, Coll. Works,* p. 438.
105. Ibid.

Parishes are lacking. The specific functions of the Phylarch are many, being enumerated by Harrington under five major headings. In the first place, the Phylarch is the Council of the Tribe. As such it governs the various assemblies, military and electoral, of the Tribe; it may review the activities of religious congregations and punish "any undue practices"; it supervises elections in Parishes and Hundreds; it arranges referenda on proposed petitions to the national legislature; and finally it has the power to pronounce marriages legitimate. In the second place, the Phylarch has certain judicial functions, described by Harrington in this way: "to receive the Judges *Itinerant* in their Circuits, whom the Magistrates of the *Phylarch* shall assist upon the Bench, and the Juries elsewhere in their proper Functions according to the more Ancient Lawes and Customs of this Nation."[106] Curiously, the constitution provides that the Phylarch may make use of whatever troops are required in the performance of this duty, leading one to suspect that what is here contemplated is some sort of police activity.[107] Thirdly, the Phylarch itself is to hear all cases involving liberty of conscience, following "such Rules as are or shall hereafter be appointed by the Parliament."[108] Fourthly, as we have noted, the Phylarch is responsible to the national legislature for the collection of taxes in the Tribe. The final, and perhaps most interesting, function of the Phylarch is to serve as the liaison between the national legislature

106. *Oceana,* p. 79.
107. Ibid.
108. Ibid. Actually, the constitution here provides that the Phylarch shall hold the "Court called the Quarter Sessions." This, as we have seen, was previously assigned to the Prerogative Troop. The fact is that in the *Oceana* Harrington does not distinguish between the Prerogative Troop and the Phylarch, although in *The Art of Lawgiving* it is clear that their composition and functions are not the same. Since *The Art of Lawgiving* postdates the *Oceana,* I have considered it as the definitive source in this matter.

and the Tribe, carrying out locally all orders from the parliament. As Harrington tells us, "these Magistrates of the Hundreds and Tribes being such wherby the Parlament is to govern the Nation . . . this Court [shall] procede in all matters of Government, as shall from time to time be directed by Act of Parlament."[109]

In addition to these general provisions concerning local government, the constitution of Oceana also provides us with valuable information pertaining to the government of Emporium (London), the capital of the commonwealth. Although distinguished by its size, its highly commercial character, and the fact that it is the capital city, Emporium may nevertheless in many respects be considered the model of municipal organization in Oceana. The very fact that the constitution includes a lengthy discussion of its government would seem to indicate that it was thought to be typical of the cities of Oceana, added to which there is Harrington's statement that "there be other Cities and Corporations throughout the territory, whose Policy being much of this kind, would be tedious and not worth the labour to insert."[110] The complexity and prolixity of this discussion make it inadvisable for us to reproduce in complete detail the governmental system of Emporium. Instead we will limit ourselves to a rather cursory outline of the more interesting and significant features.

In relation to the national government of Oceana Emporium includes three of the fifty Tribes that make up the commonwealth. For the purposes of local government, however, the city is divided into twenty-six wards, each having a Wardmot, or court, composed of all residents entitled to wear the livery of a Company. The city contains sixty of these Companies, which are defined as brotherhoods of

---

109. *Art of Lawgiving, Coll. Works,* p. 439.
110. *Oceana,* p. 161.

tradesmen, "professing the same Art, governed, according to their Charter, by a Master and Wardens."[111] Persons entitled to wear the livery of a Company are defined by Harrington as "such . . . as have attained unto the dignity to weare Gowns and Particolour'd Hoods or Tipets according unto the Rules, and ancient Customes of their respective Companies."[112] Further, we are told that of these sixty Companies twelve are "of greater dignity" than the rest: Mercers, Grocers, Drapers, Fishmongers, Goldsmiths, Skinners, Merchant Tailors, Haberdashers, Salters, Ironmongers, Vintners, and Cloth Workers. Although originally and primarily economic associations, the Companies are in fact "the roots of the whole Government of the City." This is true in the first instance because, as we have seen, participation in municipal political life is dependent upon full membership in a Company. Thus these economic groups possess absolute control over suffrage in the city; this does not, of course, apply to national elections.

As far as procedure is concerned, the liveried members of the various Companies assemble at the Wardmot and there elect aldermen and members of the Common Council of the city. Each ward elects one alderman, who thereby becomes justice of the peace of his ward, president of the wardmot and Governor of his ward; in addition the twenty-six aldermen together constitute the Court of Aldermen, or Senate of the city. Each ward also elects fifteen deputies, a total of 390 for the city as a whole. These deputies meeting together constitute the Prerogative Tribe of the city. The legislative procedure of these two bodies is simply a replica of that followed in the national parliament; the Senate debates, the Prerogative Tribe votes without discussion. It is interesting to note in passing that no man is eligible for

111. Ibid., p. 159.
112. Ibid.

election as alderman unless he possesses land, goods, or property worth the substantial sum of ten thousand pounds; the city Senate is an aristocratic body with requirements considerably higher than those of the national Senate.[113]

Finally, it should be noted that the government of Emporium, unlike that of Oceana as a whole, possesses in addition to its legislature a popularly elected executive, the Lord Mayor. All the liveried members of Companies within the city meet together annually in an assembly known as the Common Hall and there elect the Lord Mayor and two Sheriffs. The Lord Mayor acts as president of the Court of Aldermen and has the power to assemble any of the councils of the city; in addition he acts as commander of the three Tribes of the city in the performance of their functions with regard to the national government.

Other Institutions

Although we have now discussed all the major governmental institutions of Oceana there are several other significant features of the constitution to be examined, namely, education, military organization, church government, and liberty of conscience. It is not necessary to consider any of these in detail; rather, we may be content with a very brief outline of these and a mere mention of other subjects.

Although prophecy is not a necessary accomplishment of a political theorist, and the ability to anticipate developments of the distant future contributes little to the practicality of his proposals, one cannot help being struck by the modernity of the educational and military system of the commonwealth of Oceana. To give only the barest outline, the constitution of Oceana provides that each of the fifty Tribes shall have a public school, inspected by the Censors of the commonwealth, and open to all the male children of

113. Ibid., p. 160.

the Tribe. Those whose parents cannot afford to send them to this school will be publicly supported, but all male children must attend by the age of nine and remain until the age of fifteen. An exception is made in the case of only sons; they may attend, but are not compelled to do so. Upon reaching the age of fifteen, youths are free to choose between professional training, again at public expense if necessary, and apprenticeship to some trade. A youth attending one of the Inns of Court with a view to becoming a lawyer, or one of the universities in order to become a clergyman or doctor, is exempted from military service if he begins the practice of his profession upon reaching the age of eighteen.

The armies of the commonwealth are classified as marching armies, composed of the Youth of the various Tribes, and garrison armies composed of the Elders. They are chosen by an intricate system of ballots and lots which can be summarized as follows: all citizens between the ages of eighteen and thirty (Youth) are eligible for regular military service, either in Oceana itself, or in Marpesia (Scotland) and Panopea (Ireland). The term of service is one year and no person is liable for two terms in succession. Furthermore, neither professional men nor servants are liable for military service, nor are only sons or more than half the sons of any family. The standing army, or "second essay," is chosen by lot from among all eligible youths; those who can afford the necessary equipment become Horse soldiers, the remainder are Foot soldiers. Twice annually, at the Rendezvous of the Tribe and that of the Hundred, the members of this standing army assemble to participate in "games," that is, military maneuvers. Following this, they are to be ready at all times to march to the defense of the commonwealth, led by captains and ensigns of their own choosing, and under the general command of officers elected by the national legislature. The regular standing armies of Oceana consist of thirty thousand Foot soldiers and ten

thousand Horse soldiers.[114] In addition, five thousand Foot
soldiers and one thousand Horse soldiers are stationed in
Marpesia and Panopea each year. In time of national
emergency the parliament or the dictator may order the
calling up of additional groups of forty thousand soldiers,
from both Youth and Elders, following the same procedure.
Normally, the expenses of the members of the standing
army during their term of service are to be defrayed by
themselves. But, "The Services performed by the youth,
or by the Elders in case of Invasion . . . shall be at their proper cost and charges that are any wayes able to indure it,
but if there be such as are known in their Parishes to be so
indigent that they cannot march out . . . nor undergoe the
burden, in this case incumbent, the Congregations of their
Parishes shall furnish them with sufficient summes of money to be repay'd . . . by the Parliament when the action shall
be over."[115]

One may say without exaggeration that these arrangements are in many ways more "modern," or at least more
rational, than those adopted by the United States, let us
say, in the twentieth century. This is apparent in the first
place in the very fact that these two subjects, education and
military organization, are treated together in the constitution of Oceana. But beyond this, the provision for free
public education plus public support of underprivileged
students, the sweeping exemption of advanced students
from military service, and the system of regular military
training to which all are liable are considerably in advance
of current American practice. Unquestionably a substantial
part of this strikingly modern system can be attributed to
Harrington's belief that education is "the plastick art of

114. These figures may be compared with the standing army of
20,000 men suggested for France by Richelieu in 1626, and the approximately 60,000 men in Cromwell's army in 1646.

115. *Oceana,* p. 167.

Government." Although impressed by the central importance of good "orders" and good institutions, he nevertheless felt that the proper training of its citizens was requisite
to the continuing health of a commonwealth.

Just as education and military organization are interrelated in the commonwealth of Oceana, so too are church
government and liberty of conscience. The religious institutions of Occana are a strange combination of congrega-
tionalism, a national church, and almost complete toleration. This combination is well illustrated by the remarks
which follow the text of the Sixth Order in Harrington's
Oceana:

> This Order consisteth of three parts, the first restoring
> the power of Ordination unto the people. . . . The sec-
> ond . . . implyes and establisheth a nationall Religion.
> . . . The *Common-wealth* having thus performed her
> duty towards God . . . by the best Application of her
> Reason unto Scripture, for the preservation of Re-
> ligion in the purity of the same, yet pretendeth not
> unto infallibility, but comes in the third part of the
> order, establishing Liberty of Conscience. . . . to raise
> up her hands to Heaven, for further light.[116]

The specific religious institutions of Oceana are the local
congregations, the universities, and the national Council
of Religion. Those congregations which are (voluntarily)
affiliated with the national church receive their clergy from
the universities, but are able to reject probationary clergy
after a one-year trial period. Indeed, the constitution requires that two-thirds of the elders of a congregation must
approve a probationer in order for him to become the regular parson or vicar of that congregation. If such approval is
not forthcoming the elders may reapply to the universities

116. Ibid., pp. 69–70.

for another candidate. The Council of Religion, in conjunction with the two great universities, is entrusted with the determination of doctrine and ritual for the national church. But neither this method of election of clergy nor this national doctrine is in any way binding on those who do not wish to submit to it. The constitution specifically states that, "such as are of gather'd Congregations, or from time to time shall joyn with any of them, are in no wise obligated to this way of Electing their Teachers, or to give their votes in this Case, but wholly left unto the liberty of their Conscience, and unto that way of worship which they shall choose, being not Popish, Jewish, nor Idolatrous."[117]

The Council of Religion is entrusted, furthermore, with ensuring that this liberty of conscience is maintained in the commonwealth. To this end, each congregation (church) not affiliated with the national church is requested, in extraordinarily polite language, to send four magistrates of their own choosing to the Council of Religion in case any violation of liberty of conscience occurs, or is alleged to occur. The major significance of this provision for liberty of conscience, or freedom of worship and belief, is negative. Although freedom of worship is, of course, a positive value in the twentieth century, the most important result of such a law in the seventeenth century was to deny the demands of Roman Catholics, Episcopalians, and Presbyterians that a national church should enforce uniformity of belief and worship throughout the commonwealth.

We may conclude this description of the government of Oceana by noting several institutions and arrangements which do not properly belong in any of the classifications used above. In the first place, Marpesia and Panopea (Scotland and Ireland) are ruled by Councils composed of twelve Knights elected by the Senate of Oceana from among its

117. Ibid., p. 69.

own members; each Council elects a Strategus from among its members to serve as its president and as general of the provincial army. Laws for the provinces, however, are enacted by the legislature of Oceana, with the advice of the Provincial Councils. Provincial councillors are to be paid £500 each per annum, and the Strategus of each province £1500. Service on a provincial council "as to domestick Magistracies shall be esteemed a Vacation and no barr unto present Election into any other Honour, his Provinciall Magistracy being expired."[118] A certain amount of local autonomy is allowed the provinces of Oceana in those areas where the Oceanic parliament does not choose to legislate.

Secondly, there exists in the national government of Oceana a body known as the Academy of Provosts, composed of three members of each of the great Councils, twelve members in all. These Provosts serve terms of one week only, and are not eligible for re-election until every member of the Council has once been elected. The Academy serves as a link between the people of Oceana and their government. It is to meet every day, in the evening, and receive all persons who wish to address it concerning any governmental matter. The major purpose of the Academy is to overcome the reticence of the average man when confronted with an official body. Thus, "All sorts of Company that will repair thither for Conversation or discourse, so it be upon the matter of Government, News or Intelligence . . . shall be freely and affably received . . . and heard in the way of civil Conversation, which is to be managed without any other Awe or Ceremony . . . to the end that every man may be free."[119]

Finally, a few words may be said about the financial system of the commonwealth. The constitution provided that "whereas the Publique Revenue is through the late Civill

118. Ibid., p. 183.
119. Ibid., p. 111.

Wars dilapidated" a national excise tax should be imposed at the rate of one million pounds annually for eleven years. At the end of that period, we are told, although the commonwealth was in good financial condition, it was decided to continue the excise for an additional ten years. At this time, after twenty-one years, it was found that the commonwealth possessed wealth producing an annual income of one million pounds and the excise was therefore discontinued. As far as the actual incidence of taxation is concerned we know only that a man with ten children is required to pay no taxes, a man with five children pays half taxes, a man married three years without children pays double taxes, and an unmarried man above the age of twenty-five also pays double taxes.[120] This perhaps helps to explain the fact that forty-one years after the foundation of the commonwealth the Censors discovered, in their annual census, that the population of Oceana had increased by one-third.

120. It may also be noted that in Oceana bachelors are ineligible to be magistrates.

CHAPTER 6.

The Archives of Ancient Prudence

". . . how unsafe a thing it is to follow Phansie in the Fabrick of a Common-wealth; and how necessary that the Archives of ancient prudence should be ransackt."

The Commonwealth of Oceana

THE READER who wishes to identify the sources of Harrington's ideas will be delighted to discover that his works are annotated and his references cited with a thoroughness unparalleled among political theorists. Three circumstances combine to explain this happy fact. In the first place there is Harrington's considerable self-consciousness concerning his position in the intellectual history of Europe. We have already noted that the distinction between ancient and modern prudence is an integral part of his political theory. Regarding himself as a reviver of ancient political learning, Harrington continually goes out of his way to demonstrate the connection between his ideas and those of classical authors. And this is closely related to the second, less important, circumstance. Like so many writers of the seventeenth century Harrington believed in the validity and utility of proof by scientific demonstration, but was unable to liberate himself completely from the earlier tradition of proof by citation of authorities. Indeed, in most of his references to earlier writers, including the ancients, one can detect a certain element of ambivalence. Harrington has not progressed to the point where "ancient" becomes a bad word and "modern" a good one; in general his usage is just the opposite of this. Nevertheless he feels that he has something to contribute beyond a mere revival of the writings of the ancients. It seems accurate to say that in most instances, and particularly where the Bible is concerned, Harrington's appeals to earlier authorities are intended primarily to impress his readers rather than to express his own humility before the great figures of the past.[1] The third explanation of Harrington's practice of citing his sources is to be found in his characteristic honesty and candor. More perhaps than most political theo-

1. See above, Ch. 2, for an earlier discussion of this point.

rists', his ideas were derived from the work of others. And he insisted that his readers should be aware of this fact. At the same time, he was particularly jealous of those parts of his theory which he believed to be original, especially the doctrine of the economic foundation of domestic empire.[2] Having been scrupulously accurate in indicating his indebtedness to other authors, he demanded credit for those ideas which were his own.

Since Harrington himself indicates most of the major sources of his thought there is no need for us to trace them.[3] Instead, we shall attempt in this chapter to discuss the ways in which Harrington used these sources. Specifically, the procedure will be as follows: we shall take up in turn the most important authors and writings upon which Harrington relied and in each case ask three questions: What was the extent of Harrington's knowledge of this source? What was his opinion of it? And what use did he make of it? This should result in a fairly comprehensive and revealing picture of the origins of Harrington's political theory, his method of utilizing sources, and the degree of originality which he can justly claim.

The Bible

Considering all of Harrington's works, it is probably accurate to say that he quotes and cites the Bible more often and more extensively than any other single source. Such a statement would be misleading in a study of Harrington's political theory were it not modified by the observation that

2. Thus a footnote to his *Art of Lawgiving* reads, "A later Pamphlet call'd XXV QUERYS, using the Balance of Property, which is fair enough, refers it to Sir *Thomas Smith's* 15th chap. . . . where the Author speaks not one word of Property; which is very foul." *Coll. Works,* p. 431.

3. In addition, Liljegren has exhaustively annotated the sources of the *Oceana.*

at least half of these citations and quotations refer to theological questions and matters of church government. But the remaining half, which are political, still bulk large enough to deserve an important position in any discussion of Harrington's sources.

Harrington's knowledge of the Bible was extensive, to say the very least, even by the standards of the seventeenth century, and almost overwhelmingly thorough by modern standards. It is quite obvious that he was familiar with the Bible in Greek and in numerous modern languages as well. As for the first it is necessary simply to mention his frequent controversies about the proper translation of various Greek terms.[4] For the second we may cite the passage in which Harrington seeks to prove a point by referring to seven modern translations: "that of Zurich," "that of Beza," "the French," "the Italian," "that of Diodati," "that appointed by the Synod of Dort," and "that us'd in England from the time of the Reformation till the Episcopal correction of the same."[5] Whatever the occasion, it seems that an appropriate Biblical passage came to hand. Like most Protestants of his time, he was interested primarily in the Old Testament, for reasons which we shall have occasion to note below, but this did not prevent him from citing the New Testament when it served his purposes to do so.

In order to understand the manner in which Harrington used the Bible it will be necessary for us to speak briefly

4. The outstanding example of this is the entire second Book of his *Prerogative of Popular Government,* which is devoted to a lengthy dispute over the proper translation of the words *"chirotonia"* and *"chirothesia."* See *Coll. Works,* pp. 325–82. See also above, p. 40, n. 61.

5. *Prerogative of Popular Government, Coll. Works,* p. 376; we do not mean to argue that Harrington had actually read each of these seven, for it is quite apparent that he has simply looked up the disputed passage in each translation. On the other hand, he had read both the Vulgate and the King James, which are not included in the list.

of his general attitude toward the Scriptures. This will have
the further advantage of throwing additional light on the
disputed question of whether his leanings were fundamentally secular or religious.[6] As might be expected, Harrington viewed the Bible in two distinct lights. He believed
it to be a divinely inspired work, recounting the works of
God on earth. And he treated it as an historical source and
also as a text in comparative government. Harrington
began his discussion of ancient prudence by noting that it
had been "first discovered unto mankind by God himself,
in the fabrick of the *Common-wealth* of *Israel*."[7] Therefore
it is unquestionably true that for Harrington a special importance, indeed a transcendant importance, is attributed
to the Bible as the embodiment of the Word of God. But
at the same time, as the above passage indicates, the Bible is
also the source of our knowledge of the so-called "Commonwealth of Israel," a system of government which may be
treated in the same way as any other system of government.
Thus in Harrington's *Seven Models of a Commonwealth*
the government of the Old Testament Jews is discussed as
simply one possible polity.

But does this not imply an inconsistency in Harrington's
presentation? If the government of the Jews is in fact divinely inspired, why is it necessary to go any further? The
answer seems to be that Harrington was attempting to appeal to all varieties of opinion. For those who were prepared
to accept the argument of divine inspiration—and this
surely included the vast majority of Puritans—he provided
proof from the Old Testament. For those who remained
unimpressed—and there were doubtless many—he proceeded to "appeal . . . unto the *World* in the universal *Series*
of *ancient prudence*."[8] The most interesting indication of

6. See above, pp. 165 ff.
7. *Oceana*, p. 12.
8. *Oceana*, p. 26.

Harrington's technique here is provided by a passage in his *Art of Lawgiving*, "observing that the Principles of Human Prudence being good without proof of Scripture, are nevertheless such as are provable out of Scripture."[9] Thus in effect Harrington says to his reader: you may take your choice, I have shown you the government of the Old Testament Jews and you are free to treat it either as divinely created or as simply another example of human wisdom, but in both cases it will support my position.

Harrington was interested in the Bible for both political and religious reasons. Politically, he believed that the form of government described in the Old Testament corresponded in all essential points to his own "equal commonwealth." Thus he writes, "The *Common-wealth of Israel* consisted of the *Senate,* the *People,* and the *Magistracy.*"[10] Furthermore, the political system included elections by ballot and something approximating an agrarian law.[11] Thus, taken as either secular history or the Word of God, the government of Israel provided a valuable example of the successful operation of the sort of political system which Harrington wished to see introduced in England and a vindication of the theory on which this system was based. As far as religion was concerned, Harrington was interested in the Bible as the final authority on questions of church gov-

9. *Coll. Works,* p. 395. The order of the arguments here is interesting.

10. *Oceana,* p. 26; the "Senate" was the Sanhedrin, the "People" the synagoga magna or ecclesia, the "Magistracy" a Council of Priests and Levites. His citations are chiefly from the following Books: Numbers, Judges, Deuteronomy, I Samuel and Exodus.

11. Merritt Y. Hughes is mistaken in believing that Harrington wished to introduce in his commonwealth the custom of periodic cancellation of debts and sales of land. It was the effect of this device rather than its details which he admired. See *John Milton, Prose Selections,* ed. Merritt Y. Hughes (New York, 1947), Intro., p. civ.

ernment.[12] He attempted at great length to demonstrate that the religious organization of the Jews was congregational, that is, that the clergy were ordained by popular assemblies, and that no provision was made for bishops, presbyters, or popes. His position here, and his method of argument, are both so typical of the Independents of his time that further comment is really unnecessary.

We may conclude this discussion by noting one further fact: although Harrington shared with the Puritans the view of the Bible as an embodiment *in detail* of the divine will, he did not go to the extremes characteristic of the so-called Fifth Monarchy Men. That is, he did not advocate or look forward to the terrestrial rule of the Saints. Although admitting that Jesus prophesied the earthly rule of "the soules of them that were beheaded" for Him, Harrington insists that this must be interpreted literally. Therefore the rule of the Saints will only occur as a result of divine intervention through a miracle, and has no present political significance whatsoever. Thus, "it is not lawfull for men to perswade us that a thing is, though there be no such *object* of our *sence,* which *God* hath told us shall not be, untill it be an *object* of our *sence.*"[13] Here again Harrington contrives to take a position combining an apparent faith in the divinity of the Scriptures with a certain skepticism and mundane practicality. The general explanation of this position, at least insofar as it relates to things political, is best expressed by Harrington's assertion that "neither God, nor Christ, or the Apostles, ever instituted any Government Ecclesiastical or Civil upon any other Principles than those only of Human Prudence."[14] Thus in the absence of a miracle it is unnecessary to recognize any special category of knowledge relating to divine intervention in human af-

12. Here, of course, he treats the Bible as the Word of God.
13. *Oceana,* p. 56.
14. *Art of Lawgiving, Coll. Works,* p. 427.

fairs. On the contrary, by mastering the principles of human prudence—that is, the laws of political life—one serves both God and man.

Classical Sources

Although Harrington's persistent references to "ancient prudence" would lead one to expect that he relied heavily on the writings of the Greeks and Romans of the classical age in constructing his political theory, this is actually not the case. It is quite apparent that Harrington was familiar with the writings of all the major figures of this period. To mention only the most important classical sources he cites, we know that he had read Plato, Aristotle, Livy, Virgil, Horace, Thucydides, Xenophon, Cicero, Ovid, and Plutarch. If one attempts to distinguish among these various sources in terms of the frequency of Harrington's references to them it will be discovered that Livy and Plutarch are by far his favorites, with Aristotle and Virgil ranking next. Thus Thucydides and Xenophon, the two professional historians whose works were unquestionably familiar to Harrington, were very seldom cited by him.

His knowledge of Greek and Latin was sufficient to make it highly probable that he read all these authors in their native tongues. Indeed, as we have seen, he had actually translated large portions of Virgil into English, and was always prepared to enter into a dispute over the proper rendering of a passage in English. Therefore we may conclude that Harrington was well equipped to make extensive use of these classical authors. Why did he not do so?

The answer is that Harrington, like almost all "historians" before the nineteenth century, treated history not as a complex of interrelated developments through time, but rather as a disjointed collection of facts from which one was free to choose instructive, useful, or attractive items. And,

like virtually every other historian, he selected the evidence
that was relevant to the particular problems which concerned him. Thus he used Livy because Livy's view of the
Roman Empire was similar to his own; he used Plutarch
primarily because Plutarch gave him information about
Lycurgus, a figure particularly fascinating to Harrington;
he used Aristotle because Aristotle shared his interest in
the relation of economics and politics; and he used Virgil,
one suspects, simply because Virgil was so familiar to him.
And this observation, it should be emphasized, is not intended as a criticism of Harrington or as tantamount to an
accusation of garbling ancient history. On the contrary, he
was exceptionally successful in defending his presentation
of the facts against his many critics. Thus he did not falsify
Plutarch's account of Lycurgus, but simply chose to empha-
size Lycurgus rather than some other figure because Lycurgus illustrated a point he was anxious to make.

It must be added that he used these writers with very little
discrimination and rather low critical standards. A poet is
considered to be as good a source as an historian, a literary
figure as accurate as a political "scientist." The classic example of this, of course, is Harrington's political commen-
tary on Virgil's *Eclogues*. Here, although the poet was
clearly speaking loosely and with little sense of responsibility for the historical accuracy of his political statements,
Harrington treats his verse as a reliable account of the practices of several late Roman emperors.[15]

Harrington was primarily interested in the political history of Sparta and Rome. The former he considered to be
a commonwealth distinguished by an "equal agrarian" but
an "unequal" system of rotation. Thus he was able to use
it time and again as an illustration of the central importance
of the principle of rotation. "Here," he says in effect, "is a

15. See above, p. 179, n. 11.

commonwealth which lacks only one feature in order to achieve equality. In its history we may observe the consequences of this shortcoming."[16] Even more interesting, Harrington believed, was the origin of the Spartan commonwealth. We have already noted the passage from the *Oceana* in which he describes his reaction to Machiavelli's account of the founding of this commonwealth. This was to him the classic example of rational political creativity and he never tired of citing it.[17]

Harrington's view of Rome, the other ancient "commonwealth" with which he was most concerned, is very different. Unlike Sparta, it serves primarily as an illustration of political pathology rather than a model of good government. Here in a fairly brief compass one can observe the entire range of political life, from popular government to tyranny with frequent intervals of anarchy. Harrington was fascinated by the ever changing quality of Roman politics, just as he had been impressed by the stability of Sparta. Summarizing Roman history, he concludes: "All these tumultuously, and to the alteration of the Government, with so frequent Changes under so divers shapes, as make a very *Proteus* of the Commonwealth."[18]

In general, it might be said, Harrington believed that the wisdom of the ancients is expressed more fully in their political arrangements than in their political theory. Although both Plato and Aristotle were on the side of the angels, particularly in their advocacy of government under law and their view of government as an embodiment of morality, the fact remains that Harrington's real hero is Lycurgus. Therefore the devoted student of ancient pru-

---

16. Actually, Harrington argues that the Spartan commonwealth was finally destroyed as a result of the prior destruction of its agrarian law. See *Prerogative of Popular Government, Coll. Works*, p. 287.

17. See, for instance, the *Corollary* of the *Oceana*, pp. 207 ff.

18. *Seven Models, Coll. Works*, p. 529.

dence will spend relatively little time on the writings of
classical political theorists and a great deal of time on the
investigation of the *polis* and the Roman empire.

There are two possible exceptions to the statement that
Harrington used the classical authors chiefly as useful compendia of illustrative material. The first is suggested by his
attitude toward Aristotle. It is unquestionably true that he
found in Aristotle's *Politics* many handy examples with
which to buttress his general theory, but he also found
more. The mere facts of ancient history and political life
could be taken from more modern writings, and indeed
there is much evidence to support the view that a considerable part of Harrington's knowledge of Greek and Roman
institutions was derived from precisely such works, notably
Nicholas Cragius' *De republica Lacedœmoniorum,* Ubbo
Emmius' *Grœcorum respublicae* and Justus Lipsius' *De
magistratibus veteris populi Romani Commentariolus.*[19]
But in addition to whatever factual evidence Aristotle may
have contributed, he also offered a theoretical explanation
of Greek politics which in some respects was similar to
Harrington's. Harrington himself believed that this similarity was apparent in two respects. First, Aristotle said
many things about the relation of economics and politics
which Harrington found very convincing. Specifically, he
quotes with approval the Philosopher's dictum that "Husbandry or the Country way of life [is] the best stuffe of a
Commonwealth," and in defending his theory of political
balance notes that "you have Aristotle full of it in divers
places."[20] In the second place, Harrington regularly appeals

19. The first was published in Copenhagen in 1593, the second in
Leyden in 1632, and the last in Leyden in 1629. In some instances
Harrington himself cites these works; Liljegren's edition of the *Oce-
ana* indicates further evidence of Harrington's reliance on them.

20. *Oceana,* pp. 10 and 17. Harrington quotes the first passage,
Politics, VI, 4, 1f., in Latin as "Agricolarum democratica respublica
optima." The second, *Politics,* V, 3, 4f., is quoted in English.

to Aristotle for support of his assertion that the most desirable government is that which unites empire and authority. This, Harrington says, is precisely what Aristotle had in mind when he argued "that a Common-wealth is an Empire of Lawes and not of Men."[21]

With respect to the first similarity, the argument that a rural life is the best suited to democratic government was not unusual in the seventeenth century. The fact that Machiavelli stressed this idea leads one to suspect that he is a more likely source than Aristotle. Again, expressions of the desirability of government by law rather than by men can be found in the writings of virtually every political theorist between Aristotle and Harrington. One suspects that in both these cases Harrington quotes the *Politics* primarily to gain for himself some of the prestige associated with Aristotle's name.

But the connection between Harrington's theory of political balance and Aristotle's theory of revolution cannot be dismissed so lightly. A recent writer has stated that Aristotle's theory of revolution "may be reduced to the proposition that whenever political and economic power are separated, a revolution is likely to occur." And on the basis of this he goes on to conclude that "the first noteworthy attempt to revive the theory must be attributed to . . . James Harrington."[22]

As we have seen, Harrington himself was not unwilling to acknowledge his debt to Aristotle in this connection. Actually, he took a rather casual view of the whole matter in a way that is revealing of his attitude toward all his sources. Matthew Wren accused Harrington of basing his theory of political balance on very scanty evidence.[23] In reply Har-

21. *Oceana*, p. 21. The most obvious reference is to *Politics*, III, 6, 13.

22. Fred Kort, "The Quantification of Aristotle's Theory of Revolution," *American Political Science Review, 46* (1952), 487, 486.

23. *Considerations*, p. 73.

rington cited the passage in which Aristotle explains the
origin of ostracism in Greece.[24] This, he added, "will go
nearer than any thing alleg'd . . . to deprive me of the honor
of that invention" of the principle of political balance.[25]
In other words, if anyone other than Harrington deserves
credit for the discovery of this principle it must be Aristotle. But Harrington is really not very much concerned
about the question of his originality here: "If the Con-
siderer thinks that I have strain'd courtesy with Aristotle
(who indeed is not always of one mind) further than is
warrantable, in relation to the Balance, be it as he pleases;
I who must either have the more of Authority, or the less
of Competition in the point, shall lose neither way."[26] Perhaps Aristotle did recognize this principle; in that case Harrington has the advantage of being able to cite an impressive authority. Perhaps Harrington is being too generous
in giving Aristotle this credit; in that case his claim to
originality is undisputed.

It is interesting to compare Harrington's bantering tone
here with his response to the suggestion that Sir Thomas
Smith had recognized this principle before him.[27] The explanation of this difference may lie in the fact that Smith
was a "modern" writer, or in the fact that Harrington stood
to gain more prestige from an association with Aristotle, but
it undoubtedly also reflects Harrington's genuine feeling of
indebtedness to the great classical theorist. He is obviously
unclear, however, as to the exact degree of this indebtedness, as evidenced by the fact that he accuses Aristotle of
uncertainty on the question of political balance.[28] And it
is here that one sees more precisely the relation between the

24. *Politics*, III, 13.
25. *Prerogative of Popular Government, Coll. Works*, p. 292.
26. Ibid.
27. See above, p. 278, n. 2.
28. ". . . who indeed is not always of one mind."

two theorists. Aristotle recognized the connection between politics and economics, between political stability and the economic order. His theory of revolution, his account of Greek political history, and his explanation of the institution of ostracism all illustrate this fact. In all probability it was Aristotle more than any other theorist who was responsible for the fact that Harrington sought to explain political phenomena in terms of economic developments. And, furthermore, the general direction of Harrington's economic investigations may well reflect Aristotelian influence. But it is also undeniable that Harrington did not simply "revive" Aristotle's theory of revolution. On the contrary, having adopted the Aristotelian outlook here, he then modified it considerably by making it both more systematic and more central to his general theory of politics. Whereas Aristotle's theory of revolution was only a coordinate part of his general political theory, Harrington makes it the keystone of his entire theoretical structure. And it must be recognized that the same theory used in these two different ways becomes in effect two rather different theories. By thus assigning it a position of central importance Harrington really alters the fundamental significance of the theory. It is now no longer an explanation of certain political phenomena (i.e. revolutions and ostracisms), it is *the* explanation of all political life, and the guide to all intelligent political activity. Harrington made of this general insight a systematic principle of political theory. By applying it in a systematic fashion to all political experience he went considerably beyond Aristotle.

It may be argued, of course, that by thus broadening and systematizing Aristotle's original insight Harrington was erecting too weighty an edifice on so slight a foundation. Indeed if Harrington may be said to have had one predominant fault it was surely his tendency to go too far with his rationalistic system-building. But in any case, whether it is to his credit or not, it is clear that he did more than simply "revive" Aristotle's theory of revolution.

A second, and considerably more puzzling, exception to our general statement about Harrington's use of classical writings concerns Plato's *Laws*. The relation between this dialogue and the *Oceana* is such that it is at best only partially revealed by any enumeration of specific similarities between the two. Such a detailed comparison can merely serve to suggest the real core of the matter, which is that Harrington seems to have attempted in his *Oceana* to write a modernized version of the *Laws*. The parallels are striking and a few should be noted simply as examples of the general pattern. In the first place, of course, both books are in essence exercises in constitutional legislation; that is, they take the form of written constitutions based upon, and justified by reference to, an explicit general theory of politics. In both cases the constitutional provisions and the theoretical principles are clarified and defended by a dialectical process, a dialogue (in Plato) or a debate (in Harrington). Furthermore, both systems contemplate some public regulation of property, tending toward the elimination of undesirable extremes of wealth and poverty. Again, both systems are designed to embody and combine the peculiar virtues of several "pure" forms of government. Thus Plato explicitly claims that his proposed constitution combines the best features of monarchy and democracy, while Harrington argues that the government of Oceana will contain elements of monarchy, aristocracy, and democracy.[29] In other words, both works embody the theory of "mixed" government. And, along the same lines, both authors are concerned to introduce into their constitutions an element of balance which will lead to the achievement and maintenance of political equilibrium. Thus the statement that

29. *Laws*, 693–94 and *Oceana*, p. 25.

"this was the principle of the 'mixed' state, which is designed to achieve harmony by a balance of forces, or by a combination of diverse principles of different tendency in such a way that the various tendencies shall offset each other," can be applied with equal accuracy to either the *Laws* or the *Oceana*.[30] More specifically, the role of the popular assembly in both states is strictly limited, and electoral procedures are elaborately arranged to combine elements of chance with direct and indirect elections. Finally, to give a single instance of the more detailed sort of parallel, both constitutions provide that army officers shall be elected by the rank and file.

If this is sufficient to indicate the close relation between the *Laws* and the *Oceana*, we must now consider the curious fact that Harrington never in all his writings explicitly referred to the *Laws*. Since we have already had occasion to observe his penchant for full—indeed, exhaustive—citation of sources, this unique omission would seem to require some explanation. We know that Harrington was not averse to quoting and even praising Plato's *Republic*, but evidently he had some reason for preferring to remain silent about the *Laws*. In the light of these facts, it is difficult to avoid the apparently perverse conclusion that he does not refer to the *Laws* precisely because his reliance upon it was so great. In other words, it was possible for him to quote innumerable other sources without casting doubt upon the originality of his general system and of the enterprise in which he was engaged; but his debt to the *Laws* was so substantial and so fundamental that he was reluctant to reveal it. Indeed, it may further be suggested that Harrington's profound and often-declared admiration for "ancient prudence"—an admiration that is difficult to account for

---

30. George Sabine, *A History of Political Theory* (New York, 1946), p. 77; Sabine is speaking of Plato.

on the basis of the evidence he offers—is to a considerable extent a reflection of his attitude toward this "private" source. It may also be noted that on the whole Harrington's policy of silence has succeeded in achieving its presumed purpose of obscuring the relation between his own work and Plato's dialogue. Of all the students of his political thought, only Russell Smith has recognized the significance of this relation—and even he treats it rather perfunctorily.[31] Zera Fink, the tireless and intelligent tracer of classical influences, concludes rather lamely that the influence of the *Laws* on Harrington is "indeterminable."[32]

Although in a sense Harrington's reticence does make the whole question of his debt to Plato indeterminable, it may be suggested that the *Laws* was quite literally the model for his *Oceana*. Clearly, he did not simply choose to imitate Plato; many, if not most, of the proposed institutions of the Cretan colony are absent from the Oceanic constitution. Even the voting arrangements themselves look very much like the origin of what Harrington condemned as an "optimacy."[33] Rather, Harrington chose to copy Plato in the only sensible manner, not by reproducing his very words, but by attempting to do for his own age and country what the Athenian had done for his. The purpose is the same: to combine virtue and stability in a functioning constitutional order. And the technique is remarkably similar: if one were to seek a general statement of the program followed by Harrington in the *Oceana*, the words of Cleinias would do very well, "Let us make a selection from what has been said, and then let us imagine a State of which we will suppose ourselves to be the original founders. Thus we shall proceed with our enquiry, and, at the same time, I may

31. *Harrington and His Oceana*, pp. 14 and 73.
32. *The Classical Republicans*, p. 63, n. 58.
33. See above, p. 203.

have the use of the framework which you are constructing, for the city which is in contemplation."[34]

Apart from his use of Aristotle and the *Laws,* we must conclude that Harrington's reliance on the classics is of considerably less importance than his constant allusions to "ancient prudence" would seem to indicate. It might be pointed out that his apparent veneration of the classics was highly characteristic of the age in which he lived. The republicans of seventeenth-century England, as Zera Fink has shown in *The Classical Republicans,* looked always to the ancient world for inspiration and illustration. And thus, in following this pattern Harrington made use of the most impressive possible authorities. His state of mind and that of his contemporaries is expressed vividly, although perhaps rather cynically, by Selden in his *Table Talk:* "To quote a modern Dutchman where I may use a classic author, is as if I were to justify my reputation, and I neglect all persons of note and quality that know me, and bring the testimonial of the scullion in the kitchen."[35]

Machiavelli

The compiler of the index for an eighteenth-century edition of Harrington's collected works, after citing twelve references to "Macchiavel," abandoned the task and simply wrote, "quoted—*passim.*" Considering the high esteem in which Harrington held Machiavelli and the extensive use which he made of his writings, one can sympathize with this man. Although no precise count has been made, a thorough study of Harrington's works leaves one with the impression that the Florentine is the political writer whom he quotes and cites most frequently. And certainly there can be no doubt that he is the writer whom Harrington most

34. *Laws* (Jowett trans.), 702.
35. John Selden, *Table Talk,* Ch. 9 ("Books. Authors"), para. 9.

admires. He is "the onely Polititian of later Ages" and "the onely Politician that hath gone about to retreive" ancient prudence.[36] Furthermore, "he that will erect a Commonwealth against the Judgment of *Machiavill,* is obliged to give such reasons for his enterprize as must not go on begging."[37] In other words, Machiavelli's writings provide a standard against which all other political theory is to be measured. The mere fact of disagreement with Machiavelli creates a presumption of error which can only be removed by very convincing arguments. The only thing comparable to this in all of Harrington's writings is his attitude toward the Bible, and the reasons for this are obviously very different. To those of the twentieth century who are accustomed to viewing Machiavelli as the incarnation of political evil, Harrington's admiration will surely seem strange. What can Harrington, a moral man and a firm believer in republican government, find attractive about the author of the infamous *Prince?* A somewhat more sophisticated and balanced view of Machiavelli's position in the history of political theory will go far toward providing an answer to this question. It seems unnecessary here to comment on "the other Machiavelli," the author of the *Discourses.* Rather, it will be more profitable to try to discover in some detail the relation between Harrington and Machiavelli. Quite apart from the question of the Florentine's morality or immorality, the near-worship which Harrington accorded him requires some explanation.

Perhaps the most sensible way of arriving at such an explanation will be to consider briefly those specific aspects of Machiavelli's theory which Harrington admired and copied. Of these, two come to mind immediately: the idea of political creation by an omnicompetent and omniscient Legislator, and the institution of dictatorship. Now it is

36. *Oceana,* p. 13.
37. Ibid., p. 133.

apparent that these two aspects of Machiavelli's thought have much in common, notably their classical origin, their relation to a constitutional order, and the view of human nature which they imply. The first of these needs little further comment, since we have already noted that the two theorists shared an admiration for the ancient world. Machiavelli claimed he was opening "a new route . . . not yet . . . followed by anyone" in studying and commenting upon the political history and theory of the classical world.[38] This, he says explicitly, is to be the political counterpart of that veneration of classical art and literature which characterized the Italian Renaissance. And Harrington willingly accepts the claim of his distinguished predecessor, according him the honor of being the only political theorist since the fall of Rome who has truly appreciated and understood the wisdom of the ancients.

More interesting is the constitutional aspect of these two institutions. It is quite clear that the raison d'être of the Legislator is the need for an explicit and permanent constitution which will fix once and for all the form of government. Similarly, the essential point about the dictatorial power is that it must be a *constitutional* power; if emergencies necessitate the recourse to extraconstitutional devices, all is lost. Is it, then, a mere coincidence that Harrington should have relied most heavily upon Machiavelli in precisely those areas which are most closely related to constitutionalism? The answer, of course, is no. The most basic similarity between the two theorists is their pessimistic, or "realistic," view of human nature. This is nowhere more clearly reflected than in their common reliance on what Harrington termed "good orders." For both theorists it is necessary, so far as possible, to create an unchanging and unchangeable political system in order to restrain

38. *Discourses,* Preface to Bk. I.

and control all human beings, none of whom is to be trusted
without such restraint.

But that variety of constitutionalism which is characterized by faith in a Legislator and in dictatorial power
also implies that at certain times certain individuals must
be entrusted with enormous power. And here we find in
both Machiavelli and Harrington a commitment to what
we may describe, following Burckhardt, as the notion of
"the state as a work of art." Living as they did in times of
political crisis and instability, the Florentine and the Englishman shared a somewhat extreme opinion of the power of
human creativity. Impatient with failure and confusion,
they insisted that a wise and powerful man could, as it
were, cut the Gordian knot and with one stroke bring
peace and order.

At this point we may recall for a moment the passage in
the *Oceana* in which Harrington describes the "deepe impression" made by Machiavelli's account of Lycurgus.[39]
Surely it is most significant that the dramatic impact of
Machiavelli on Harrington should have come in connection
with the Spartan Legislator. Indeed, as the previous discussion indicates, this one incident reveals the essentials of
the relation between the two theorists: admiration of the
classical world and constitutionalism with all its implications.

It is interesting in the light of what we have been saying
that in his *Oceana* Harrington argued with Machiavelli
more than with any other political theorist save Hobbes.
The argument concerns Machiavelli's belief that enmity
between nobility and people is inevitable in a commonwealth. This, of course, directly contradicts Harrington's
ideal of a commonwealth in which popular and aristocratic
elements are to be combined. And Harrington was fully

39. *Oceana,* p. 58.

aware of the difficulty; having quoted at great length Machiavelli's discussion of this question,[40] Harrington adds: "*My Lords,* I do not know how you hearken unto this sound, but to hear the greatest Artist in the modern World, giving Sentence against our Common-wealth; is that, with which I am nearly concerned."[41] He then proceeds to argue, using Machiavelli's own evidence, that the enmity between the Roman nobility and people resulted rather from bad orders than from an inevitable conflict of interest, and concludes with these highly characteristic words: "as the people that live about the Cataracts of *Nilus* are said not to hear the noise; so neither *Roman* writers, nor *Machiavill* the most conversant with them, seem among so many of the Tribunitian storms, to hear their natural voice."[42]

The interesting point, of course, is that Harrington's veneration of Machiavelli should have persisted despite this fundamental disagreement. This is to be explained by two factors. First, the difference of opinion on this question did not destroy the fundamental similarity noted above; thus in a sense it was precisely because they were so close that Harrington was tempted to dispute Machiavelli's view at such length. The identical statement in any other writer would doubtless have been dismissed with a few scornful words. But, even more important, Harrington seems to have felt an almost irrational sympathy with Machiavelli, a sympathy strong enough to create a predisposition to accept the opinions of the Florentine unless the arguments against them were insuperable. And although most of us have at some time experienced a reaction of this sort its existence is always difficult to explain in a convincing way.

Returning for a moment to the passage from the *Oceana,*

40. *Discourses,* I, 6.
41. *Oceana,* p. 135.
42. Ibid., p. 137; the reference to the Nile is taken from Pliny's *Natural History,* VI, 29.181.

one may construct a hypothetical explanation: profoundly depressed and discouraged by the execution of Charles I and the failure of Cromwell's attempts to create a stable and legitimate government, Harrington took to his study and there began to read the *Discourses;* in the very first Book of this work he came upon Machiavelli's account of Lycurgus, a true statesman who had created order out of chaos; noting Machiavelli's enthusiasm, tempered always by a strain of pessimism, Harrington must have felt that here, at last, was a man who understood politics and who offered hope of a happy solution for England's problems; from this day forward, and despite certain weaknesses in his analysis, Machiavelli became Harrington's master.

In conclusion we may note that Harrington's admiration of Machiavelli was not confined to the Florentine's discussion of the Legislator and the dictatorial power, nor to the work which first inspired it. On the contrary, Harrington cites with approval Machiavelli's treatment of Roman history and his theory of provincial government. The latter, he tells us, is the greatest of Machiavelli's insights: "It is upon this point where the writings of *Machiavil* having for the rest excelled all other Authors, come as far to excel themselves."[43] We have already had occasion to note Harrington's acceptance of Machiavelli's discussion of the virtues of a hardy rural existence. Harrington also models his treatment of military organization deliberately on Machiavelli's *Art of War:* "Machiavel discourses upon these Particulars in his Art of War, to admiration: by whom I shall therfore steer."[44] And he even goes so far as to praise the infamous *Prince* on one occasion:

As in the privation of Virtue, and in Beggary, men

43. *Oceana*, p. 188; the reference is to *Discourses*, II, 4, in particular.
44. *Prerogative of Popular Government, Coll. Works*, p. 277.

are Sharks or Robbers, and the reason of their way of living is quite contrary to those of Thrift; so in the privation of Government, as in Anarchy, Oligarchy, or Tyranny, that which is Reason of State with them is directly opposit to that which is truly so: whence are all those black Maxims set down by som Politicians, particularly Machiavel in his *Prince,* and which are condemn'd to the fire even by them who, if they liv'd otherwise, might blow their fingers.[45]

In other words, unlike many later students, Harrington recognized that the "black Maxims" set forth by Machiavelli were in fact appropriate to an anarchic and corrupt political state. But, like the Florentine, he insisted that a better form of government could and should be created.

Venice

As Zera Fink has said, the three chief bases of Harrington's thought were "ancient prudence, Machiavelli the retriever, and Venice the exemplifier."[46] And Harrington leaves no doubt that of these three he considers Venice the most nearly perfect. Although the greatness of Venice may be said to result from her adoption of the principles of ancient prudence, it is nevertheless true that she has "attained to a perfection even beyond her Copy."[47] Somewhat startling, however, is his assertion that "the Orders [of this Common-wealth] are the most *Democratical* or *Popular* of all others."[48] In view of the fact that in the year 1581 only

45. *A System of Politics, Coll. Works,* p. 514.
46. *The Classical Republicans,* p. 54. We are indebted to Fink for much of the material used in this section. See also his brief article "Venice and English Political Thought in the Seventeenth Century," in *Modern Philology, 38* (1940), 155–72.
47. *Oceana,* p. 12. "Copy" here means, of course, "model."
48. Ibid., p. 19.

1843 persons out of a total population of 134,890 were allowed to participate in the political life of Venice, it seems difficult (if not impossible) to make any sense of Harrington's opinion. Surely a government limited to less than two per cent of the population will not impress the modern reader as outstandingly "Democratical or Popular."[49] What is the explanation of Harrington's view?

The answer is that Harrington was apparently unaware that the closing of the Great Council in the year 1297 and the publication of the Golden Book in 1315 changed the Venetian government from a democracy with a popularly elected executive to an extreme oligarchy. After this time, only direct descendants of members of the Council between the years 1293 and 1297 were allowed to participate in Venetian politics, and thus the vast majority of the population was completely excluded. In Harrington's opinion, as in the opinion of many of his contemporaries, the original Venetian constitution had extended citizenship to all residents of the "Lagoon commonwealth"; and for "two thousand years" their descendants continued to enjoy the privileges of citizenship. Thus the only people excluded are those who have voluntarily chosen to become subjects of the commonwealth despite the fact that they could not hope to become citizens, or those conquered by the arms of Venice. As Harrington puts it: "The Government . . . is usually mistaken: for *Venice,* though she do not take in the people, never excluded them. . . . they that now live under the Government without participation of it, are such as have since either voluntarily chosen to do so, or were subdued by Arms."[50]

49. The figures are given by J. A. Symonds in his *Renaissance in Italy,* Modern Library ed. (New York, 1935), *1,* 100. They are substantially the same as those available to Harrington in Lewkenor's translation of Contarini.

50. *Oceana,* p. 19.

But, one may ask, how does this justify the statement that a government open to only two per cent of the population is "Democratical and Popular"? Harrington's answer would be that only those eligible to sit on the Grand Council should properly be considered natives of Venice. Thus he refers to "the 3000 now governing" as constituting the "National interest" of Venice.[51] The remainder of the population is therefore relegated to the status of provincial subjects, either voluntarily or by conquest. Consequently for Harrington the Venetian commonwealth *means* this group of three or four thousand citizens and no one else. And therefore the government is "popular" because it is based on the participation of these citizens.

The primary explanation of Harrington's inaccurate and overly sympathetic view of the constitution of Venice is to be found in the writings of Cardinal Gasparo Contarini, whose *De magistratibus et republica Venetorum* was first published in 1543, was republished in Venice in 1589, and appeared in English under the title *The Commonwealth and Government of Venice* in 1599.[52] It is almost certain that this, along with the works of Machiavelli and Giannotti, was part of the "Collection of all the valuable Books in the Italian Language, especially treating of Politics" that Harrington acquired during his stay in Venice. And it is equally certain that he read it thoroughly and was deeply impressed by its account of the Venetian commonwealth. Some indication of this can be seen simply by comparing the general terms of praise which Harrington and Contarini use in speaking of Venice. But much more revealing is the fact that Contarini first asserted "the changelessness of the Venetian constitution," that very fallacy which underlies Harrington's entire interpretation. As Fink points out, his

51. Ibid. The figure is that given by Contarini.
52. In all, Zera Fink lists 19 editions in various languages between the years 1543 and 1722. *The Classical Republicans,* p. 39, n. 50.

De Magistratibus either omits or obscures such crucial
events as the *Serrata del Maggior Consiglio,* the publication
of the *Libro d'Oro,* and the establishment of the Council
of Ten. And in thus distorting history Contarini gave rise
to the belief that every feature of the Venetian constitution
as it appeared in the sixteenth century was the result of the
wisdom of those who had originally created the government. In this respect his words are echoed by Harrington.
We may note again Harrington's declaration that in the
seventeenth century, after a thousand years, Venice is "as
fresh, and free from decay . . . as shee was born." Thus for
both the Venetian Cardinal and the English theorist, Venice
represents a striking instance of the advantages to be gained
from the application of "prudence" or human wisdom to
the creation of a political order.

But the mere fact that Harrington considered the Venetian constitution to be "popular" is hardly sufficient to explain the enthusiasm which it aroused in him. Much more
important from his point of view was the apparent stability
of the government. This he attributed to a happy combination of circumstances, without implying, however, that
mere chance was mainly responsible. He did once admit
that the geographical location of the commonwealth was a
factor in its political life: "if *Venice* be defended from external causes of commotion, it is first, through her situation,
in which respect her Subjects have no hope (and this indeed
may be attributed unto her fortune)."[53] But he also argued
that this was really incidental and applied only to external
security: "There is another thing, though not so materiall
unto us, that my Lord will excuse Me, if I be not willing to
yield, which is that *Venice* subsisteth only by her situation;
It is true, that a man in time of Warre, may be more secure
from his Enemies, by being in a Citadell; but not from his

---

53. *Oceana,* pp. 136–37. Cf. Machiavelli, *Discourses,* I, 5 and 6.

Diseases; wherefore the first cause, if he live long, is his good Constitution, without which his Citadell were to little purpose; and it is no otherwise with *Venice*."[54]

Thus the fundamental cause of the stability, indeed the immortality, of the Venetian government was the perfection of its constitution. And Harrington is quick to point out the source of this perfection. In a passage which nicely summarizes his attitude toward Venice he writes: "there never happened unto any other Common-wealth, so undisturbed and constant a tranquillity and peace in her self, as is that of *Venice;* wherefore this must proceed from some other cause then Chance. And we see that as she is of all others the most quiet, so the most equal, Common-wealth."[55] In short, for Harrington Venice represented the only existing "equal commonwealth." The fact that virtually every institution proposed by him in the *Oceana* is to some extent a copy of a Venetian model makes it unnecessary for us to discuss at length the constitution of Venice. We may note, however, the fact that he particularly admired the arrangement whereby the Doge was made little more than a figurehead while the Grand Council exercised the actual sovereign power. Thus he writes, "The great Council of Venice has the Sovrain Power, and the Duke the Sovrain Dignity."[56] Furthermore, Harrington believed that the Venetian Council of Ten constituted the best possible model of a well-ordered dictatorial power and explicitly copied it in creating his Dictator Oceanae: "Now for our imitation in this part, there is nothing in experience like that of the *Council* of Ten in *Venice*."[57] Finally, and perhaps most

54. *Oceana*, p. 102. The view that the stability of the Venetian government was due to the location of the state was put forward by Sir Robert Filmer in his *Observations upon Aristotle's Politiques* in 1652.

55. *Oceana*, p. 137.

56. *Art of Lawgiving, Coll. Works*, p. 390, marginal note.

57. *Oceana*, p. 114; Harrington here cites Giannotti as his source.

significant of all, both the system of rotation and the ballot which Harrington stresses so heavily in his *Oceana* are copied from the Venetian constitution.

In view of these striking parallels one may conclude that the major source of Harrington's constitutional proposals was unquestionably the government of Venice. It will be remembered that as a youth Harrington traveled to Venice and was deeply impressed by what he saw there; he was apparently quite unaware that the greatness of Venice had severely declined by the time of his visit. The physical beauty of the city, its position as a bastion of the West, its defiance of the papacy so dramatically symbolized by Paolo Sarpi, and finally the fact that its government did function with remarkable smoothness and efficiency all combined to commend it. Particularly interesting in this connection is the treatment of the Venetian government in Shakespeare, notably in *Othello* and *The Merchant of Venice*. "When Brabantio in *Othello* says to Roderigo, 'What tell'st thou me of robbing? this is Venice; My house is not a grange,' he expresses an attitude which the facts of the time seemed to warrant."[58] And the entire plot of *The Merchant of Venice* depends for its force upon the assumption that justice will be done according to established law regardless of which party suffers; "it is impossible . . . to believe that as Shakespeare portrayed these things he was unaware of the contemporary reputation of Venice for justice."[59] Thus we may say that Harrington arrived in the Italian city predisposed to admire what he saw there. And indeed he admired the Venetian government so much that he determined to read all the available books about it, thereby falling under the influence of those two ardent partisans Contarini and Giannotti.

The result of all this was that Harrington possessed a

58. Fink, *The Classical Republicans*, pp. 35–36.
59. Ibid., p. 43, n. 65.

picture of an ideal Venetian constitution which only slightly resembled the true state of affairs in the seventeenth century. The outstanding feature of this ideal constitution was its supposed stability. Thus when Harrington became interested in English politics, and particularly in the problem of creating a stable government in England, it is only natural that he should have turned for inspiration to Venice and the Venetian constitution. But it should be noted that he did not advocate for England a slavish adoption of every feature of that constitution. Rather, he sought to generalize from the successful history of Venice, to create a theory of politics which would account for the stability of her government. And in so doing Harrington went much beyond his model. His proposed agrarian law, and the entire theory which justifies it, is almost completely unrelated to Venice. Again, as we have seen, he deplored the fact that Venice was a commonwealth "for preservation" and insisted that this made it unfit to serve as the sole model for English government. It was in the realm of specific political institutions that Harrington relied most heavily on the Venetian constitution. But in fitting these into a theoretical system of his own creation, and in adapting them to English requirements, Harrington surely did more than simply "put himself under the Protection of the most serene Republique of Venice."[60]

Contemporary Sources

Harrington's general attitude toward contemporary writers, with the obvious exception of Machiavelli and the Venetian historians, is best expressed by his observation that "there is a difference between having the sense of a thing, and making a right use of that sense."[61] As we shall have

60. The words are those of Wren's *Considerations*.
61. *Art of Lawgiving, Coll. Works,* p. 389.

occasion to see, Harrington relied very heavily upon the
writings of several contemporary historians for his knowledge of "modern prudence" and the "Gothick ballance."
But in every case he believed that these historians had failed
to understand the true meaning of the facts and events
which they recorded. Thus, like many of the classical authors whom Harrington consulted, they provided him with
the raw materials for a theory of politics but not with the
theory itself.

The most important of these historians were those from
whom Harrington derived his knowledge of the development of the English constitution. The first of these was John
Selden, author of *Titles of Honor* first published in 1614.
The extent of Harrington's debt to Selden is indicated by
a marginal note which occurs at the beginning of that portion of the *Oceana* devoted to the history of England[62]:
"For the proof of the ensuing discourse out of Records and
Antiquities. See *Selden's* Titles of Honour, from page 593
to page 837." Even without this acknowledgment something
of Selden's influence might be apparent simply from the
highly formalistic and legalistic manner in which Harrington treated the history of England. As is well known, Selden
was primarily a legal historian and an antiquarian, and was
noted rather for his erudition than for his critical abilities.
His work for the parliamentary cause in the early seventeenth century, and his attempt to prove from history that
the claims of the Stuarts were unwarranted, and indeed un-
constitutional, must certainly have prejudiced Harrington
in his favor. But it should be emphasized that Harrington
was not influenced by Selden to the extent of adopting the
conservative constitutional position which characterizes the
work of the latter. It should be clear by now that Harrington was not concerned with English history in order to

62. *Oceana,* p. 43.

justify the return to any form of medieval constitutionalism. Therefore, although he used Selden's facts, he used them for his own purposes. And pre-eminent among these purposes was Harrington's wish to demonstrate the nature of the politico-economic balance as it developed through English history. In this connection he tells us explicitly that "in Mr. Selden's Titles of Honor, he has demonstrated the *English* Balance of the Peerage, without making any application of it, or indeed perceiving it there."[63]

Speaking of his second major source of information about English history Harrington adds, "the like might be made apparent in . . . my Lord Verulam."[64] For it was Francis Bacon, and particularly Bacon's *Historia Regni Regis Henrici VII*, which Harrington relied upon for the details of the crucial reign of the first Tudor monarch. And here again it is quite clear that Harrington's interpretation of the facts is purely his own. Whereas Bacon is unstinting in his praise of Henry, Harrington, as we have seen, finds in his policies the seeds of the destruction of the English monarchy.

Among the contemporary authors most often cited by Harrington one must surely list the name of Thomas Hobbes. So often, in fact, does Harrington refer to Hobbes that Richard Koebner was led to conclude that "Der Gedankengang der *Oceana* in ihrem theoretischen Teil ist, Punkt fur Punkt, eine Kritik an dem . . . Leviathan."[65] Although this is unquestionably an overstatement, and one which has the unfortunate effect of denying to the theoretical portions of the *Oceana* a systematic structure of their own, Koebner's view is understandable. Harrington does use the *Leviathan* as a kind of whipping boy, constantly contrasting his own wisdom and Hobbes's foolishness. In this

63. *Art of Lawgiving, Coll. Works*, p. 390.
64. Ibid.
65. "Oceana," p. 364.

connection, one finds under Hobbes's name in the index of
the 1747 edition of Harrington's works such listings as
these: "goes about to destroy ancient Prudence," "misrepresents Aristotle, Cicero and Livy," and "his Mistakes concerning the Constitution of Rome." But, as we noted in
our discussion of methodology, Harrington very seldom
troubled to argue with Hobbes in any detail. His inductive
approach was so completely different from Hobbes's deductive method that there was virtually no common ground
between the two, and no agreement sufficient to make disputation possible. On matters of detail, and particularly
where historical interpretation is concerned, Harrington
does attack Hobbes. But in general he is content simply to
prove his own points and then mention scornfully Hobbes's
very different conclusions.

Perhaps the most interesting aspect of the relation between these two theorists is that Harrington profoundly
admired Hobbes as a philosopher, while disagreeing completely with his theory of politics. Thus in *The Prerogative
of Popular Government* he wrote:

> It is true, I have oppos'd the Politics of Mr. Hobbs,
> to shew him what he taught me, with as much disdain
> as he oppos'd those of the greatest Authors. . . . Never-
> theless, in most other things I firmly believe that Mr.
> Hobbs is and will in future Ages be accounted the best
> Writer, at this day, in the world. And for his Treatises
> of Human Nature, and of Liberty and Necessity, they
> are the greatest of new Lights, and those which I have
> follow'd, and shall follow.[66]

It is clear that in Harrington's opinion the method used by
Hobbes, whatever its virtues might be when applied to psychology and epistemology, was inappropriate to the study
of politics.

66. *Coll. Works,* p. 259.

The remaining contemporary authors to whom Harrington refers have either been mentioned above in the text or listed in the bibliography. Actually, nothing would be gained by entering into a discussion of any of these men. We may note in passing that Harrington supplemented his knowledge of English history from the writings of Coke, Bracton, and Fortescue, and that he relied upon the series published by the Elzevirs in the seventeenth century for information concerning the governments of continental Europe. As its title indicates, Sir Walter Raleigh's *History of the World* proved a storehouse of miscellaneous but useful historical information; much the same purpose was served by Sandys' *Travailes*. The works of Hooker and Grotius supplied impressive quotations to buttress Harrington's argument from natural law, though they certainly were not followed in any systematic fashion. In conclusion, then, we may say that Harrington used his contemporary sources rather as compendia of factual information, or what passed with him for factual information, than as sources of theoretical insights. This is surely not surprising in the light of his opinion that political wisdom died at the fall of the Roman empire.[67]

67. The customary exceptions must be made for Machiavelli, the "retriever," and Venice, the "exemplifier" of ancient wisdom.

CHAPTER 7.

"If this Age fails me . . ."

"If this Age fails me, the next will do me Justice."
The Art of Lawgiving

THE UNFEIGNED JOY with which the people greeted the restoration of the Stuart monarchy in the spring of 1660 can hardly have been shared by England's republican political theorists. For ten hectic but exhilarating years they had believed that their country's destiny rested in their hands. The Civil Wars and the dismantling of the traditional constitutional structure had left a *tabula rasa* upon which they might inscribe the formulas of a new order, a rational and moral order superior to any the world had seen. If the unexpected strength and stubbornness of Oliver Cromwell had proved frustrating to their hopes, the year of near-anarchy following the Protector's death raised their excitement to new heights—surely now, if ever, England cried out for a theorist to lead her in the ways of stability and civic virtue. But within eighteen months of Cromwell's death all opportunities had seemingly vanished, all hopes had been dashed; in their misery and confusion the English people had welcomed the return of the King, turning their backs upon the disciples of republicanism.

If this turn of events was disappointing to all republican theorists, it was perhaps peculiarly gloomy for the greatest of them, James Harrington. Like the others, he had seen his proposals rejected by his countrymen; but this was only part of his sorrow. In addition, he believed with absolute assurance that the restored monarchy was doomed to failure. Thus he was forced to sit by, Cassandra-like, while the English eagerly attempted to achieve the impossible: the erection of a monarchy in a country suited only for a commonwealth. Although, as we have seen, Harrington could (and did) comfort himself with the knowledge that time would inevitably prove him right, his love for his country and concern for its well-being were too deep to allow him to view the Restoration with anything like equanimity, to say

nothing of joy. It was, in his opinion, an unmitigated dis-
aster for his country. Soon it was to prove personally disastrous as well.

The collapse of the Protectorate seemed at first to have
very little effect upon Harrington's life. True, it led to the
dissolution of the Rota Club, but apart from this the pattern of his activities remained substantially unchanged. In
about 1657 he had moved into a house which overlooked
Westminster Hall; "he had a pretty gallery, which looked
into the yard . . . where he commonly dined, and medi-
tated, and tooke his tobacco." Here Harrington continued
to live, visited by his friends and others who sought his views
of the exciting events of the time, and devoting his energies
to the writing of yet another political treatise—the collection of aphorisms that was posthumously published as *A
System of Politics*. In Toland's words, "Not concern'd in
the excessive fears and hopes of those that favor'd or oppos'd
the Restoration of CHARLES the Second, [he] continu'd
to live in a peaceable manner at his own house, demeaning
himself as became a person blindly ingag'd to no Party or
Factions."[1] It would seem that Harrington, now in his fif-
tieth year, responded to the disappointment of his hopes
with an unwonted, but appropriate, air of calm and resigna-
tion. But perhaps his quietness was due rather to a prudent
discretion; it remained to be seen what would be the fate
of England's leading republican theorist under the monarchical government he had so strenuously opposed.

Late in 1661, Harrington received a visit from a man
who is described by Toland simply as "an eminent Royalist."[2] The ostensible purpose of this visit was to persuade
the author "to draw up some instructions for the King's
service, whereby he might be able to govern with satisfac-

1. *Coll. Works,* p. xxx.
2. Ibid.

tion to the people and safety to himself." In view of Charles
II's professed determination "not to go on his travels again,"
this explanation has a certain plausibility. But subsequent
events indicate that it was almost certainly false and that
Harrington's visitor was in fact an *agent provocateur* using
the story of the "instructions" in order to trap the theorist.
Machiavellian as he was in the technical sense of the word,
Harrington was anything but Machiavellian in the popular
sense. Trustingly he set to work preparing the memoran-
dum for the King; unfortunately, no copy has survived and
we do not know what advice Harrington gave to the son of
his beloved Charles I. Whatever it was, it was apparently
sufficient to arouse the suspicions of the Royalists. Having
delivered his suggestions in writing to one of the ministers
of Charles II, Harrington turned again to the unfinished
System of Politics.

"While he was putting the last hand to this System, as an
innocent man apprehensive of no danger, he was by an Order from the King, on the 28th of *December* 1661, seiz'd by
Sir WILLIAM POULTNEY and others, and committed to
the Tower of *London* for treasonable designs and practices."[3] His papers were seized and sent to the Council,
among them the *System of Politics,* which he was permitted
to stitch together before he was taken to the Tower. In the
Tower he was kept incommunicado, presumably while the
authorities studied the evidence. His sisters, learning somehow of the arrest, were distraught, particularly since it was
not clear what the charge was. One of them who was ac-
quainted with the king pleaded for her brother's release,
pointing out that the warrant under which the arrest had
been made was in the name of *Sir* James Harrington; surely

---

3. Ibid. Actually, the date of Harrington's arrest would seem to
have been Nov. 26, 1661, as given in the 1737 edition of the *Coll.
Works,* p. xxxi.

this must have been her cousin, Sir James of Swakeleys, regicide and president of the council under the Protectorate. The King was unimpressed: "tho they might be mistaken in his Title, he doubted he might be found more guilty of the Crimes alleg'd against him, than he wish'd any Brother of hers to be."[4]

What were these crimes? This is the question that Harrington must constantly have asked himself during these dark days. Soon he was to discover the nature of the accusation. Prompted by the plea of Harrington's sister that if he could not be released he at least be given a speedy trial, the King sent Lord Lauderdale, Sir George Carteret, and Sir Edward Walker to the Tower to examine the prisoner. Harrington wrote down from memory an account of this examination, which was preserved by his sister and later printed by Toland.

Much earlier in 1661 the government had been given reason to suspect that anti-Royalist plottings were being carried on in Nonesuch House in London. Mary Ellis, a servant in that coffeehouse, testified that John Wildman, a notorious trouble maker, had been meeting there regularly with Harrington, Praisegod Barebones, Nevill, and others.[5] In November the government began to arrest the suspects. Wildman was interrogated on November 26, 1661, the day of Harrington's arrest. He was asked first whether he knew of any "present design to disturb the peace of the nation or to alter the Government." When he denied any such knowledge, he was asked, "When were you last in Mr. Harrington's company? Where was it? And what company was present?"[6] The interrogation of Harrington followed the same pattern:

4. *Coll. Works,* p. xxxi. "Doubted" here means "supposed."
5. See Maurice Ashley, *John Wildman, Plotter and Postmaster* (New Haven, 1947), Ch. 14.
6. Ibid., pp. 177–78.

Lauderdale: Do you know Mr. Wildman?

Harrington: My Lord, I have som acquaintance with
him.

Lauderdale: When did you see him?

Harrington: My Lord, he and I have not bin in one
house togethcr these two years.

Lauderdale: Will you say so?

Harrington: Yes, my Lord.

Lauderdale: Where did you see him last?

Harrington: About a year ago I met him in a street
that goes to Drury-Lane.

Lauderdale: Did you go into no house?

Harrington: No, my Lord.

Carteret: That's strange!

Lauderdale: Com, this will do you no good: Had you
not, in *March* last, meetings with him in
Bowstreet in *Covent garden?* Where
there were about twenty more of you;
where you made a speech about half an
hour long, that they should lay by distinguishing [i.e. secret] Names, and be-
take themselves together into one Work,
which was to dissolve this Parlament, and
bring in a new one, or the old one again.

Harrington: My Lord, you may think, if these things
be true, I have no refuge but to the mercy
of God and of the King.

Lauderdale: True.

Harrington: Well, then, my Lord, solemnly and deliberately, with my eys to Heaven, I renounce the mercy of God and the King,
if any of this be true, or if ever I thought
or heard of this till now that you tell it
me.

Carteret: This is strange![7]

7. *Coll. Works*, p. xxxii.

Actually, the whole proceeding was not nearly as strange as Sir George Carteret seems to have felt it to be. Clearly the government had been given information, correct or not, that led to suspicions of a republican plot. Even if Harrington had not been directly implicated, his whole career was surely sufficient to make him suspect. He was, after all, a convinced and active republican; he had dedicated his first book to Oliver Cromwell; he had openly predicted the downfall of the restored monarchy within seven years. What more natural than that he should be involved in a conspiracy to overthrow Charles II and establish his beloved "equal commonwealth"? In fact, such a view is not consistent with what we know of Harrington's personality, but it is hardly to be expected that the harassed servants of a newly restored King would have troubled themselves unduly over such niceties.

In retrospect it seems that Harrington's conduct during his examination in the Tower was exemplary, and that his repeated protestations of innocence were sincere. After categorically denying all the specific charges of conspiracy, he proceeded to discuss the more fundamental points at issue. One rather lengthy statement, addressed directly to Lord Lauderdale, seems worthy of inclusion in its entirety:

> My Lord . . . you charge me with being eminent in Principles contrary to the King's government, and the Laws of this Nation. Som, my Lord, have aggravated this, saying, that *I being a privat man have bin so mad as to meddle with Politics: what had a privat man to do with Government?* My Lord, there is not any public person, not any Magistrat, that has written in the Politics worth a button. All they that have bin excellent in this way, have bin privat men, as privat men, my Lord, as my self. There is PLATO, there is ARISTOTLE, there is LIVY, there is MACHIAVEL. My Lord, I

can sum up ARISTOTLE'S *Politics* in a very few
words; he says there is a barbarous Monarchy (such a
one where the People have no Votes in making the
Laws) he says there is the Heroic Monarchy (such a one
where the People have their Votes in making the Laws)
and then he says there is Democracy; and affirms that
a man cannot be said to have Liberty, but in a Democracy only.

(My Lord LAUDERDALE, who had thus far been
very attentive, at this shew'd some impatience.)

I say, ARISTOTLE says so [Harrington continued]; I
have not said so much. And under what Prince was it?
Was it not under ALEXANDER, the greatest Prince
then in the world? I beseech you, my Lord, did ALEX-
ANDER hang up ARISTOTLE, did he molest him?
LIVY for a Commonwealth is one of the fullest Authors; did not he write under AUGUSTUS CAESAR?
did CAESAR hang up LIVY, did he molest him? . . . I
have don no otherwise than as the greatest Politicians,
the King will do no otherwise than as the greatest
Princes. But, my Lord, these Authors had not that to
say that I have; I did not write under a Prince, I wrote
under a Usurper, OLIVER . . . Som sober men came
to me and told me, if any man in *England* could shew
what a Commonwealth was, it was my self. Upon this
persuasion I wrote; and after I had written, OLIVER
never answer'd his Officers as he had don before, therfore I wrote not against the King's Government. And
for the Law, if the Law could have punish'd me,
OLIVER had don it; therefore my writing was not
obnoxious to the Law. After OLIVER the Parlament
said they were a Common-wealth; I said they were not,
and prov'd it; insomuch that the Parlament accounted
me a Cavalier, and one that had no other design in my

writing, than to bring in the King; and now the King
first of any man makes me a Roundhead.[8]

Harrington's plea for freedom of expression is eloquent,
although his attempt to suggest that Cromwell had suspected him of being a monarchist is rather farfetched. Making
due allowance for the fact that Harrington himself is our
sole source for this speech, one must at least admire the
felicity with which he expressed his views. In fairness to his
interrogators it must be noted that Lord Lauderdale answered this speech by saying, "These things are out of doors;
if you be no Plotter, the King dos not reflect upon your
Writings."[9] This recognition of the distinction between
subversive *activities* and anti-monarchical *writings* is extraordinarily enlightened even by modern standards, to say
nothing of those of the seventeenth century. Indeed, it is
so enlightened that one wonders whether it was in fact
shared by all of Harrington's monarchical enemies. Although perhaps they thought they were acting against a
suspected plotter, it is clear that their suspicions were
aroused and sustained by their knowledge of what Harrington had written. Charges that might otherwise have been
dismissed as unsupported were credited because Harrington's overt republicanism lent them a certain credibility.
In any case, all of Harrington's eloquence and protestations
of innocence were in vain.

After his interrogation Harrington remained imprisoned
in the Tower. Although no new evidence had been discovered, Clarendon insisted at a conference of the Lords and
Commons that he was one of the thirty-one leaders of a
conspiracy against the King. On the fourteenth of February, 1662, the Council granted a petition of Harrington's
sisters: "Petition of Elizabeth, Lady Ashton, and Anne Eve-

8. Ibid., pp. xxxiii–xxxiv.
9. *Coll. Works,* p. xxxiv.

lyn, sisters of James Harrington, who has been eleven weeks
a prisoner in the Tower, for permission to themselves and
his tenants to have access to him, as the tenants refuse to
pay their rent, unless they see him sign acquittances; the
fortunes of the petitioners, since the death of their mother,
Lady Harrington, depending chiefly upon him, they are in
danger of ruin."[10] Finding upon arrival at the Tower that
their brother was being badly treated, the two women proceeded to bribe the Lieutenant with fifty pounds. When
they left they took with them a petition from their brother
pleading not for release, but for a speedy trial at which he
might prove his innocence. Finding no one willing to present this petition in Parliament, they next set out to procure
a writ of habeas corpus. After considerable delay this was
granted—probably on April 23, 1662[11]—but on the very
same day, at two o'clock in the morning, Harrington was
hastily and secretly removed from the Tower. After a mysterious sea voyage he found himself once more in prison,
this time on St. Nicholas Island, a small rock off the coast
near Plymouth. By this underhanded maneuver his enemies had prevented both his release and his trial.

The change in locale was most unfortunate for Harrington. Although he had quite naturally protested his imprisonment in the Tower, he seems to have been tolerably well
cared for after his sisters had bribed the Lieutenant. Now
the climate and the added confinement of St. Nicholas Island led to a rapid deterioration of his health. So bad did
his condition become that he soon petitioned to be allowed
to move to the city of Plymouth. After his brother William,

10. Calendar of State Papers (Domestic), 1661–1662, p. 273.
11. The date is that of a document listed in the Calendar of State
Papers (Domestic), p. 347, as "Warrant to Sir John Robinson, Lieutenant of the Tower, to receive James Harrington into close custody,
for endeavouring in several meetings to promote a change in the
government."

a prosperous merchant and a fellow of the new Royal Society, and his uncle Anthony Samuel had posted a bond for five thousand pounds, this request was granted.

In Plymouth Harrington's lot was considerably improved; he was allowed to walk about freely and he enjoyed the friendship of Sir John Skelton, the deputy governor of the fort, who "much lov'd his Conversation." Among his other acquaintances in Plymouth was a certain Dr. Dunstan, a physician. Seeing that the prisoner was suffering from scurvy, the doctor prescribed a medicine containing guaiacum. This Harrington took in his coffee, and very soon it was observed that his "Fancy was much disorder'd."[12] When his sister heard of this she sent word to the chief governor of Plymouth, the Earl of Bath, requesting that some action be taken. Upon investigation, the Earl sent word to Charles II that Harrington's life would be endangered if he were not immediately removed to London. "And the King was accordingly pleased to grant a Warrant for his Release, since nothing appear'd against him supported by good proof or probable presumptions." This would seem a reasonable indication that no reliable evidence had existed at the time of Harrington's arrest; apparently his enemies felt that he was no longer a threat and consequently had no objection to his release.

On the day following the issuance of the royal warrant, Lady Ashton and Mrs. Evelyn traveled to Plymouth, where they found their brother in a shocking condition. "He was reduc'd to a Skeleton, not able to walk alone, slept very little, his Imagination disturb'd, often fainted when he took his drink, and yet so fond of it that he would by no means be advis'd to forbear it." Dr. Prujean, the eminent friend of William Harvey, attended Harrington and blamed his disorder on Dr. Dunstan's prescriptions, particularly the gua-

12. *Coll. Works,* p. xxxvi; Toland is the source for this episode in general.

iacum, which begot "Melancholy or Phrenzy"; to modern eyes, the disorder looks suspiciously like dipsomania or some form of addiction. Lady Ashton was quick to conclude that her brother had been the victim of a plot designed to prevent his writing "any more Oceanas," but this is wholly unsubstantiated. After a month of care Harrington was able to leave Plymouth. He journeyed slowly to London, stopping on the way at Ashstead in Surrey to drink the Epsom waters, and finally settled once again in his house in Westminster.

In London it was discovered that Harrington was the victim of a curious mental disorder. Aubrey has described it in this way:

> [It] was not outragious, for he would discourse rationally enough and be very facetious company, but he grew to have a phance that his perspiration turned to flies, and sometimes to bees . . . and he had a versatile timber house built . . . to try the experiment. He would turne it to the sun, and sitt towards it; then he had his fox tayles there to chase away and massacre all the flies and bees that were to be found there, and then he shut his [window frames]. Now this experiment was only to be tryed in warme weather, and some flies would lye so close in the cranies and the cloath (with which it was hung) that they would not presently show themselves. A quarter of an hour later perhaps, a fly or two, or more, might be drawen-out of the lurking-holes by the warmeth; and then he would crye out, "Do not you see it apparently that these come from me?" 'Twas the strangest sort of madnes that ever I found in any one: talke of any thing els, his discourse would be very ingeniose and pleasant.[13]

13. *Brief Lives* (Dick ed.), p. 125.

More interesting than the illness itself was Harrington's reaction to it, particularly his rather crude attempt to demonstrate by the experimental method that he was perfectly sane. In addition to performing the experiment that Aubrey describes, he undertook to write a treatise simultaneously demonstrating the reality of his hallucinations and the fact of his sanity. This work, which was never completed, bears the title *The Mechanics of Nature;* its subtitle describes it as "An Imperfect Treatise written by James Harrington during his sickness, to prove against his Doctors that the notions he had of his own Distemper were not, as they alleg'd, Hypochondriac Whimsys or Delerious Fancys." This, Harrington's last known work, is a truly curious mixture of Cartesian physics, alchemical symbolism, and the remnants of Scholastic philosophy.[14] In it Harrington argues that nature "furnishes herself with innumerable ministerial Spirits, by which she operates on her whole matter," and that these spirits manifest themselves in various corporeal forms. The flies and bees which he perceived were simply manifestations of evil spirits. In assessing Harrington's malady it is well to recall that such bizarre beliefs were by no means uncommon in the seventeenth century; many of the leading figures of the age, including scientists of great distinction, continued to believe in alchemy and witchcraft.

This puzzling combination of delusion and rationality was to characterize Harrington for the remaining years of his life. Soon it was augmented by other purely physical ailments, especially gout and palsy. Despite all this—or, as Toland believed, because of his mental instability—Harrington at the age of sixty-four married his childhood sweetheart, the daughter of Sir Marmaduke Dorrell of Bucking-

14. The text of the treatise came into Toland's possession along with many of Harrington's papers; he printed it in his collection of Harrington's works, pp. xlii–xliv. It is printed at the end of this volume as Appendix I.

hamshire. Aubrey informs us that, since "he could not enjoy his deare in the flower and heate of his youth, he would never lye with her, but loved and admired her dearly." By 1676 Harrington was a chronic invalid, enfeebled in mind and body. On the seventh of September, 1677, he died at his home in Westminster, bequeathing his property to the children of his brothers. It can hardly be doubted that his last years were darkened and his death hastened by the political persecution he had suffered; in a very real sense he died a martyr for the republican cause to which he had devoted his life. He was buried in St. Margaret's Church, beside the grave of Sir Walter Raleigh. Even at the moment of his burial he was pursued by his peculiar nemesis: an epitaph which his friend Andrew Marvell had written for him was not used for fear it might give offense to the authorities. In its place, these unexceptionable words were inscribed on his tomb:

> Nec virtus, nec animi dotes (arrha licet
> aeterni in animam amoris Dei) corruptione
> eximere queant corpus.

One may ask, finally, whether this is a story of success or failure, of fulfillment or frustration. In human, personal terms, there can be little doubt that Harrington's career was a tragic one. In the last twenty years of his life the high hopes of his youth and early manhood were shattered; those in power in his country would not heed his warnings or accept his counsel, and all his labors seemed to have been in vain. Viewed in broader perspective, however, the picture is not so grim. Within a century of his death, many of the institutions of the "equal commonwealth" that had been rejected by his contemporaries as a matter of choice had come into being in England simply as a matter of gradual historical evolution. At the same time, thoughtful men in America and France as well as in England, had come to recognize the merits of Harrington's analysis. No less a figure than John Adams credited him with the discovery of an "infallible" law of politics; the eminently sensible David Hume described the *Oceana* as "the only valuable model of a commonwealth that has yet been offered to the public"; legislators in America and would-be legislators in France made wide-spread use of his proposals, root and branch.[15] In short, Harrington's hope that he might contribute significantly to the development of political thought and political institutions has been amply fulfilled.

15. The best account of Harrington's "influence" is still that in H. F. Russell Smith, *Harrington and His Oceana.*

Appendixes

Appendix I

THE MECHANICS OF NATURE: *or*

An imperfect treatise written by James Harrington during his sickness, to prove against his doctors that the notions he had of his own distemper were not, as they alleged, hypochondriac whimsies or delirious fancies*

The Preface

HAVING been about nine months, some say in a disease, I in a cure, I have been the wonder of physicians, and they mine; not but that we might have been reconciled, for books (I grant) if they keep close to nature must be good ones, but I deny that nature is bound to books. I am no studied naturalist, having long since given over that philosophy as inscrutable and uncertain: for thus I thought with myself; "Nature, to whom it is given to work as it were under a veil or behind the curtain, is the Art of God; now if there be Arts of Men who have wrought openly enough to the understanding (for example that of Titian) nevertheless whose excellency I shall never reach, how shall I thus, sticking in the bark at the Arts of Men, be able to look thence to the roots, or dive into the abyss of things in the Art of God?" And nevertheless *si placidum caput undis extulerit*, should Nature afford me a sight of her, I do not think so meanly of myself but that I would know her as soon as another, though more learned, man. Laying therefore arts wholly, and books almost all aside, I shall truly deliver to the world how I felt and saw nature; that is, how she came first into my senses, and by the senses into the understand-

---

**Coll. Works*, pp. xlii–xliv. I have modernized the spelling.

ing. Yet for the sake of my readers, and also for my own, I must invert the order of my discourse. For theirs, because till I can speak to men that have had the same sensations with myself, I must speak to such as have a like understanding with others. For my own, because being like in this discourse to be the monkey that played at chess with his master, I have need of some cushion on my head, that being in all I have spoken hitherto more laid at than my reason. My discourse then is to consist of two parts: the first, in which I appeal to his understanding who will use his reason, is a platform of nature drawn out into certain aphorisms; and the second, in which I shall appeal to his senses who in a disease very common will make farther trial, is a narrative of my case.

A Platform or Scheme of Nature

1. Nature is the *fiat,* the breath, and in the whole sphere of her activity is the very word of God.

2. She is a spirit, that same spirit of God which in the beginning moved upon the waters, his plastic virtue.

3. She is the providence of God in his government of the things of this world, even that providence of which it is said, that without it a sparrow cannot fall to the ground.

4. She is the *Anima Mundi,* or soul of the world. [Here follows a long passage from *Aeneid,* I, 6]

5. She is infallible; for the law of an infallible lawgiver must needs be infallible, and nature is the law as well as the art of God.

6. Though nature be not fallible, yet she is limited, and can do nothing above her matter; therefore no miracles are to be expected from her.

7. As defects, redundancies, or other such rude qualities of matter ought not to be attributed to the Artificer or his art, so neither is nature, or the art of God, to be charged with monsters or imperfections, the things so reputed being

the regular effects both of the matter and the art that forms it.

8. Nature is not only a spirit, but is furnished, or rather furnishes herself with innumerable ministerial spirits, by which she operates on her whole matter, as the universe; or on the separate parts, as man's body.

9. These ministerial spirits are certain ethereal particles invisibly mixed with elementary matter, they work ordinarily unseen or unfelt, and may be called animal spirits.

10. As in sound bodies there must needs be good spirits managing the economy of health, so in unsound bodies, as in chronic diseases, there must needs be evil spirits managing the economy of distempers.

11. Animal spirits, whether in the universe or in man's body, arc good or evil spirits according to the matter wherein and whereof they are generated.

12. What is a good spirit to one creature is evil to another, as the food of some beasts is poison to man; whence the gentleness of the dove and the fierceness of the hawk.

13. Between the animal spirits of the whole universe and of the parts, as man's body, there is an intercourse or cooperation which preserves the common order of nature unseen; and in some things often foretells or discovers it, which is what we call presages, signs and prodigies.

14. The work of good spirits, as health for example, is felicitous and as it were angelical; and that of evil spirits, as in diseases, is noxious, and as it were diabolical, a sort of fascination or witchcraft.

15. All fermentation is caused by unlocking, unbinding, or letting loose of spirits; as all attenuation is occasioned by stirring, working or provoking of spirits; and all transpiration by the emission or sending abroad of spirits.

16. Nothing in nature is annihilated or lost, and therefore whatever is transpired is received and put to some use by the spirits of the universe.

17. Scarce any man but at some time or other has felt such a motion as country people call the Lifeblood; if in his eye, perhaps there has flown out something like a dusky cloud, which is a transpiration or emission of spirits, perhaps as it were a flash of fire, which was also an emission of spirits—but differenced according to the matter wherein and whereof they were wrought, as choler, etc.

18. Animal spirits are ordinarily emitted streaking themselves into various figures, answerable to little arms or hands, by which they work out the matter by transpiration, no otherwise than they unlocked it, and wrought it up in the body by attenuation; that is, by manufacture, for these operations are perfectly mechanical, and downright handiwork as any in our shops or workhouses.

19. If we find nature in her operations not only using hands, but likewise something analogous to any art, tool, engine or instrument which we have or use, it cannot be said that nature had these things of men, because we know that men must have these things of nature.

20. In attenuation and transpiration, where the matter of the disease is not only copious but inveterate, the work will not as I may say be inarticulate, as in the trembling called the Lifeblood; but articulate, and obviously so to the sense of the patient by immediate strokes of the humor upon his organs, which sometimes may be strong enough (though not ordinarily) to reach another's.

21. Nature can work no otherwise than as God taught her, nor any man than as she taught him.

22. When I see a curious piece from the hands of an apprentice, I cannot imagine that his master was a bungler, or that he wrought not after the same manner as his servant learned of him; which I apply to God and nature.

23. Physicians sometimes take the prudence of nature for the frenzy of the patient.

24. If any man can show why these things are not thus, or

that they may be otherwise, than I have done, and there is said in this part already more than enough. But if they can neither show that these things are not thus, nor know how they should be otherwise, then so far I stand my ground, and am now armed for my narrative *cap a piè*.

Appendix II

Expenditures connected with the Senate of Oceana, calculated annually*

The Lord Strategus	£ 2,000	
The Lord Orator	2,000	
The three Commissioners of the Seal	4,500	(at £1,500 each)
The three Commissioners of the Treasury	4,500	(£1,500 each)
The two Censors	3,000	(£1,500 each)
The remaining 290 Knights	145,000	(£500 each)
The four ordinary Ambassadors	12,000	(£3,000 each)
Council of War, for intelligence	3,000	
The Master of Ceremonies	500	
The Master of the Horse	500	
Substitute Master of the Horse	150	
Twelve Ballotines (for Livery, board, and wages)	840	(£70 each)
For keeping of State coaches	1,500	
For Grooms, etc.	480	
The Twenty Secretaries	2,000	
Coats for twenty Door Keepers	200	
Board and Wages for same	1,000	
Twenty Trumpeter–Messengers	1,200	
Ornaments for Musters	5,000	

TOTAL   £189,370

*See *Oceana*, pp. 150–51, for these figures. The figures for the Prerogative are not round figures because in the original they are quoted on a weekly basis and here they have been figured annually. Harrington gives an incorrect Grand Total of £287,459.

Expenditures connected with the Prerogative Tribe, calculated annually

The two Tribunes of the Horse	£ 728	
The two Tribunes of the Foot	624	
The three Captains of Horse	780	
The three Cornets	468	
The three Captains of Foot	624	
The three Ensigns	364	
The remaining 442 Horse Deputies	45,968	(at £104 each)
The remaining 592 Foot Deputies	46,176	(at £78 each)
The six Trumpeters	390	
The three Drummers	117	
TOTAL	£96,239	

Grand Total, Senate and Prerogative   £285,609 per annum.

Bibliography

I: Harrington's works listed in order of publication
II: Contemporary works of direct relevance to Harrington
III: Modern works dealing with Harrington

I.

A. Individual works (all published in London)

The Common-wealth of Oceana. 1656; also 1658.

Pian piano, or, intercourse between H. Ferne, D.D. and J. Harrington, Esq.; upon occasion of the Doctor's censure of the Commonwealth of Oceana. 1657.

The Prerogative of Popular Government. Being a political discourse in two books. 1657 or 1658.

The Stumbling-Block of Disobedience and Rebellion . . . 1658.

An Essay upon Two of Virgil's Eclogues, and Two Books of His Aeneis (if this be not enough) towards the Translation of the Whole. 1658.

Seven Models of a Common-Wealth, or brief directions shewing how a fit and perfect model of popular government may be made, found, or understood. 1658.

Politicaster, or a comical discourse, in answer to Mr. Wren's book . . . 1659.

Pour enclouer le canon. 1659.

A Discourse upon this Saying: The Spirit of the Nation is not yet to be trusted with Liberty . . . 1659.

Virgil's Aeneis (Books 3–6, translated). 1659.

The Art of Law-giving. 1659.

The Humble Petition of Divers Well-affected Persons, deliver'd the 6th of July 1659, with the Parliament's answer thereto. 1659.

A Discourse Shewing, That the Spirit of Parlaments, with a Council in the Intervals, is not to be Trusted for a Settlement . . . 1659.

Political Aphorisms. 1659.

A Parallel of the Spirit of the People with the Spirit of Mr. Rogers . . . 1659.

Valerius and Publicola: or, the true form of a popular commonwealth extracted ex puris naturalibus. [Includes: *A Sufficient Answer to Mr. Stubs.*] 1659.

The Rota, or a model of a free state or equal commonwealth . . . 1660.

The Ways and Means Whereby an Equal and Lasting Commonwealth May be Suddenly Introduced . . . 1660.

A Word Concerning a House of Peers. 1660 (?).

Political Discourses. 1660.

The Use and Manner of the Ballot. 1660.

A System of Politics. [Written c. 1661; published posthumously by Toland.]

The Mechanics of Nature. [Written c. 1676; published posthumously by Toland.]

B. Collections

The Oceana of James Harrington and His Other Works; som whereof are now first publish'd from his own manuscripts. The whole collected, methodiz'd, and review'd . . . *by John Toland.* London, 1700.

———————another edition of the Toland volume, with an appendix containing eleven additional works. London, 1737, 1747, and 1771.

—————another edition of the Toland volume, with Henry Nevill's *Plato Redivivus* added. Dublin, 1737 and 1758.

The Political Writings of James Harrington (selections), ed. C. Blitzer. New York, 1956.

II.

Baxter, Richard. *A Holy Commonwealth*. London, 1659.

The Censure of the Rota upon Mr. Milton's Book . . . London, 1660.

Decrees and Orders of the Committee of Safety of . . . *Oceana*. London, 1659.

R. G. *A Copy of a Letter from an Officer of the Army in Ireland*. London, 1656.

Heylyn, Peter. *Certamen Epistolare*. London, 1659.

—————. *The Stumbling Block of Disobedience*. London, 1658.

Milton, John. *The Readie and Easie Way to Establish a Free Commonwealth*. London, 1660.

Nevill, Henry. *Plato Redivivus*. London, 1681.

The Plain Case of the Common-Weal . . . London, 1658.

Prynne, William. *An Answer to a Proposition* . . . London, 1659.

Rogers, John. *Diapoliteia, or, a Christian concertation* . . . London, 1659.

—————. *Mr. Harrington's Parallel Unparallel'd*. London, 1659.

Sprigg, William. *A Modest Plea for an Equal Commonwealth*. London, 1659.

Stubbe, Henry. *The Commonwealth of Oceana put in the Ballance, and found too light*. London, 1660.

Vane, Sir Henry. *A Needful Corrective or Ballance in Popular Government*. London, 1660.

Wren, Matthew. *Considerations on Mr. Harrington's Common-wealth of Oceana* . . . London, 1657.

――――. *Monarchy Asserted* . . . Oxford, 1659.

III.

Ashley, Maurice. *John Wildman, Plotter and Postmaster.* London, 1947.

Bernstein, Eduard. *Cromwell and Communism.* Translated by E. Stenning. London, 1930.

Dwight, Theodore. *James Harrington and His Influence upon American Political Institutions and Political Thought.* Boston, 1887. Reprinted from *Political Science Quarterly* for March 1887.

Fink, Zera. *The Classical Republicans.* (Northwestern University Studies in the Humanities, No. 9) Evanston, 1945.

Firth, C. H. *The Last Years of the Protectorate.* 2 vols. London, 1909.

Friedrich, C. J. *Constitutional Reason of State.* Providence, 1956.

Gooch, G. P. and Laski, H. *English Democratic Ideas in the 17th Century.* Cambridge, 1954.

Gough, J. W. "Harrington and Contemporary Thought," *Political Science Quarterly, 45* (1930), 395–404.

Grimble, Ian. *The Harington Family.* London, 1957.

James, Margaret. "Contemporary Materialist Interpretations of Society in the English Revolution," in *The English Revolution,* ed. C. Hill (London, 1949).

――――. *Social Problems and Policy During the Puritan Revolution, 1640–1660.* London, 1930.

Jordan, W. K. *The Development of Religious Toleration in England.* 4 vols. Cambridge, Mass., 1932–40.

Judson, Margaret. *The Crisis of the Constitution.* New Brunswick, 1949.

Koebner, Richard. "Die Geschichtslehre James Harringtons" in *Geist und Gesellschaft* (Breslau, 1927–28), *3,* 15–19.

————. "Oceana" in *Englische Philologie* (Leipzig), *68* (1933–34), 364–68.

Levett, A. E. "James Harrington" in *Social and Political Ideas of the 16th and 17th Centuries,* ed. F. J. C. Hearnshaw (New York, 1949).

Liljegren, S. B. "Harrington and Leibniz" in *Studies in English Philology* (Minneapolis, 1929).

———— (ed.) *James Harrington's Oceana.* Heidelberg, 1924.

————. "Some Notes on the Name of James Harrington's Oceana" in *Probleme der Englischen Sprache und Kultur.* 1925.

Petegorsky, D. *Left-wing Democracy in the English Civil War.* London, 1940.

Pocock, John. *The Ancient Constitution and the Feudal Law.* Cambridge, 1957.

Polin, R. "Economique et politique au xviie Siècle: L'Oceana de James Harrington," in *Revue Français de Science Politique, 2* (1952), 24–41.

Robbins, Caroline. *The 18th Century Commonwealthman.* Cambridge, Mass., 1959.

Russell Smith, H. F. *Harrington and His Oceana . . .* Cambridge, 1914.

Schenk, W. *The Concern for Social Justice in the Puritan Revolution.* London, 1948.

Shklar, Judith. "Ideology Hunting: The Case of James Harrington" in *American Political Science Review, 53* (September 1959), 3.

Tawney, R. H. "Harrington's Interpretation of His Age" in *Proceedings of the British Academy, 27* (London, 1941).

Trevor-Roper, H. R. "The Gentry 1540–1640" in *Economic History Review Supplements, 1* (Cambridge, n.d.).

Wershofen, Christian. *James Harrington und Sein Wunschbild vom Germanischen Staate.* Bonn, 1935.

Wormuth, F. D. *The Origins of Modern Constitutionalism.* New York, 1949.

Zagorin, Perez. *A History of Political Thought in the English Revolution.* London, 1954.

Index